OFF THE BEATEN PATH

‹‹‹‹‹‹‹ • ›››››››

WITH WALTER HESMAN

HOMESTEAD PRESS

Off The Beaten Path
By Walter Hesman
Published by Natural Heritage/Natural History Inc.
P.O. Box 69, Postal Station H
Toronto, Ontario
M4C 5H7
Copyright © March, 1989

Cover Design: Derek Chung Tiam Fook
Printed in Canada by T.H. Best Printing Company Ltd.

All photos provided by the author.
The publisher acknowledges with thanks
the use of photographs by Dr. A. C. Johnson, H.A.P.T., and W.C. Horrigan.
Commanda General Store Museum photo courtesy The Highland Herald.

Canadian Cataloguing in Publication Data

Hesman, Walter, 1908-
    Off the beaten path with Walter Hesman

ISBN 0-920474-54-3

1. Hesman, Walter, 1908-   .   2. Outdoor life –
Ontario – Biography.   3. Little River Lodge (Ont.).
4. Hunting guides – Ontario – Biography.   I. Title.

SK17.H47A3 1989   799.292'4   C89-093854-7

CONTENTS

If I had to rank on outdoor ethics and sheer ability the sportsmen of my acquaintance, Walter Hesman would hold down top spot. It has been both a pleasure and privilege to share the same trails and fishing spots with Walter over a great many years.

Few outdoorsmen can truthfully claim the unlimited wilderness living adventures that Walter Hesman has known. To the many former guests at Little River Lodge, Walter will always be remembered as the ideal host, guide and companion. If he has an equal, it would be his devoted wife, Mary, a wonderful partner.

Readers of Off The Beaten Path will quickly discover what so many acquainted with Walter have always known. Namely, that he is, in outdoor terms, "The Real McCoy"!

Dr. Alan Secord,
Toronto

INTRODUCTION

During my 60 years trapping and guiding in this off-the-beaten-path area, especially the 50 years developing Little River Lodge, many guests had urged me to write a book with details of the many special and unusual experiences I had to succeed. I finally decided to start after I sold the lodge, and took on a trap partner. However I soon realized I was not a "Ralph Bice" when it came to writing. Then my manuscript was delayed over three years at a publisher who failed, and many guests who had urged me to do this have passed away. I am going ahead with it, and hope their children and grandchildren, who have the many pictures taken here by their seniors, will be interested. I will start from the period I left school at age 14, 1924. My school education was limited, but not my practical education and knowledge of this area. So please bear with me and I hope you will find it interesting.

Walter Hesman

Mary Hesman

CHAPTER 1

THE EARLY YEARS — OFF THE BEATEN PATH

"Either apologize or pack your books," Mr. Hooper said laying down an ultimatum.

"In that case," I replied, "I had better pack my books."

At fifteen my high school days were over, and because of this incident my life no doubt took an entirely new turn, which may not have happened otherwise. At that age it took some courage to stand up for my rights before my peers, and this courage would be needed in later adventures of my life. I was born November 9th, 1908, in Windsor, Ontario, in the County of Essex, which is the most southern point in Canada.

My dad purchased a farm in 1914 near Maidstone, about fourteen miles from Windsor, but due to the first world war, instead of farming, dad was needed at the Ford factory in Highland Park, Michigan, a suburb of Detroit. He was a tool and die maker and a valued employee. He commuted back and forth once a week on an interban railroad, that ran between Windsor and Kingsville. The farm was worked on shares by a man named Mr. Little. Dad began purchasing livestock. Due to his lack of farm knowledge he became a victim of smart horse traders, with the result that we had a number of bad experiences. Mother suffered the most, as the horse and buggy was our only means of transportation. It was a miracle she was not killed or injured during several runaways. On one occasion the horse became frightened by the commuter train, bolted across a deep ditch and over the tracks, then jumped a page wire fence, leaving the buggy just a few inches from the track as the train went by.

The years on that farm were very beneficial to me; my health improved and I began to take part in doing the chores. I learned to milk a cow and tend to the chickens. That was one thing my dad knew something about.

1

Early in 1919 dad had a good offer for the farm and sold it. Although he had never farmed the place, he still had the yearning to farm. With his chronic bronchitis, factory work was the worst possible thing he could do.

A realtor talked him into looking at a dairy farm near Burgessville, which was just a few miles from the town of Norwich, where he was born.

We made the trip by train to Woodstock and it was a big thrill for me, as it was my first train trip. We were met at the station by the realtor who drove us out to the farm. The trip impressed me very much as I had never seen such scenery; beautiful rolling hills and valleys, with streams winding through the farms; also the many orchards that were in full bloom and spreading their fragrant perfume in the soft spring air. I was bewitched by beauty I had never in my young years come across before.

Essex county where I had been raised was very flat and so level that the farms had to be tiled and drained into the ditches, in order to work the land in the spring.

When we arrived at the farm I was more impressed than ever. The lane leading from the road to the house was lined on both sides by beautiful spruce evergreen trees. Never had I seen evergreen trees around a home before.

The house was a low rambling home surrounded on three sides by an orchard in full bloom, like a picture postcard! Some of the limbs were touching the house. It was a sight to see, and hard for me to understand how this fairy-land had been left vacant for three years!

Apparently the owner's son had been a war casualty and the land had been worked by a neighbour. The barns were huge and very modern for the period and had been occupied by a large dairy herd before the war.

As the realtor was showing us around, I was hoping my dad would tell him he would buy the farm. I could very nearly taste it, never dreaming that that was where my heart longed to be; as close to the land as it could get. Land that was pleasing to the eye as well as a challenge.

The spring crops had already been planted, but the salesman said, "You can move in anytime; the final closing and full possession will take place after the harvest." Dad finally agreed to this, and we returned to our home on the farm near Windsor, and I could hardly contain the joy that kept flooding over me.

I am sure it was I that convinced mother to agree to make the move to Burgessville. I bragged to the kids at school until they were all envious of our moving. Ferne remained at Maidstone with a neighbour until her school exams were over. I had never taken into consideration that this was the fifth move we had made during my ten years. My poor mother had to clean up all these places; all her life she had been an extremely meticulous French woman, and known to all as a "lint picker." All our homes were very immaculate, due to her constant scrubbing and cleaning. You could literally "eat off the floor."

After hearing both our glowing reports of this new farm, mother wasn't prepared for what she found in this fourteen room house. The fact the house was so close to the orchard, and the squirrels so numerous, plus the house being vacant for three years, the squirrels and bats had taken over in the walls and attic. The first night we spent in the new house was a nightmare. The following month almost put mother in the hospital, as she tried to put that vacant house back in order. Dad, in the meantime, was unaware of the chaos, as he was back in Detroit working in the factory.

That summer turned out to be the high point of my life so far. When I began school and acquainted with boys my age, and in particular with Joe, who became my best friend. He knew all the local places of interest to boys our age. The first thing he showed me was the swimming hole; it was a wide place in Otter creek, about fifteen feet from one bank to the other and four feet deep. He taught me how to swim using the dog paddle stroke. I was elated the first time I paddled across the creek without touching bottom, and when I made my first dive and came up on the opposite bank.

During one of my exploring trips along the bank of the creek, I spotted a school of fish lying in the shade of an overhanging willow tree. I rushed home and on to Joe's to see if he had any line or hooks. His grandad said, "Those fish are suckers and you will waste your time with fish hooks."

We watched as he made several brass wire snares and he instructed us to put them on a pole. "Now you will be able to reach over the bank and slowly slip the snare over their heads, then jerk

3

the pole up to tighten the snare." We were so eager it took awhile before we got the nack of doing it properly. The first few times the snare cut the fish in half, or we lifted too high and our fish would be tangled in the willow branches. This was a lot of fun, until we took them home to mother.

All she said was, "I can't cook them like that, go and clean them."

When we tried eating them we soon learned about sucker bones. This knowledge rather dimmed our future fishing trips along with the cleaning.

On our way home from school one day Joe took me into a dairy farm where his dad was cultivating corn; the owner was just putting his cows into the milking barn. It was the first time I had seen the modern stanchions for holding cows in the stalls. Joe helped the owner by closing the stanchions as the cows put their heads through.

The owner, Mr. Price, heard me telling Joe that I had learned to milk back in Maidstone and he turned to me and asked, "Walter, would you like to try milking one of my cows?" When I hesitated, he said, "You can try one that doesn't kick, how about it?"

So I proceeded to show off my milking skills, but I thought that cow would never run out of milk. I had never seen that much milk from one cow.

Mr. Price laughed and asked how old I was. When I told him ten years, he said, "Well, I don't know any local boy your age that can do as well." After a pause he asked me, "Would you like to earn some money before and after school by coming in each morning on the way to school to stir the milk in the cans to cool and again after school as well as the evening milking?"

I said I would like to try it, so he took us into the milk house. This was a stone building with cold spring water running through a stone and concrete trough. The milk cans were submerged in the trough and he stirred the milk with a long-handled paddle. My job would be to keep the milk in motion until the natural animal heat had cooled. This procedure was required by the Borden Milk Company, to bring the milk up to proper test.

I took the job and was payed fifty cents a day. I soon learned that milk tasted much better when cooled this way, rather than

4

allowing it to cool slow. Also, when I arrived at the milk house in the morning, the milk cans from the previous night would have as much as six inches of cream on top. I would drink a small dipper of cream before I began my work, and this certainly gave me energy that helped to carry me through my long day.

Some times I would milk one or two cows while I was waiting for Mr. and Mrs. Price to bring the milk to the milk house, and I usually received a bonus for this. There were no milking machines or even hydro in that area, and they were milking forty-six cows. Due to the war it was very difficult for them to hire anyone, so no doubt my small contribution must have been greatly appreciated.

One day Mr. Price asked me, ''How would you like to work steady during the summer holidays?'' Then he added, ''I can pay you two-fifty a day.''

When I told mother and dad of my offer dad said, ''Well, first I would like to meet Mr. Price.'' Then dad went over one weekend and after talking with the Prices, he agreed to my working there.

I got along fine and was eventually milking as many as eight cows night and morning. During the period of putting in the hay and alfalfa, my job was driving a horse on the fork lift or slings, that took the hay off the hay wagon up into the hay mow or stack. When they were thrashing grain, I operated the straw blower. When we were blowing the straw in the mow inside the barns, I soon got sick from the dust. That had been one of my health problems in Maidstone. In fact my nasal problems had greatly improved here in Burgessville.

I was back on the job in two days but from then on I was very careful and avoided the straw blower when it was inside the barn. When the corn began to get high, I used a single horse cultivator between the rows. I got along really well with Mr. and Mrs. Price, and they treated me like their own son. They were also thoughtful enough to keep our home supplied with milk, butter and eggs.

When it was time to pick fruit in our own orchard, I was needed at home to help my mother and Ferne and had to quit my job at the Price's. It was an old orchard and had not been properly cared for during the war; however, it produced much more than we could use ourselves. Of course the birds and squirrels took their share, and were welcome to it. Dad was forced to shoot a number of squirrels, as they were a real nuisance. They were beautiful grey squirrels with a huge bushy tail, but they had taken over the house in its three year vacancy and made such a racket between the walls it was impossible to sleep. They probably resented us as "THEE" interlopers. Nature abhors a vacuum and the squirrels were just filling in the void left by humans. And in the true sense of the word, they did have squatter's rights and they did all in their power to hang on to those rights. All the noise they made may have been just their way of saying "We were first, YOU get out."

The last week in October, dad stopped in Woodstock on his way home to settle the final closing with the realtor. You can imagine our surprise when dad came home and said, "Well, I have sold the farm!" We children did not know all that our parents may have discussed between themselves. Mother may have given an ultimatum. She was living a very lonely life with three small children; a fourteen room house that needed extensive cleaning; her work was endless and dad was in Detroit most of the time.

Not comprehending all this at the time, it was really a very sad day for me, as I had enjoyed this place so much and learned so much. However, I did know it had been extremely rough on mother with dad away so much. Ferne, being older, had missed her Maidstone friends. And as I look back now I realized dad would have never made a farmer. His entire life had been factory work. He started young to be a brass finisher, making the fittings for ships. Later, he was a self-taught pattern maker; eventually a tool and die maker. He managed to stay in the tool and die department at Ford's until he was past seventy years of age. They permitted him to work from a stool.

I had one experience of trapping before we moved away. That entire area was over-run with ground hogs, and more so during the war years, as fewer hunters were available to keep them under control. They were a nuisance to farmers and their numerous holes in the fields were a hazard to horses and cattle.

On this occasion Joe and I decided to trap some. He came over with one of his dad's traps and we set it at one of the holes where we had seen a ground hog duck in. We looked at it several times without success, then one morning as we approached the trap we not only saw a skunk but we could smell it long before we got close. We decided we would kill it with stones, as we couldn't get close enough with a club; but we misjudged and both got some spray before we had succeeded in killing it.

We were so excited we struck up the road proudly carrying our catch, still in the trap. Several people passed us in their horse and buggy holding their noses, even the horse shied away from us. When we got home, mother was already outside to meet us. "Get to the barn and change," was our homecoming greeting. Later she informed me, "That is the beginning and the end of your trapping!"

However, she was wrong as future events in my life will reveal.

The Hesman clan at Burgessville, Ontario, 1919.
Walter was ten years of age at the time.

7

CHAPTER 2

BACK IN THE CITY AGAIN

We arrived back in Windsor November 8th and the next day was my eleventh birthday, 1919. My cousin Orval, who I had not seen much of in four years, came by and informed me the Border Cities Star had a paper route open.

The circulation department had asked him to find them a good boy and I was his choice. Sitting on the crossbar of his bike he pedalled us to the office and I was hired.

I handled 70 papers and the route was the full length of Goyeau Street and I pedalled happily on my Black Beauty bike that dad had bought used for $25.00. The tires were a tubeless type filled with some kind of glue that was supposed to plug a leak. That was the last time dad had to spend money on me.

I managed to clothe myself and occasionally had a little money in the bank. Although Orval was three years older than I we became very close chums. Most of our week-ends were spent across the Detroit River by ferry boat to the amusement park known as Electric Park, located at the entrance to Belle Isle Bridge. Belle Isle was also a great place to spend a week-end canoeing on the canals. A number of the more romantic adults stored their fancy decorated canoes on the island, and had them equipped real plush with fancy cushions and victrolas.

At our tender age we looked on with envy as the couples glided by, reclining on the cushions listening to their soft music drifting out over the canals. With drugs, alcohol and raucous music how different the scene and sound would be today.

On some occasions, a group of the most daring would rent canoes and go out beyond the canal barriers, paddling out into the freighter ship channel to ride the swells as the ships passed. Knowing what I do now about canoes, we were darn lucky we never had an accident, and I realize how very foolish we were and the danger we were in. However, those were pleasant times when hot dogs and hamburgers with real meat cost five cents as well as coke and soda pop.

Another special treat while in Detroit was Vernors Gingerale plant, located at the bottom of Woodward Avenue across from the ferry boat dock. I wonder if their famous sign is still on the river front where it can be seen from Windsor.

I don't think anyone ever managed to match their sodas they served in their spacious lounge. They were so busy on week-ends you had to buy tickets from cashiers in a booth and waiters served you like they do in taverns today. You had a choice of nickel or dime servings. Then you boarded the ferry boat for a leisurely quiet trip across the river to home. Today they drive across through the tunnel but it isn't as relaxing although it is faster.

In the spring of 1920 I was offered the chance to set up a news stand at the main gate of the new Ford Plant in Ford City, to handle the Detroit Free Press paper, a morning paper like our Globe and Mail as it published all the sports results and stock market news. This meant leaving home at 5:00 a.m., riding my bike to the plant gate, then setting up a box with change, so the men in a hurry to punch the time clock could make their own change. The were docked a full half hour if they punched their card after the bell rang.

The first morning the plant opened I only handled 30 papers. As the different departments became active, my sales increased to 300 within two weeks. I was usually at the gate by 6:30 a.m. and the early bird men who wanted the late race results were always waiting for me. The gates opened at 7:00 a.m. and the bell would ring at 7:30. During that half hour I passed out 300 papers that cost me 3 cents each and I would collect from 5 cents to 25 cents for each paper, depending on how much time each man had left to get to his particular time clock to punch in, before the 7:30 bell. Many men came in on the run the last ten minutes and dropped whatever coin they had in hand without stopping for change, as some had to travel up to half a mile to their time clock. I really believe that was the most money I made in such a short time.

As soon as the gates were closed I would pick up and head for the chinese restaurant on Druillard Road to have my much-needed breakfast. This always consisted of a piece of Boston cream pie about 3 inches thick. Thus fortified I would ride off across Ford City and Walkerville to my school in Windsor.

I missed all the before and after school activities, as my morning Free Press and Windsor paper at night after school kept me on the jump. However, all this bicycle riding kept me in better shape than many who took in all the school activities. I don't think the Boston cream pie contributed a darn thing, except fill my belly.

When our annual track and field meet was held, I took the medal for the 100 yard dash, the broad jump, high jump and won the start of the relay race to enable our class to win it. At the end of the meet our coach asked me why I did not turn out for practice after school. He said he was surprised to see me competing in so many events and felt I could benefit with some coaching, as he felt I had over done it that day and had not cooled off properly.

My cousin Orval had been a news boy for years, not only with a paper route, but he also handled the Detroit Sunday papers as well as his regular customers and had a good corner stand near the Ferry Dock. He had saved regularly and had a good savings account. We both earned extra money doing special favors for some of our elderly customers. We must remember there were other news media at that time and we did have a little competition to keep us on our toes.

When Orval bought a new CCM bike, I suddenly decided to have one too. Mother and dad were away for a week, so Orval and I rode off to Maidstone. I managed to sell my bike for $25.00 the same as dad had paid for it. Orval did not want to ride back to Windsor alone, so I rode his cross bar the 14 miles on a gravel road.

I was almost a cripple when we got back to Windsor, but the next morning I was at the CCM dealer when he opened his door and purchased my new bike for $65.00, using the $25.00 as my down payment.

I rode directly to one of my paper customers who made homemade donuts. I had delivered some for her before and now with my new ''wheels'' I made a deal with her. I asked for a commission of 5 cents a dozen for all I could sell. By soliciting all my paper customers I managed to pay off my bike in two weeks. In fact I had got so many donut customers, my supplier had to get help. I purchased a wire basket for the front and rear of the bike to help carry the donuts and my papers. I was forced to taper off the project when school started again.

The last two years I attended public school I took a summer job with a negro tailor on Lincoln Road in Walkerville. He was a former master tailor in the British Navy in Bermuda. At that time the City of Walkerville had a by-law which forbid negroes to live in the city. However, they gave Mr. Baisden a special permit to operate his tailor shop and to take in dry cleaning and pressing within the city, providing he did not have his residence there. The majority of his customers were among Walkerville's professional men — the doctors, lawyers, etc. They came to him to have their suits made. Also the Dowler's men's store had a branch there and depended on Mr. Baisden for all suit alterations.

There was a garage across the street that serviced a number of bootlegger's cars, such as installing overload springs and special compartments. The owners also came to Mr. Baisden to have their suits made and their family dry cleaning done.

Rumor had it that one group had a pipe line running across the river from Hiram Walker's distillery to Detroit; and from what I was to learn later about our law enforcement, it was not hard to believe the rumor.

In the beginning my job was to pick up and deliver with my bike, later I learned to use his steam press and was soon doing complicated things like accordian pleated skirts and dresses as well as men's suits. He also taught me to do simple alterations on pants and vests for Dowler's store.

Mr. Baisden made my first long pants suit out of some excellent material he acquired from one of his customers. Bell bottom trousers were in style, but I only wore them on one moonlight boat trip to Boblo Island and back. I decided that they were not for me. Mr. Baisden very graciously did them over more conservatively. I wore that suit for the last time twelve years later.

Before I end this period I must mention that he was very strict with me about my work but he was also very kind and generous. It was not unusual for him to say, "We have had a good week, Walter, I think we deserve a bonus." He would smile and show those pearly teeth and give me an extra bonus.

11

Mr. Baisden decided to buy a Model T Ford Coupe in spite of the fact he was too nervous to drive it, so he gave me permission to drive it.

My dad also had a Model T and I had learned to drive it in our alley at first, then gradually out into traffic. I was soon making most of the deliveries with the car instead of the bike for Mr. Baisden and he even offered to let me have his car for a week-end or evening when he learned Orval and I had something special on.

One holiday week he asked me, "How would you like to drive me to Niagara Falls?" Naturally I quickly agreed, before he could change his mind!

We closed the shop Saturday at noon and arrived at the Falls early Sunday morning. After touring the Falls and the surrounding area, he suggested we tour one of the power stations. At the entrance we were stopped by a guard who refused to let Mr. Baisden enter because he was a negro even though he was a well-dressed good-looking gentleman.

Although I was only 13, I really told that guard off. Mr. Baisden never pushed himself in places he felt might reject his colour. What made me so mad, I was sure the guard was an immigrant himself. Mr. Baisden, coming from Bermuda, was as British as the guard.

This incident spoiled our trip some, however, it meant a great deal to me to say I had seen the Falls. The trip alone was worth it just to see the beautiful fruit orchards along the way. You really saw the country in those days before the Freeways and their high speed.

Mr. Baisden became ill that fall and had to close his shop. Later he opened a small tailor shop in Windsor's negro section. I stopped in to see him occasionally, but he was not well.

They found him dead one day early in the morning in his work shop. He always talked of going back to Bermuda and hoped that I could make a trip there some time. It had always pleased me that he had been respected by the City Council in Walkerville, as he certainly deserved every bit of this respect, as he was a fine gentleman. He was the only negro business man in the city.

12

CHAPTER 3

I QUIT SCHOOL

I graduated from public school when I was fourteen and I started my first year in high school at the Windsor Collegiate on Goyean Street. The Principal was a man named Mr. Hooper.

In this school the teachers of various subjects rotated room to room instead of the usual mass movement of students to different class rooms. The algebra teacher for my class was a Miss Kennedy; a short, plump, heavy footed woman. So solidly did she put down her heels that the sound of her coming was clearly audible well before she opened the door.

Usually there was a lapse of about ten minutes between the previous teacher's departure and the arrival — click-click-click of Miss Kennedy. Ten unsupervised minutes for mischief to reign among the students. The principal cut-up was a boy named Johnny.

On the day of my moment of truth — and departure — Johnny started some horseplay with another boy called Fat Parsons. They wound up chasing around and throwing books at each other. As Johnny ran by he grabbed my algebra book and heaved it at Fat Parsons, who ducked. The book went sailing out the window to land in the school yard, three floors below. This happened just as the noise of Miss Kennedy's heels announced her imminent arrival.

By the time she entered the room everyone was back at their desks. As usual, there was no visible sign of all the hoorah that had been going on before.

Hand on doorknob, Miss Kennedy said, "Class take out your algebra." Looking around with sharp eyes she noticed my book was not out. "Walter, why don't you have your book out?"

"Miss Kennedy, I can't find it," I replied.

13

Without further comment she told us to turn to a certain problem and work on it. By now she was going up and down the aisles between desks checking the work of individuals.

Coming down my aisle she approached from behind me. She wordlessly brought her fist down with a hard rabbit punch to the back of my neck, at the same time shouting, ''I told you to take out your algebra book.''

Startled out of my wits, and jumping to my feet and just as loud as she, I retorted, ''Don't ever do that again.''

I guess she thought I was going to hit her, for she jumped back and ordered me to the principal's office. Mr. Hooper told me to wait outside until Miss Kennedy arrived.

I cooled my heels until she had finished the algebra class, and came sailing into Hooper's office. What they talked about I had no idea. I was never included in their discussion and at no point was I asked one question or for a word of explanation.

In due course Hooper emerged and told me I must give an apology to Miss Kennedy. I told him, ''I would if there was any reason to do so, but under the circumstances I feel I do not owe her that courtesy.''

Still without asking me to explain, Hooper said, ''You either apologize or pack your books.''

''In that case,'' I replied, ''I had better pack my books.'' Miss Kennedy began to sniffle and weep. Hooper suggested I sit for 15 minutes and reconsider. I refused. It would have made no difference as I did not owe her an apology.

Let me say that, never at any time had I run contrary to my parents, nor would I have done so at school except for the circumstances. When I told my parents the story, my father said: ''If you are sure you are right, then you made the right decision.'' I had good, compassionate and very understanding parents.

There was a sequel to the incident a couple of years later. Driving a taxi I was sent, on a day of teaming rain, to pick up a passenger at a Giles Blvd. address. The fare was Miss Kennedy. She remembered me and began to cry and bend my ear about how sorry she now was; that she had learned the real story about the algebra book. I told her dryly she was years too late in her caring.

Anyway, this simple episode probably was the main turning point in my life, sending me down paths undreamed of.

Two days after leaving school I was downtown in Windsor and noticed a sign in the Star Taxi office asking for drivers. I applied and when asked my age I lied saying that I was nineteen. The owner took me over to the police station and I was issued a chauffeur's license. The fact that I had been a newsboy and knew the city well was a big help.

The Star Taxi was owned by Hector Goulet. It was a cheap outfit, using the old Durant-built Star touring car with side curtains. They operated with a flat 50 cent rate anywhere in the Windsor city limits for two passengers and 25 cents for extra passengers.

I was soon to learn that my education about life was just beginning. Detroiters were thirsty for the easy access to liquor and night life that the Border Cities afforded. Law enforcement, as far as liquor, prostitution and gambling was concerned, was very lax.

The taxi stand was on a lot behind the downtown street car terminal on the corner of Sandwich and Ferry Streets. Much of our business came from people who had missed the last street car or people from the liquor joints, who had no other way home. Sometimes it was difficult to find out where to take them, and would have to take them to the Police Station.

One of the my early experiences that really disgusted me was the time I picked up a couple at one of the Riverside Road Houses. I recognized the man as head of our children's Aid Society and the girl I knew from public school. When we got back to Windsor he wanted me to take the passed-out girl to a certain house and take her in. When I refused he first cussed me, then pleaded. Finally, I drove up to the house and knocked; a man who said he was a boarder came out and helped me carry her in. It was 2 a.m. It wasn't long before nothing surprised me and I was prepared to expect anything.

Windsor in 1924 was bordered by the cities of Sandwich on the west, Walkerville and Ford City on the east. They were referred to as The Border Cities. Since then they have become amalgamated with Windsor.

People coming from Detroit to Windsor came by Ferry boat, as the bridge and tunnel were not built until later. On the holiday week-ends it was not unusual to have cars lined up from the ferry dock to points completely outside the city, waiting to return to Detroit.

Some serious problems were created especially for families with babies and small children. Cars in line ran out of gas. Some cars over heated and in many cases paid gasoline vendors $5.00 a gallon, rather than lose their place in line. The hustlers who worked the line up demanded and got high prices for diapers, baby food, etc.; in fact, many items that were needed by those compelled to wait all night, as Windsor stores were closed on Sunday.

My driving for Star Taxi was very brief, due to an episode with a prostitute and her pimp. There was a bootlegging joint called Tom's Place, upstairs over the street car terminal, with the entrance to the stairway right next to our stand.

On this occasion, I was sitting in our office about 2 a.m. when I heard a ruckus outside. It turned out to be two very drunk prostitutes and their escorts from the Sunny Side Road House in LaSalle, west of Windsor. I learned later the girls had accompanied their escorts to the ferry dock, and had been left at the terminal where they had wound up their drinking at Tom's Place.

The girls got into an argument that turned into a real free for all brawl. They went at each other tooth and nail, tearing clothes off. One actually pulled the other out onto the street car tracks by the hair.

By the time a policeman came on the scene and helped get them separated they were no longer recognizable. Someone helped one girl back up the stairs, the other one left with the policeman. Apparently she got in touch by phone with the other girl's pimp, who turned out to be a rough guy from Detroit. Much of the prostitution and speakeasy joints were controlled by Detroit pimps and Montreal bootleggers.

Everything quieted down until the factory men were all coming and going at the street car terminal between 5:30 and 6:00 a.m. Suddenly there was another commotion on the stairs from Tom's Place. The girl who had been taken up there after the fight was found by her pimp, who had been given some wild story on the phone by the other gal.

16

He proceeded to beat hell out of his girl and practically threw her down the stairs from Tom's Place. Even with the help of factory workers trying to stop him, he managed to push her into my cab, which was first on the stand.

Poking me in the back (with what could have been a gun) he yelled, ''Get going buddy and FAST!'' I didn't think this was the time to argue so I started moving, but the factory men tried to hold my car. For some reason, the driver that was behind me got his bumper up against mine and he pushed me onto the street.

At the same time the pimp was knocking workmen off the taxi running board with his fists. There was a great deal of yelling and commotion as we proceeded up Ferry Street. Suddenly, I heard what sounded like two shots. At the same time the pimp was yelling and poking me in the back, ''Keep going, don't stop.'' I kept going. Ferry Street ended and I turned west out of sight of the terminal crowd.

The pimp was in a rage and began slapping the girl again. I shouted back to him. ''Leave her alone!'' and when he continued, I kept watching and hoping for the police.

As I came to the county court house and jail in Sandwich, I pulled over to the curb, intending to run in to get help. However, he anticipated my action and grabbed my arm. As I was close to the police I became brave and told him, ''This is as far as I am going.'' He argued and convinced me he would not slap her around anymore, so we proceeded on out to LaSalle and the Sunnyside Road House. It was closed.

In order to get in he had to boost me up onto the porch roof where I was able to climb through the gal's bedroom window and open the front door from the inside. He gave me a $5.00 bill for the 12 mile trip and I returned to the taxi stand.

Several police were waiting for me. It turned out that the shots had been fired in the air by a young officer. He had then called for the police flyer and proceeded to give chase, but in the wrong direction. Someone told him that the girl was from Sunnyside Hotel Road House, but the driver of the flyer mistook it to be the Riverside Hotel Road House, which was on the opposite side of Windsor.

The newspaper that night headlined the story as a 60-70 mile an hour chase. When in fact, my old Star car was going in the op-

17

posite direction and it had trouble trying to exceed 40 to 45 miles per hour.

When I told the police where I had taken the pimp, they took me along in the police flyer and drove out to pick them up. After arriving back at the Windsor Police Station, the senior officers took the couple inside. Just as I was about to return to the taxi stand, the young officer said, ''You had better come in too.''

The desk sergeant booked all of us, including the driver who had pushed my car off the stand. The charge against me and the other driver was assisting escape and resisting an officer. We were taken to the County Jail in Sandwich and we were searched. They found heroin on the other driver. His name was Art Boucher. He had come to Windsor from Montreal.

I was permitted to call home and my dad came with a lawyer. After hearing the story the lawyer soon arranged for my bail. When the case came before the magistrate, I was put on the stand as a witness and I told exactly what I had seen happen.

Then the prostitute, who was still showing bruises, refused to testify against her pimp. He got away with disturbing the peace. Art Boucher was remanded for sentence and treatment. The charge against me was dismissed and my chauffeur's license cancelled when they learned my true age. The magistrate as well gave me a short lecture.

About a week later, at the suggestion of another driver, who told me it would be a good idea if I went out west on the harvest excursion, I decided to do it. He gave me an address in Saskatchewan — a small grain elevator town called Central Butte. In 1977 C.B.S. televised a program using Central Butte as a typical western elevator town.

CHAPTER 4

GO WEST YOUNG MAN

I talked over the harvest trip with Orval, as he had just graduated from Windsor Technical School and had no immediate job to go to. He decided to come west with me. The trip turned out to be a real adventure.

We went to the C.N.R. ticket office to purchase our harvest excursion tickets. The rate for harvestors was $15.00 to Winnipeg, Manitoba, then 1½ cents a mile to points west.

The address I had been given by the taxi driver was a Mr. Alder, in a place called Central Butte, Saskatchewan. It was about 60 miles north of Moose Jaw. We boarded some old homesteader's coaches at Windsor that were not much better than cattle cars. Each set of double seats faced each other. There was a pull-down bunk overhead, with no mattress. We used the bunk to store our duffel.

By the time we got north of Toronto, we had over 30 other coaches hooked onto our train. As we got further north and west, I'll swear we frequently pulled onto sidings to let fast freight trains proceed ahead of us. The trip was a real experience for Orval and I. Many of the men had made the trip on previous harvests, and knew what to expect. The harvesters were made up from all walks of life, and also included a percentage of screwballs.

It took us a full week to get to Winnipeg. From Sudbury on west we sat on some sidings for what seemed like hours waiting for freights to pass in both directions. There were times we got off and picked blueberries as well as visiting with repair gangs along the track. At some sidings they announced how much time we had to go into the town to get food.

One bad problem was that several harvest trains had already preceded us through these northern towns and they had apparently had some rough characters on board. Because of this we found most stores and Chinese restaurants locked or boarded up. Some of them had not only been raided, but wrecked as well.

It was easy to understand, as even on our train it was all pandemonium when several hundred men suddenly jumped off a train, and all trying to be served at once. Worst of all was, that some men got hold of liquor; of course when they got drunk they were apt to do anything and none of it good.

On one occasion several mounties boarded our tain. They were looking for someone who had thrown a bottle out of a window killing someone. This may have only been a rumor.

After our arrival in Winnipeg many harvestors took off in different directions. Orval and I stocked up with food before going further, just in case our eating problems were to continue. However, when we purchased our ticket for the trip to Central Butte (our destination) we found we would be travelling on a regular passenger train as far as Moose Jaw.

The farther west we travelled the more drastic was the change in scenery. No trees of any kind and mile after mile of grain fields or prairie. There were farmers at every train stop trying to hire men. Most harvesters seemed to prefer to go further west, or were like us, knew where they were going.

The farmers were offering many inducements, such as good accommodation at $5.00 to $7.00 per day, with a bonus if you stayed, etc.

We began to see farmers using from four to eight horses to pull their equipment. Occasionally a huge steam tractor was pulling a multiple breaking plow. This was something we had never seen before back home.

After changing trains at both Regina and again at Moose Jaw, we arrived in Moose Jaw on a Saturday. This was very unfortunate as there would be no trains to Central Butte until Monday or Tuesday.

While we were debating where we would stay, we met four other fellows who were going to an elevator town next to Central Butte.

So Walter, the taxi driver, got busy contacting cab drivers, who advised me it was some 80 miles to Butte. One driver seemed anxious to make the trip. After he quoted his charged for the trip I was able to get a refund from the railroad on all our tickets. At a cost of $5.00 each we made Butte that day and saved money.

However, the taxi turned out to be as slow as our train. The overloaded taxi blew four tires before we got there. At one point the driver had to hitch a ride to get a tire. We had broken down along side of a huge wheat field that had been cut. While our driver was away we all started stooking grain. I am sure the farmer knew that some green horns had been in his field. (To stock grain, after the binder cuts and ties the sheaves, we picked them up and put them in piles of four to eight sheaves in each stook to dry until picked up.)

The Stook wagons at Central Butte, Saskatchewan, 1924.

CHAPTER 5

ARRIVAL IN CENTRAL BUTTE

It was late when we arrived in Butte, but the town was still very active; the entire town was on Main Street, the only one.

It was obvious that most of the men on the street were harvesters and most had trouble walking straight. After a few inquiries we located Mr. Alder playing poker in the rear of one of the two Chinese restaurants. He seemed pleased that we had come and told the chinaman to bring us a drink.

Orval declined and had a coke; my drink turned out to be Chinese whiskey, very red and potent. It washed out our trip in a hurry. Alder sent us to a hotel and said he would pick us up in the morning. The hotel was crude but comfortable, and after what we had endured, it was a luxury to get into a bath and bed down. We had not changed our clothes for over a week except our socks in station washrooms.

Alder never came for us until noon, so we had a good and needed rest. His car was an open McLaughlin Buick touring car with no top (seven passenger). The road to the farm was just a wagon wheel trail through wheat fields and open prairie; I never saw a fence or a tree, just sage brush. We dodged badger and gopher holes in the road all the way. It was fifteen miles to his holdings. Orval was already homesick.

When we arrived, the only buildings were a small run-down house, a stable for eight horses and a lean-to shed for implements. Alder had told us on the way that the couple looking after the place were much like share croppers.

We were informed we would take our meals in the house with Art and Betty, but our sleeping quarters was a stall in the stable, consisting of a thick bed of straw with a mattress. The horses had been kept out on the prairie all summer and would not be kept in until after the harvest. So this gave us exclusive rights such as it was and we were not jumping for joy because of them.

Our first job was to stook wheat. Art was going to start cutting grain the next day, using a Case tractor on a larger binder. Our pay was to be $6.00 a day for stooking and $7.00 for thrashing. This also included our meals. Alder jokingly said, "Boys, I won't charge you for your beds." We had been told on the harvest train to expect these kind of accommodations, so it came as no shock.

I knew for sure that Orval was not going to stay. It was his first time away from home and he had never had any experience on a farm. He informed me the first night he was going back as soon as he could get a ride back to Butte. Orval could be independent. He had money in the bank.

Betty's meals were O.K., and I soon found that I had no trouble sleeping in my stable bedroom. After a day's work in the fresh air I could have slept on a board. I also appreciated the experience that I was getting and the fact I was on my own.

Alder came back with three more men on Wednesday. As well, he had brought supplies for Betty and clean blankets for the men. He drove out to where we were working to pick up Orval. It was a very hot day and we had been drinking too much water. He had warned us not to drink too much until we became accustomed to the local water, as it sometimes made newcomers sick.

He suggested that he was not in favour of stooking grain during extremely hot periods of the day and told us to work a few hours in the morning and again in the cool of the evening. We were informed that it had reached 110 in the sun that day.

Two of the men Alder brought with him were brothers from Prince Edward Island, the other was a Polish immigrant. The brothers, Roy and Stan, were good fellows to work with, and they taught me how to use a fork to stook grain. This was their third year on the harvest. They had been lobster fishermen at home and their father had a small fox farm on Prince Edward Island.

This farm in Butte was considered to have modern equipment for that period. A stook loader that operated similar to our Ontario hay loader, except the stook loader loaded from the side of the wagon, and dumping the entire stook at one time into a wire rack on the wagon. Some large stooks would have as many as 20 sheafs. While this saved a lot of heavy lifting to load, it was much harder to pitch off into the separator, as the sheafs were badly tangled in the rack. The Case tractor was used to power the separator.

Art, the sharecropper, continued to cut the grain as much as 14 hours a day, as long as weather permitted, while the four of us tried to keep up with our stooking. I had done some of this in Ontario, where a 5 acre field would be considered large. When I could see no end in sight here, it appeared we would never finish but just go on forever.

However, there was some diversion because prairie chickens were so plentiful we could kill them by throwing our forks like a boomerang to knock them out. Roy taught me how to get close to them by walking in a circle and gradually closing in. If they were in a tight group, sometimes he got several.

Wild life was plentiful; bird and water fowl particularly; also jack rabbits, hares, coyotes, badger, a few antelope and millions of gophers. The badger and gopher holes were a real hazard to horses and cattle. Actually much of this wild life was a real nuisance to farmers and ranchers.

Ducks and geese raided large sections of the grain fields. Some evenings, ducks would fly overhead by many thousands, as they flew from grain fields to the ponds or sloughs for the night, to avoid land predators.

It was a temptation to shoot them and I yielded; Art loaned me his double barrel shot gun and I was in business. I hid in the marsh and as a large flight of ducks came in to land, I pointed the gun at them and accidently pulled both triggers. The next thing I knew I was on my back with a bloody nose and two ducks plunked down beside me. That was the end of my using a shot gun.

One week-end Alder drove in with friends from Regina. He asked Roy and I if we would flush ducks off the sloughs while his friends hid in blinds. There was continuous shooting as flocks flew back and forth between sloughs.

I was really impressed watching the two Labrador retrievers fetching the dead and dying ducks in off the sloughs. It turned out to be a real slaughter. When they were all loaded into the back seat of the 7 passenger Buick, it was full.

While it appeared to be a ridiculous slaughter, Alder informed me that due to the war years and lack of hunters, it had become necessary to reduce their numbers, as they had increased to the point they were heavily damaging crops, causing much loss of grain.

I know they still darkened the sky some evenings as they flew over. I never saw water fowl as plentiful again, until 1948 and 1949, when I made trips to Fort Albany on James Bay. I often wonder now, after 52 years have gone by, if ducks are still as plentiful in the West?

Once the wheat was cut and stooked we prepared for thrashing. Alder came in with a man to be our engineer named Ed Yerkie and another fellow called Phil.

While Roy and I rounded up the horses and broncos, Ed and Phil prepared the separator and wagons, which were to be pulled by the horses. Some of the broncos were really wild and it took much time to get them accustomed to the noise of the equipment. We had a couple of runaways and smashed equipment before they settled down.

They let the colts run along beside their mothers while we were working. Many times they interfered with our driving by trying to nurse the mare while we were moving. It was lunch on the run. Also the mares fretted when the colts were out of sight; they didn't relish being working mothers.

Art selected two old mares for me to drive, when I told him I was unable to cope with the broncos. However, it turned out I still had to cope with the interference of the colts; they were cute but a headache to me.

Eventually, we got the thrashing going fairly smooth. We had to get up, feed and harness horses at 4:30 a.m.; then have our big breakfast and we were usually in the field loading at 7:00 a.m. weather permitting. "It usually was." About 9:30 Betty or her helper would bring out our mid-morning lunch, on a two-wheel cart. The separator was not shut down; as each wagon come in with a load, a spare man would take the driver's place to throw off the load while he had lunch. We did shut down at noon to feed our horses and ourselves.

We worked steady until dark, except for our mid-afternoon lunch. The first few days of this hard work and long hours was rough, but gradually I did get used to it. I can assure you I had no trouble sleeping on my stall bed. I was almost asleep before I hit it!

Ed Yerkie, our engineer, was from Commanda, Ontario, near North Bay, about 60 miles south and west. He really did amaze me. He would grease the separator, check the belts and service and fuel the tractor. Unless a belt broke, he had nothing to do except keep fuel in the tractor.

He would lean with his head in his hands and elbows on an oil drum and fall asleep. We finally started to make bets that he would fail to wake up in time. However, the only time he failed was on one occasion when we had to move to another location. Laughing, we left the tractor running and removed the belt from the separator, before he woke up.

On another occasion we stayed in due to weather, and we were relating to each other where we came from and what it was like in our area. Phil said he was from London, Ontario, Roy and Stan from P.E.I. and Joe was an immigrant from Poland. Ed told us about the excellent deer hunting around his homestead at Commanda, and invited Phil and me to stop at his place for the hunt in November. (From this invitation I eventually would come across the site where I built my lodge.) I often wonder what would have happened had I not accepted? In life, we never know what lies around the corner in making a simple decision.

The wheat crop was a good one that year. When the thrashing was over, Alder asked for a couple of men to stay and haul grain to the elevators in Butte. Phil and I volunteered until the end of October. We wanted to be free to accept Ed's invitation in November.

The only hard work was shovelling the grain into the grain tanks on the wagons. The grain had been piled out in the open, as there were not enough sheds to store the crop, and it would spoil if left too long exposed to the weather. In fact there was considerable spoilage in wet weather.

It was about 15 miles to Butte, and we were hauling with a four-horse team, which I personally found quite interesting. The daily trips also provided more study of the varied wild life; they being used to horses, paid little attention to the grain wagons. Frequently, I would see the coyotes in pursuit of rabbits; I know they caught them at times but I never did actually see it.

Roy and I managed to get a couple of badger while stooking. As soon as the badger saw us they would duck in if we got close, and would come out when we went back to work. Roy had learned in previous years to rush over and stand behind the hole entrance with his fork poised to strike. I would continue working and when the badger thought it was safe he would come to the entrance. At this point, Roy would block the hole with his fork tines and occasionally catch the badger around the neck.

Badgers are fierce fighters if caught away from their hole. They have been known to fight off a coyote. And they gave us a good bit of trouble, too.

The grain haul was over the third week in October, and, we made our preparations to return east.

A Swedish cook and her daughter prepared meals
in a wooden trailer pulled by horses.

Harvesters at Central Butte came West from Ontario
and Prince Edward Island.

27

CHAPTER 6

EAST TO COMMANDA AND DEER HUNT

The Trip back to North Bay was much faster and more comfortable, as we were travelling first class, blowing some of our hard-earned money.

At North Bay we took the south bound C.N.R. to Trout Creek Station arriving at 11:00 p.m. Oliver Moore's stage would be leaving at 7:00 a.m. for Commanda, Golden Valley, Arnstein and Port Loring. We spent the night at Hugo Evers Hotel; his father had been the original hotel keeper in Commanda, during the early river log drives, when the virgin pine of this area was floated all the way to Georgian Bay, through series of dams right from the head waters of the Pickerel and the Magnetawan Rivers. I was to hear many tales regarding these now famous log drives.

We met Oliver, the stage driver, at breakfast the next morning. He informed us, "Ed is not at Commanda, as I saw him in his shop at Loring." He finished his bacon and said, "Ed does blacksmith and machine shop work for the area lumber companies and his home is in Loring."

All this seemed strange to us as we were sure he had said his home was in Commanda; still, we had no choice but to take the stage to Loring and see Ed himself.

The stage stopped frequently along the way, as Oliver delivered purchases he had made for the settlers. Some of the people would be standing on the road waiting. Oliver also delivered messages and medicine from the only doctors in the area. Their offices were in Powassan about 9 miles north of Trout Creek. Dr. Harcourt and Dr. Delaine had all of the north part of the Parry Sound District and much of the Nipissing District to look after. Oliver said, "It is not unusual for them to travel over 40 miles by horse and buggy to attend a patient; and occasionally by horseback." How times have changed!

28

The stage was a covered Model T Ford truck which he could only use during the summer and dry months. He went on to explain, "I use horses and a covered wagon or sleigh during bad road periods. I keep several teams, which I use in relays by changing to a fresh team at my father's homestead at Golden Valley which is half way."

It was 46 miles from Loring to Trout Creek and Oliver, made three trips each way, out and back each week, if the weather permitted. There were many tales told about him and his stage trips, as he was noted for the lively horses he kept. He was also full of information as he knew everyone's business that travelled on his stage. If he didn't know he had his way of finding out. He would tell you something absolutely false and naturally most people were quick to correct him, telling him exactly what he had been trying to find out in the first place.

Our first mail stop was at Commanda P.O. It was in Ben Schwart's general store; the second was at Jim Hamilton's home in Bear Valley; the third was at Mel Cameron's store in Golden Valley. When we were half way to Arnstein we met the first car since leaving Trout Creek and it turned out to be Ed Yerkie, with his car loaded with furniture, etc.; he was taking it to his homestead about 5 miles south of Commanda, on the north road.

He had moved his family there the day before, but there was no room for us in his car. Oliver said he could take us back after he delivered the mail to Loring. When he came back he took us to what he said was the north road. (See map.) It was the road all the first lumbermen and settlers came in on before the railroad. It started at the Parry Sound harbour and ran north through Dunchurch to Maple Island and joined up with the Nipissing trail at Commanda.

The Nipissing trail was an original Indian trail that ran from Scotia Junction to Lake Nipissing. Early settlers came by boat to Parry Sound, then by ox cart up the north road, to eventually settle on their homesteads.

When Oliver left us off it had been snowing hard since noon, and now there was a good 4 inches of wet snow. That was the first snow of the season, October 23rd, 1924. He said, "This is a short and heavily timbered way to Ed's place, but not possible to travel by car and it is about 4 miles." Before we got there I was sure it was much further. It was the first house we came to and in the darkness and cold it was a very welcome sight. We were really grateful to get into a warm house and into dry footwear; we were not prepared to walk in wet snow. But best of all was the good home-cooked meal put on by Mrs. Yerkie.

Ed and his wife had three children, two girls and a boy. They made us feel so welcome, and it was great to be once again living in a comfortable home after our stable experience in Butte.

The Yerkies had homesteaded here years before and as Ed was mechanically inclined, he had set up a small portable steam-powered saw mill on a little lake on his property. Then later on when he moved to Loring, he had established his blacksmith shop along with the machine shop.

His skills were much in demand by all local lumbermen. He only returned to the homestead when he wanted to take out logs, which I was soon to learn, was his main reason for his inviting Phil and me for the deer hunt. He needed two men to help take out logs that winter.

The deer season was the first two weeks of November, and I learned that most everyone in the area stopped whatever they were doing to go deer hunting. A number of hunters from Southern Ontario came up for the hunt as well, having their own camps back in a remote area.

Deer were plentiful around Ed's place. The clearing of the land by the settlers after the war years and the recent removal of much mature pine plus extensive burned-out areas had permitted new growth, making ideal brousing for deer. It was not unusual to stand out on the porch at night and hear the snorting and clashing horns of bucks fighting during their rutting season.

A couple of days later deer season opened; October snow had disappeared leaving the ground bare. The only way to hunt, Ed explained, would be to make chases with some of us standing on deer runs. Herman showed Phil and me where to stand; Charlie and Ed picked their watches and Charlie's three boys made the chase.

I heard several shots and saw a deer coming in the distance. I froze, apparently having my first case of buck fever, and unable to get my gun up, the deer saw me and it turned off.

When the chaser came through they had a good laugh at my expense.

30

Charlie and Herman each got a deer, Phil had wounded one and Ed had gone with him following it, they found it dead at the foot of the hill. Charlie got his with a single shot 22 rifle. He said, "I use the 22 rifle because I don't like spoiling a lot of meat." I was to learn later that Charlie would not shoot at a running deer, taking a chance of destroying a large portion of meat, which was what he was hunting for.

The rest of that week the same group made several more organized chases each getting another deer. The younger boys and myself tried some still hunting covering miles. We startled several deer and fired a number of shots and did manage to kill a few porcupines which were numerous.

The highlight of the week was the hunter's dance at Commanda. There were more hunters around the community hall than local folks. Most of the action was outside where liquor was flowing freely and the participants absorbed enough to overcome their shyness to take part in the square dancing with much zeal. As a spectator I really enjoyed the square dances.

The hall could accommodate four square dance sets, each set consisted of four couples. They tried to follow the caller's directions and keep time to the fiddlers' music, but it was a series of confusion and stumbling, except for the few experienced couples, and their smoothness was nice to watch.

Naturally we had a couple of minor drinking brawls quickly brought under control by their friends. The fiddlers left the hall about 1:30 a.m. and we all headed for home. The five mile walk seemed more like ten. We were lucky to have Henry Yerkie's carbide head lamp to show us the way, as the road was very muddy. I had no desire to hunt the next day.

Before I left Commanda I took in a few more dances. After the Yerkie girls had given some home lessons on how to swing my partner and do the dosy-doe, I finally had nerve to try it in public and discovered it was my favourite type of dancing.

Living at the Yerkie's was much like home; Mrs. Yerkie was a good cook and housekeeper like my mother, and while the furniture was mainly home made, it was comfortable. Their three children were well behaved. Pearl, the eldest, was twelve and considerable help to her mother. She wasn't going to school while I was there, but her brother Clarence and two of Bill Yerkie's girls walked the five miles to Commanda school daily, excepting bad weather.

31

My wife Mary is one of a family of six girls and one boy who were born and raised three miles from the same school. Mary tells me that Charlie Yerkie had four daughters, Leta and Gertie were not around when I was at Ed's place. Mary says, "Leta never did attend school and Gertie came to school for the first time when she was 21 years old, and she sat with the first graders. The teacher, Mr. Simms, who, Mary says, was the best teacher Commanda school ever had made a special effort to teach Gertie to read and write.

The following September when the new term began, Gertie was missing. Her brothers told Mr. Simms that Gertie was now married.

During the winter and bad weather the children would often miss several days to a week of school, Mary tells me.

One thing I have observed during my time is that a school education alone does not always make one more intelligent than knowledge developed through practical experience.

Ed made it clear after the first week of the deer hunt that he wanted to work at his logging, which was the reason he had invited us there. So I settled down to logging and naturally I had a lot to learn. I won't go into detail regarding all the trials and tribulations I encountered on the job, that would be a book in itself. Ed had patience with me more so than Charlie's sons, who delighted in making fun of my awkwardness. By observing old Charlie I soon learned to handle my axe and keep it sharp, so that I didn't have to spend so many evenings turning the grind stone while he or someone else sharpened my axe or fixed a broken handle.

Everything went along fairly well through the balance of November and most of December. I had my 16th birthday November 9th, and as Christmas approached I became more and more conscious of my growing home sickness, as this would be my first Christmas away from home.

Three days before Christmas I decided I was going home. Ed paid me off and I walked out to Commanda and took Oliver's stage to Trout Creek. The stage at that time was a sleigh with a caboose built onto it especially for the women passengers and pulled by a team of horses.

His headquarters and home was in Loring. During the winter months he would start from Loring with a fresh team and come as far as his father's homestead at Golden Valley and there he would change to a fresh team. When he reached Commanda he gave his team a quick feed of oats and watered them before going on to Trout Creek, where that team got a night's rest in the hotel stable to be ready for the return trip the next day.

There were many interesting tales about this stage trip; Oliver's lively and some times wild horses, severe weather and the number of interruptions between Trout Creek and along the road to Loring. So the time schedule for leaving and arriving on Moore's stage was quite flexible. Many people depended a great deal on Oliver. It was no wonder he knew so much about so many.

Getting back to my trip home for Christmas, I caught the midnight train to Toronto and was on my way!

Photo: The Highland Herald

The historic Commanda General Store Museum.

CHAPTER 7

HOME FOR CHRISTMAS

I arrived in Toronto early in the morning and had time to purchase some needed clothes before I took the train on to Windsor. I got off the train at the Walkerville Station, as it was only two miles from my home. I had $2.00. I felt rich! because of the valuable experience I now was master of and carried with me wherever I went and it was a light and happy load. No one could steal it from me.

Full of the joy of being home again, I sneakily slipped through one of the cellar windows, then creeping up the stairs to the kitchen where my surprised mother almost fainted, as I swept her in my arms.

It was a glorious and happy Christmas, one I shall never forget. There is no place like home and our loving parents and a child must go away to find this out. My mother was not a "liberated mother." Her career was her children and her home and she excelled in both. She was always THERE! Our home reflected her constant presence, spick and span and well-cooked meals and love!

After Christmas was over and I had made the rounds of visiting close relatives, I had to think about a job. Finding one was not easy, especially at my age, and with my qualifications. Driving was the only definite one I could say I had much experience in, in the city. In the hope I might get a job where I would require a driver's license, I went to the police station to get mine renewed, now that I was 16. The fact I had not had any traffic violations and was now of legal age, my license was renewed. However, my parents didn't want me to go back to cab driving. With this in mind I got a job at the Detroit Gear and Machine Works and commuted back and forth from Windsor to Detroit. Finally this job was cut to three days a week (like 1979 and 1980) and I started to drive independent cab for Bill Mechanic on my days off.

Bill's independent taxies were all seven-passenger Hudson cars with no special markings to identify them. I was soon driving steady for him and he treated me like a son.

At that time the Yellow Cab Company was operating from all the city public taxi street stands, with only competition from the Checker Cab Company. Bill Machanic then purchased six special built cabs by the Reo Car Company. The driver's seat was open and separated from the closed passenger section. These cabs had a special paint job and Bill called it the Seven Eleven Cab Company.

We soon took over the hotels and railroad stations, and this created some friction with other companies, especially when Bill established call-in phone boxes at several east and west end locations, where drivers could call in and wait for a return trip from that direction, which gave us more pay miles on our meters. Bill paid his drivers 30% of the total meter take, which was considered good pay for the time, and I was doing quite well.

Bill put a Michigan license on my cab and this permitted me to cross the border into Detroit with passengers and also livened things up quite a bit. I had several interesting trips into Detroit's underworld and night life areas and I always had my car crank beside my driver's seat in case of an emergency. However, thankfully I never had to use it. A few times I did have to pick it up and let them know I had it.

The Star Taxi Company had changed hands since I drove for them. It was taken over by Leo Meyhew, a man I knew quite well. He approached me one day saying he wanted to get rid of the old Star touring cars. "Walter, would you be interested in purchasing a half interest in a seven-passenger Studebaker with a California Rex top?"

It was equipped with the first four wheel brakes and had balloon tires. It had been repossessed from a bootlegger, who had been jailed for alien smuggling. This was very prevelant around the Border Cities. More on that later.

Leo's proposition was for us to operate on a 50-50 basis under his company's license. The fact the two Windsor race tracks were going to open for the season made it appear a good deal for me, as it was a seven-passenger car and we would be charging one dollar per person to drive seven miles from the ferry dock to the Devonshire and Kenilworth race tracks with Detroit race fans.

I discussed it with Bill Mechanic and he said, "I can't blame you for switching, but you are always welcome to come back here anytime."

Immediately I contacted Leo, telling him I would accept and rushed out to borrow my share of the down payment. Excited with the prospect of my new business, I went a bit crazy.

During the period the races were on I worked night and day. Leaving home at 11:00 a.m. I would rush to the C.P.R. station on the outskirts of Windsor, meet the train bringing immigrants from Montreal and Halifax. I tried to pick passengers who were going in one direction, which was usually clear across town to Ford City. I was well paid for my time before I was due at the ferry dock.

At times I was able to squeeze in eight passengers. On a good day I usually made four or five trips to the track.

Due to heavy race track traffic, the police designated special routes. All cabs and busses were required to take these routes and at times this caused problems when a slow driver was in front of you on a two lane road, causing you to lose an extra trip.

Walter's Checker Cab in 1927, across from Detroit, Michigan.

36

Some drivers took radical chances to get by a slow driver and one incident really put fear into me. A Yellow Cab driver called Bummer came up behind me when I was being held up and unable to pass. Bummer sounded his horn a few times, then got his solid steel bumper against my rear one and began pushing my cab. All I could do was apply my brakes enough to forestall hitting the car ahead. My brakes almost took fire before I could get away from him, and I had a car full of scared passengers as well.

Bummer's taxi driving days ended when he violated the designated taxi route. A motorcycle policeman gave chase but he made a stupid mistake trying to force Bummer's cab into the curb by cutting in front of the cab.

Fortunately for the officer the incident happened in front of the Hotel Dieu Hospital. When the cab knocked him off his cycle he was quickly carried into emergency.

Bummer claimed, in his defense, that he applied his brakes but was uanble to avoid hitting the cycle unaware he was being stopped.

During our wait for return passengers, some of the cabbies would place a few bets at the track. My best entertainment was facing the grandstand and watching the antics and emotions of the spectators during a race. There was considerable contrast between the winners and losers; I decided the race track patron was a terrific actor.

While snoozing in my cab a small man came over and started a conversation about my cab, as it certainly was different. I thought he was a jockey but he was a trainer.

He said, "If you are for hire this evening come to stable 0 at 8:00 p.m. and take me to town." "I'll be here," I replied. "If you hurry," he said, "place a small bet on Ramona, in the next race she is ready." She was and paid $8.00.

This meeting with Jim C. really turned into a long association and a very interesting one, as he turned out to be a race Tout. Jim was not like the average Tout as he did have some principles.

During the racing season and after we both finished with our duties I became Jim's private chauffeur. He liked my cab because it lacked taxi markings.

I was surprised to learn Jim could not drive. I let him drive one Sunday on a back road and he ditched the cab when another

37

car passed us. With the help of some negro boys we managed to get back on the road and that ended Jim's driving.

Jim had started out to be a jockey but was unable to keep his weight down because of his drinking, and that he would not give up. However, due to his knowledge of horses and his size he was in demand as an exercise boy.

In our early association, Jim handled his liquor well. Most of his customers were bootleggers and small joint operators, which he said were the biggest gamblers and suckers as well. It was people who had made him a Tout. This was proven true as I accompanied him around the joints at night. Patrons would fall all over him soon as they learned he worked at the track. They plied him with drinks and the women gushed over him hoping to get inside information.

Jim would brush many of them off and do it in a nice way, but if he felt he had one worth while, he would arrange a meeting, usually before a certain race. To avoid some bettors from killing the odds he would ask how much they intended to wager, then ask them to let him place the bet. If it was very large he would spread it at several mutual wickets and not release the tickets until the horses were going to the post and the wickets were closing.

He told me, "If I permit them to know the horse and bet themselves, they will signal the number to friends who could kill the odds." Jim differed from most Touts, he did not try to have people betting several horses in one race. When he happened to have a winner he would ask for 25 to 50% of their winnings.

Patrons with whom he became well acquainted, especially those from Detroit, he would phone them just in time so they could place bets with a Detroit bookie. Jim's horses were fairly consistent winners.

He befriended many stable hands and grooms when they were down in their luck. They would compensate him by telling him when their stable had a horse that was ready. This information, plus his own knowledge of horses, gave him a good average of winners. Jim always said that there was not as much collusion between horsemen as the public believed. He said, "It is far more prevalent at very small tracks."

He had one patron, a dentist's wife in Toronto, who had befriended Jim in the past. They nursed him in their home for

38

several weeks when he was injured by being thrown into the rail while working a horse at Long Branch, Toronto.

Since that time, out of gratitude, he phoned them twice a week no matter where he was. After telling me about them he asked, "Would you consider driving to Toronto over the week-end, Walter, I want to visit with them."

"Sure, Jim, the track is closed Monday and I'd like to meet your friends. Besides," I added, "I like to drive."

We were treated royally and it was a pleasant weekend. I kept in touch with them for years. Later they came up to Camp Caribou a few times while I was there.

Driving Jim around at night was never dull and I was well paid for the few miles I put on. Much of the time I was parked at one place or another. At times Jim barely made it back in time to exercise his horses in the morning.

Many incidents happened, but this one stands out. Jim had to come into the city at noon and when he called I was out on a trip, so he hitched a ride with a New York dress salesman at the track gate. On the way the salesman indicated he would like to attend the races that afternoon but he did not want to unload his samples to bring his car.

Jim left a message for me to pick up the man at the Prince Edward Hotel and to contact him before the first race. I left the salesman in the grandstand and went to see Jim.

Jim briefed me on how he had met the salesman and marked a horse in the first race for him to bet. I was to see Jim again before the second race so he could mark the second bet, etc., for the rest of the afternoon.

The first horse won, also the second and third. When I went to see Jim for the fourth race, the salesman said, "Ask Jim how much I should bet?"

When I did, Jim replied, "Tell him it is not a question of how much to bet, tell him to bet ALL HE'S GOT."

This performance went five straight races. Jim could not do one thing wrong! But silly me, I bet against him after the third race. I could not believe he would connect after three in a row.

He gave me his pick for the sixth, but before the race came up there was a real cloudburst and the Devonshire track quickly turned to slop. I told the man, "I'm sure Jim wouldn't want us to bet his horse after the rain. Blue Boy is a mudder, let's try him." We did and he won.

Later when I told Jim, he said, "Let's not press our luck, Walter, tell the man to quit and meet us tonight in time to go to dinner." The salesman agreed and suggested we bring our girl friends and one for him. He said, "It will be my treat."

I alerted the girls as soon as I got back in the city and after my last trip rushed home to clean up for the evening of celebration and pick up Jim. I asked him, "Did you ever pick five winners in a row before?" He smiled, "Not in my memory, Walter."

Only one of the horses paid $12.20, the rest were all favorites or second choice on the odds board. I never did find out how much the salesman bet or won but it must have been considerable and I'll wager he would never have another day like it again.

Our night out at the Ledo Venice was one to remember for all of us. The salesman spent freely and it was an expensive evening for him. He never offered any commission to Jim but he invited us all up to his room, where he outfitted each girl with a dress, a great finale for a spectacular day and night.

When the season ended in Windsor, I said goodbye to Jim and soon got back into my pre-race schedule. This lasted a short while, then Leo was having an affair and frequently wanted the car to go out of town for long week-ends. I soon saw that this partnership would not work out. We had a showdown and I sold him my interest.

CHAPTER 8

SECOND TRIP WEST

Since my purchase of the Studebaker I had been overdoing it, especially after meeting Jim. My hours had been ridiculous and there were times I never went home to bed for a couple of days. The little sleep and rest I got was in the car at the track.

My parents counselled me to take stock of myself and I considered it good advice and did some serious thinking. So when my problem with Leo came up, I decided to go out West for the harvest again. I had made money driving the cab but I paid for it healthwise.

While job hunting one of my cousins had been staying at our home. When he heard of my plans he wanted to go with me. After calling his parents they thought it would be good experience for him.

We arrived in Central Butte around the end of August, 1925. The same man I had worked for the previous year hired me again; as for cousin Dick, I was already sorry I had taken the responsibility for him. He was not mature enough to take care of himself on an adventure such as this.

I finally got him a job on a neighbouring farm. But several times I had to help settle problems they had with him. I was pleased to find Roy Getson working again with me. He had stayed instead of returning to Prince Edward Island. He had a married brother living in Moose Jaw.

Roy was a big strong fellow and easy to get along with. He had been a lobster fisherman at home and his father had a small fox farm.

Roy had acquired an old Model T car and converted it to a dune buggie, which was ideal for the prairie. We both enjoyed hunting and when time allowed we hunted and explored the prairie. I rode the back of the dune buggie like a saddle horse, shooting prairie dogs and jack rabbits.

Once in a while we could get close enough to a coyote, but they usually moved too fast for me to hit. One week-end we found a slough or lake with a huge flock of Canada Geese on it. We had a 12 gauge shotgun and a 22 rifle, we circled around the slough until we could approach the geese from behind a knoll. But as soon as we poked our heads over the knoll a goose would give a signal and they would all move out of range of our guns.

We played this cat and mouse game for an hour and the geese refused to fly; they just kept moving out of range. They had learned their lesson from other hunters.

Another time we saw four coyotes run into a gully as we came along. Investigating, we found the gully was a real jungle of undergrowth, making excellent cover for them. We decided if one of us chased through the undergrowth from one end, while the other watched the other end, we might get a coyote.

I was doing the chasing while Roy covered the outlet. When I got down in the gully it was so thickly matted with brush and vines that the animals had made a net work of tunnels throughout it. I struggled my way through for some distance before Roy called to me to give up. The entire gully was a mess of holes and dens, a perfect hiding place, which they well knew.

Roy and I spent most of our free time in this manner and I learned much that would benefit me in the career that lay waiting in the future for me.

Other excitement we found lay in an occasional trip into town on Saturday nights, usually some fights by those who drank too much booze. There were two Chinese restaurants; one served drinks and had card tables in a back room. It was here that we had met Adler the year before. The main customers were town business men and men who owned large sections of wheat land. The card games were usually much too high stakes for us. We could usually find Adler there when he was not in his store office.

One night I will not forget. We had gone to town early as it had rained and was too wet to work. Many harvesters had come in earlier and were drunk when we arrived.

They had separated into east and west groups. One group yelling, "We are from the east," the other yelling, "We are from the west." They met in the middle of Main Street, which was a sea of mud by then and proceeded to fight each other. It was a terrible sight to behold as they wrestled each other down into the mud, toppling over and over each other. Some had fallen face down and were too drunk to get up.

We were afraid they would smother, so some of us tried to pull them to the sidewalk and had to be careful to avoid being pulled into the melee ourselves. There was no police in town as the area came under the Mounted Police Protection. Thankfully, the fight died down of its own accord and those we had managed to pull on the sidewalks were saved from being trampled on.

I had seen some very wicked brawls around Windsor's night spots, but never anything like this. Roy and I decided to avoid Central Butte on rainy days.

Saskatchewan's liquor laws were different than ours in Ontario, but I can't remember enough to quote here. However, I feel sure the Chinese made their own brands. For my age, I had probably drank more liquor than most, as it had been pushed at me as I taxied people around the night spots in Windsor. Fortunately, I somehow never reached the stage where I had to drink myself silly. Yes, on several occasions I did get drunk before I drove a cab, when I was with older fellows and thought I was smart if I could drink as much as they did. However, the aftermath soon made me realize how stupid I had been.

To get back to Central Butte. We had an early fall snow storm that put a stop to thrashing grain. So Roy and I went to town to get our pay. Roy had planned for us to spend the week-end visiting his brother in Moose Jaw. But Alder had decided to let his harvest crew go as he expected the snow to last for some time.

This made Roy angry as it meant we had to return to the farm to pick up our duffel. Before we left town, we happened to meet the Peterson Brothers. They owned several sections of land about five miles out of Butte. They knew Roy from the previous year. When Roy told them we were through at Alder's Place, they said they had a job for him.

Roy turned to me and said, "What do you think, Walter?

The Petersons quickly spoke up before I had a chance to answer, saying they only needed one. Roy replied, "That's too bad, because Walt and I are together." When they realized he meant it, they said, "In that case we will take you both." It was

43

very apparent they wanted Roy, under any circumstance, because they knew his qualifications; Roy not only looked strong, he was powerful.

Returning to Alder's farm we picked up our duffel and happily moved to Petersons. This was a very big outfit, their separator was powered by a large straw-burning steam engine. It could handle four men pitching in grain at one time. They had 16 stook wagons, but no loaders, you had to load your own from the ground. This I had not done before.

At their headquarters they had a huge stable to house twenty teams. The teamsters were not required to feed or harness their horses as long as they were working at their headquarters. They had men that were responsible for the stable and horses.

I was most grateful to the stable man, as he was good enough to tell me which was the most gentle team in the stable. I did not want a wild team if I were going to load my wagon from the ground and drive at the same time. Driving a taxi cab and a horse are just not the same.

We were housed in a large bunk house, adjacent to a cookery and diner. A Swedish woman did the cooking, with her daughter as helper. The food was excellent and it was plentiful.

We had arrived at Petersons Saturday evening; on Sunday, we had one of those chinook winds that made the snow disappear like magic and it was dry enough to thrash on Monday morning. Even Petersons were a bit surprised.

Due to the number of men employed by them, there naturally were some coming and going much of the time, as a result I was given no instructions. Roy tried as best he could on how to load the grain from the ground onto the wagon. He said, "Just work as close to me as you can, see how I do it."

We were working in an area of rolling hills and he tried as much as possible to keep his wagon on the low side of each row of stooks. He would keep his wagon as close as it was possible to the stooks, and put his fork into as many sheafs as he could lift and properly place on the outside edge of the rack. Then he would bind that row by filling in the center. With one side built high enough to suit him, he worked from the opposite side of the rack and repeated the procedure until the load was completed.

44

There was a considerable judgement required, especially when working a side hill. If you happened to lose part of your load on the way back to the separator that marked you as a novice.

As I watched Roy, I noticed there were times he would lift an entire stook onto his wagon with one forkful as his team was moving to the next stook. Most of these horses were so used to this work they knew when to move without being driven. If the grain had been properly stooked, and the field level enough, Roy and a few others seldom had to stop their team from moving along the stook row to complete their loading.

When you arrived back at the separator, and it was your turn, you were to drive the load in as close as possible to a conveyor belt that fed the sheafs into the separator. Two wagons would unload at the same time, with two men pitching off each load; as spare, pitch off men were ready to climb onto your load as soon as you pulled into the conveyor. It was a dangerous operation in several ways, and you had to be alert constantly to avoid falling off your load and onto the fast-moving conveyor and into the cutting knives, just waiting to make mincemeat out of you.

My first day loading was a rough and tough one for me, and several other newcomers as well. On our first load, I had the distinction of being the last one in, which meant from then on that would be my place and turn to unload; also, leaving me the last one in at night. However, after three days I was able to keep up with much less effort.

With Roy it was just the opposite. He would get his laod on and back to the separator in time to have a good snooze while waiting his turn. He also was credited with usually having the largest load. There was one incident when he had a chance to prove his strength and his worth to any employer.

Roy had pulled into the conveyor and had part of his load pitched off, when some one yelled fire; a spark or sparks from the steam engine had been blown into his load setting it on fire. It was fast engulfing his entire load.

The spare pitch-off man jumped clear. Roy, instead of jumping off, grabbed for the reins and whipped his team into a gallop away from the outfit. When he was well clear he jumped off, and while still running got his shoulder under one corner of the rack and forced his team to turn sharply. As they did he was able to tumble the burning rack off the wagon and pull clear of the fire.

45

Everyone cheered him and the boss ran over to shake his hand saying, "Roy, your quick thinking has proably saved the outfit from being seriously damaged or destroyed and the horses being burned, thanks man!" The only thing lost was the wagon rack.

Peterson gave Roy a $50.00 bonus, and said, "We sure would like you to stay on as a permanent employee."

We learned later that it was not unusual for these straw-burning outfits to catch fire. The engineer always tried to set up the steam engine so the sparks would blow away from the separator; however, sometimes swirling winds would suddenly change. It was not unusual to have the wheat stubble catch fire a number of times each day, but these fires could be beat out easily.

After Petersons finished thrashing their own grain, they went out to do custom thrashing for farmers lacking their own equipment. They had two large bunk cars, trailers and a cook car trailer, both on wheels. We would move from one section to another. At each location we would set up the cook car and bunk cars wherever water was available.

Each night we made a circular corral, using our stook wagons, and tie our horses inside the circle, to the racks, and put the harness under the racks. We had bankets for the horses as the nights were becoming cold. They were fed by placing the feed on the wagon racks.

The men had three meals served in the cook car each day and two lunch breaks in the field, but none of us grew fat. We worked every daylight hour as long as weather permitted. Some mornings we had to break the ice in our wash water. This always woke you up real fast and kept your skin nice and firm. Several times I had to shake the snow out of my shoes before putting them on. The snow we were having was mostly dry and drifted through the cracks in our bunk car. As long as the snow stayed dry we continued to thrash.

We did have several days when we stayed in and kept busy playing poker or black jack for small stakes. On one occasion I had a streak of luck. It seemed I could do no wrong. We had played all night and I was terribly weary; I became careless — it still made no difference. Gradually, all but one engineer had dropped out of the game. He indicated he wanted to continue to see if he could make a comeback. His statement was, "I sure as hell hate to lose to a lousy kid."

46

I actually bet foolish, this seemed to confuse him, and he let me win with nothing, or, he would call when I was pat. On the final hand, he had drawn aces back to back and a jack, and I had kings back to back and a deuce.

I raised him once. He called my raise and raised me. I called and we took another card. He drew the second jack and I another king, which let me know I had him beat so far. The best he could have was three jacks or two pair.

With my pair of kings showing, I bet first. He raised. I called and raised. He called and we drew our fifth card. He drew the third ace and I, my fourth king. After several raises by both of us, he had to wake a friend and borrow money to call me.

When I turned my fourth king, he said, "Damn, that's enough, I can't beat that kind of luck."

Really, as far as that last hand was concerned, he was the one playing careless. My winnings for that session was $280.00. I gave Roy $200.00 to keep for me and told him under no circumstances to let me have it until we left, as I was sure they would expect me to play again to give them the opportunity to get some back. The next time we played Black Jack and during one perod that I was banker I made another $60.00.

Our cook put up such wonderful meals and her pies were like my mother's; I ate so much pie that I developed boils, even where I sat, before I had enough sense to lay off. But, even today pie and ice cream are my weakness and probably will be my downfall, according to my sister in Ventura, California. When I visit her, she loads me up with fruit and vegetables with nary a cookie in sight. She makes me go out and buy my own ice cream and then helps herself!

I had told Roy, all about my experience the previous year at Ed. Yerkie's; about the deer and trapping. He then suggested that we go back to Commanda after we finished with Peterson. He had trapped some in Prince Edward Island and thought it was an excellent idea and so did I. We enjoyed each other's company and hated to part.

We finished at Peterson's around October 15th. The dune buggy had broken down and Roy sold it for $25.00. We made the mistake of stopping in Central Butte, where Peterson was giving the men a farewell party.

47

Unfortunately, Roy, had a little too much to drink, although he was still in his usual good humor. I finally persuaded him to leave and go to the other cafe to get some needed food into him.

The owner of this cafe had in the past, much trouble with harvesters who went crazy on drink and had damaged his place. Therefore, he was always expecting trouble from anyone drinking.

When I got Roy over there he was just in a happy mood and walked back to the kitchen to kid with the chinaman. The chinaman, however was in no mood for that and told him to get out. At first, Roy, tried to convince him that he meant no harm. Turning around he started back to our table.

Before he reached the table, the chinaman came running out of the kitchen with a dipper of hot water and threw it on Roy's back.

That, "was a mistake," because Roy, let out a roar and went completely berserk. He wheeled around knocking a coal heater over with his arm, then picked it up and threw it through the kitchen swing doors, knocking over a dish rack.

I got hold of him and with difficulty steered him out the door; at the same time he swung out his arm breaking one of the windows. You can imagine the racket all this was making.

The druggist from next door heard all the commotion; he came running out and helped me get Roy, into the hotel and up to our room. By this time he had calmed down and he realised what he had done. We got his wet clothes off and into bed. The druggist then told me, "that chinaman is a bit crazy." A year before he had thrown a cup at him, badly cutting his head. He even showed me the scars.

Later, he came back with a bottle of coffee and some sandwiches for us. I asked him, "Will it do any good if we pay for the damages?"

He said, "Walter, someone has already sent a wire to have the Mounties come in, and they no doubt will be on the train tomorrow. I suggest that you stay in your room and I will try to find someone to drive you to Tugaskie." He explained that was an elevator town on another rail line, about thirty miles away.

Next morning, Roy, was really upset about what had happened, and worried. The druggist finally came up with more coffee for the fugitives. He was all excited and said, "Get your duffel together, the hotel keeper and I have arranged for a car to get you guys to Tugaskie, so get moving."

Roy and I were offering our thanks but he brushed that off with, "No time for that just hurry." He tried his best to help us pack, but the three of us were falling all over each other in our haste.

They led us out the back door and into a car just as the train pulled in and two Mounties got off and walked up Main Street. Believe me, we were scared we wouldn't get away in time.

I can't remember the man's name who drove us to Tugaskie, and maybe he never told us, but he refused payment. He said, "Boys, that has already been taken care of."

I feel sure now, that Petersons had done this for Roy, but did not want to get the other Cafe involved, as they could have been prosecuted for selling liquor, for the party.

As long as I associated with Roy, he never drank that much again. I also still think there was no reason for the chinaman to throw hot water on Roy, for even a cold sober man would have had a violent reaction. I have always been grateful to the druggist for the part he played, and the risk he took for us.

Roy and I purchased two tickets to Moose Jaw, then we asked the stationmaster what time the next train was due. "Well, boys you just missed one an hour ago, and the next one is due here in two days."

This really floored us, as we wanted to get out of the area as fast as possible and far away from the Mounties.

While we were feeling sorry for ourselves, we heard a train whistle and soon a freight train came in sight and to our amazement stopped at the water tank to take on water.

I said to Roy, "Let's go!" We ran along to box cars until we came to an empty coal car and crawled up and in. The train soon started up and we relaxed, quite pleased with ourselves, in spite of the crude accommodations.

After we had travelled some distance the train began to slow down, and we saw a trainman coming along the cat walk on top of the box cars. My first thought was. "This is it." However, as

49

he climbed down to go through our coal car, I pulled out our tickets. "We have tickets to Moose Jaw." I said, almost proudly.

His only comment was, "What in the hell are you doing here, get back to the coach at the end of the train before we get moving again." As we scurried off, he yelled after us, "And KEEP your tickets."

At the end of the train, instead of a caboose they had an old but very comfortable coach. There must have been a dozen harvesters, besides the trainmen, riding in perfect comfort. We felt absolutely ridiculous for our glaring stupidity, and it took time before we could have a good laugh at our silly mistake.

As we entered the freight yards in Moose Jaw, Roy pointed out his brother's house. We grabbed our duffel and jumped off the train as it slowed down, crossed a few vacant lots and arrived at the house.

When his brother came home from work, I would have never guessed they were brothers, there was certainly no resemblance whatsoever.

I noticed that Roy never mentioned the escapade in Butte.

We spent the night with his brother and wife and it felt good to wash after our ride in the coal car and we all had a good belly laugh.

After Roy and I had changed jobs and gone to work for the Petersons, I only saw Dick, my cousin, in town a couple of times. Then due to the incident of our last night in Butte and our hurried exit, I left word with the druggist to get word to Dick, to meet us at the Moose Jaw Station, and to come on the next train out of Butte.

Luckily we spotted him coming down the street with a tall fellow who steered him into one of the many joints that flourished in the western cities, and fleeced the harvesters out of their hard earned money.

We let them get seated and as we walked in, one of the girls was already at their table taking their wine order. (Wine was all these places were permitted to sell openly.) And it was the cheaper wine that they charged 50 to 75 cents a small glass for. The girls would usually ask the suckers to buy them a drink and if there was any chance the guy might go further, they would seat themselves at the table hoping to lure them to their room.

Dick looked surprised when I spoke to him, he said, "I met my friend here at the Station and we just came in for a drink." I said, "Dick, come outside, I want to talk to you."

Outside I informed him, "Your friend in there happens to be a Pimp, who specializes in hooking suckers just like you, as they get off the train." That knowledge had been part of my cab driving education.

We went to a restaurant for dinner and then I took Dick to the Station to purchase his return ticket to Windsor. We had to use our original ticket stub in order to receive the harvester reduced fare.

Dick, wanted to come to Commanda with us but I was not going to be responsible for him any longer. We did travel as far as Winnipeg with him, where Roy and I wanted to do some shopping at Eaton's department store.

I learned from Mother's letters that Dick arrived safely but broke, and he returned to his home in Coldwater Michigan. He immediately joined the U.S. Navy and left after his first term.

He surprised me by walking into my shack in the fall of 1934, when I was starting to build my Lodge. He spent one year with me, then joined the U.S. Army in World War II and was killed in Belgium on Christmas day.

CHAPTER 9

BACK IN THE BUSH AT COMMANDA

We picked up our refund on the tickets purchased in Tugaskie, but we ran into a problem with Roy's year old harvestor ticket, which was required to obtain the reduced return fare. It had expired after a year.

When the C.N.R. turned us down, I took Roy's ticket over to the C.P.R. and told a good story about how very important it was for me to get back home, and that I did not have enough money for the full fare. The agent said, "Well, that is a pretty good story; most of the time they come in here saying they lost their ticket or someone has stolen it," and, he drawled, "I sure wouldn't want your poor mother to worry, so you can have the reduced fare and give your mother my best regards."

In fact, there was a lot of these return ticket stubs lost or stolen, and some were traded for wine or booze. It meant a considerable savings to get the reduced fare, as none of us were exactly rolling in money.

We left Moose Jaw that night and Dick stayed with us as far as Winnipeg, where Roy and I did our shopping. We bought 30-30 rifles, high top shoes, clothes and books on trapping, two large pack sacks and numerous incidentals. We hoped to be expert trappers by the time we reached Commanda via our books.

Our trip from Winnipeg to North Bay was uneventful, except that about six of the coaches on our train were off limits to the passengers, as they were carrying a couple hundred Chinese coolies from the west coast. They were destined for the sugar cane fields in Cuba. (How times have changed. I am writing this in 1980, fifty-five years later and television is broadcasting the fact that 50 to 60 thousand Cubans are leaving their country and pouring into Key West, Florida.)

I was taken through the coaches by the conductor to get my trunk out of the baggage car, as it was in the wrong car and on its way to Montreal. The coolies were all in their native garments; most had the very long-braided pig tails. Many were taller and bigger than most Chinese we see here.

As I was escorted through they were eating their ration of rice. I found it interesting to see so many chop sticks working in unison. Some I assumed were smoking opium pipes. I had seen several old Chinese smoking their opium when I was driving cab in Windsor.

We had to change trains at North Bay and take the C.N.R. to Trout Creek, arriving at 11:00 p.m. It was good to be back in this beautiful country of Ontario bushland. In the fall the riot of colour is unsurpassed.

Checking in to the Evers Hotel for the night we planned to meet Oliver Moore at breakfast and ride his stage to Commanda. There we began our five mile walk to Yerkie's, lugging our heavy packs and wearing our new high top boots. Only I forgot to turn onto the Yerkie road at the cemetery and we walked three miles in the wrong direction, then three miles back to Yerkie's road.

By this time Roy called a halt! As tough as he was he said, ''Walter, these boots are killing me, either you carry me or we rest.'' Sitting on a road side rock we took off our boots only to discover the nails were protruding right through the soles into our feet. We managed to pound the nails with rocks and bend them over; then by inserting another pair of insoles we somehow finished the five mile walk to Yerkies. By now I imagine you have come to the same conclusion that we did. Our new high-top boots were not the type that we needed.

The Yerkies made us welcome until they learned we were planning to trap. We were staying at Charlie Yerkie's as Ed. was back at his Loring home, but it became obvious they didn't want us near the place, so they suggested several places we should go and even offered to direct us.

We made another trip back to Commanda to get supplies, which included first off the proper type of boots. We had many miles facing us in the future and mostly on foot.

The Yerkies were kind enough to let us spend one more night, then early in the morning Henry guided us to our trapping location. We travelled south on the old north road about eight miles to the Little Pickerel River. We crossed the river and travelled another five miles, then turned off east and south on a bush trail for about two miles arriving at Raganooter Lake (see map).

It was a long narrow lake with an island at the west end. Henry told us it was part of the big Pickerel chain of lakes that drained into Georgian Bay; this is the very beautiful body of water east of Lake Huron. Georgian Bay has beaches similar to Daytona Beach in Florida.

The entire distance we had travelled from Yerkies was all Crown Land and no settlers. I am sure we must have seen at least 100 partridge or rough grouse along the road. We shot six to have for our supper and Roy killed one by throwing a stick, like he did prairie chickens.

It was a beautiful sight to see the male grouse strut around his covey, with his tail fanned out. Some would charge at us to scare us away from the covey. It was very obvious they had not been shot at much.

There was a small log shack on the shore of Raganooter Lake; it was about 8 ft. x 10 ft. with a split cedar roof. There were two pole bunks one over the other. Roy rigged a stone fireplace to broil our partridge. We had both broiled and burnt but tasty partridge for supper and bread spread with lard; corn syrup for dessert.

The only utensils were; two small frying pans, two tin plates and cups, four knives and forks and spoons.

By the time we had finished our banquet it was very dark and we were bone tired from the miles of walking. We had no trouble falling alseep on our pole bunks.

In the morning Henry was busy cleaning all the porcupine dirt out of the shack; it hadn't bothered us the night before. I unpacked our gear and tried to find a place for the contents. Roy was busy gathering enough firewood for two days of cooking, as well as improving the outdoor fireplace. We had no landlord breathing down our necks, no first and last month payment to come up with, no waiting for utilities to be hooked up nor a cleaning deposit. Life can be simple and beautiful, especially when you spend most of your time outdoors where the true beauty is all around you.

Walter and his first trap shack in 1925.

Roy Getson, Walter's trapping partner in 1925.

After lunch, on our twelve-inch board fastened to the wall that was our table, Henry and I went to gather some beaver hay for our bunks, then he left for home.

We walked with Henry as far as the north road and he directed us to Hummel's hunt camp, located on roaring creek a short piece off the north road. This camp was well equipped for a hunt camp of that period. We found a few jars, some large cans to store our food in, and a can of rusty nails that came in very useful.

This was the 20th of October, 1925, and I was 17 years of age. It would be another 9 years before I would start my biggest adventure, Little River Lodge, but I was gaining valuable experience and I was going to need all of it.

Deer season was to open the first Monday in November. We had seen many tracks around the lakeshore, especially in the marshy bay where we had gathered beaver hay.

I made a list for our next trip out for supplies as our present supplies were limited. We killed several of the porkies that appeared around our shack. The third day we went back to the north road and followed it south to the Pickerel River.

We could see what looked like an old clearing with some fallen down building across the river, so we crossed over on the stringers of an old bridge to explore the buildings. We saw there had been a large settlement at one time. Later we learned it was known as the Miller Lawson settlement, back before the railroad came through to North Bay. It was abandoned about 1905 after the railroad and No. 11 Highway was built.

Prior to that, the settlers and lumber men came to Parry Sound by boat, then followed the north road to the old Nippissing trail at Commanda and settled the east Parry Sound District.

In poking around the old buildings we found an old box stove. We carried the top and the door and front frame back to our camp. Roy said, "I can make us a dandy stove with this." I didn't doubt him for a minute.

Roy with weasel skins at the second trap camp in 1925.

56

On our way back we also picked up a few lengths of pipe at the Hummel camp. The moment we arrived home Roy began building our inside stove. I was instructed to gather flat rocks along the lakeshore, while Roy located some suitable clay, besides making a paddle to dig it.

Had we had a stern boss standing over us with a whip, we couldn't have worked harder or faster. With winter coming soon that was enough incentive, "to get moving." We were enjoying ourselves at the same time and proud of our being on our own.

By nightfall we had the foundation ready. The following day we completed the job. Although it was very crude it did fullfil our needs and there was no one we had to impress. It really was a stone stove with a two lid iron top and front door with a pipe through the roof. But at the time it looked to us like a brand new Tappan range fresh out of Sear's catalogue, and we stood there admiring our joint handiwork.

Roy was anxious to explore the area, but I suggested we should go back to the Lawson settlement and carry enough boards from the old buildings to at least cover the portion of the floor we had to walk on, between our bunks and the shelf we called our table. He decided if we both went one trip would do it.

Some of the boards were pine and had been cut by hand before there were saw mills, and they were as much as 20 inches wide.

In our exploring we found a couple of carrying yokes in one of the stables. They had been used to carry water from the spring to the horses. By using pieces of discarded harness we were able to fashion four slings, two for each yoke. By putting one end of the board in each sling, and leaving the other end to drag, we were able to bring four boards back to our shack. Roy was an expert at improvising, so we managed to make our shack livable.

A few days later Roy went back to his exploring urge down the river below the blue shute. It was a series of falls and rapids that drained our lake.

When he returned he said casually, "I met two fellows below the shute. They have a tent set up high on the ridge above the falls and they called down to me to ask what I was doing." He went on, "I told them we were staying in a shack on the lake and I invited them to drop by."

I really didn't believe him, as he was in the habit of pulling my leg but I went along and said, ''Sure and I bet they are trapping too.'' He turned quickly and with surprise written all over his face said, ''Yes, they are but how do you know so much?''

''Oh, I get around'', I said, and let it go at that.

The next day I went exploring roaring creek to see if I could find signs of beaver and I set a few traps. Roy had already returned and was cleaning some partridge for supper when I came back.

Up to that time he had been doing all the cooking, as I had never done any. I started the fire and put water and bean soup on to heat.

I noticed Roy had started to prepare supper and I also saw that he had not washed his hands after cleaning the partridge. When I mentioned this to him he stopped what he was doing, turned and said, ''You can do the cooking from now on.'' By the tone of his voice and the look he gave me, I knew he meant it.

Well I struggled through that meal and I ended up with a lot more respect for a cook then I had had previously. But neither of us died of indigestion but it was nip and tuck. Conversation all through the meal was a bit strained as Roy didn't appreciate my checking on him. I felt I was eating with a perfect stranger, and he didn't compliment me on my first dinner.

After so-called dinner, I put some prunes on to cook, like a real housewife, trying to please her husband. I even rigged up a double boiler to make some oatmeal porridge for our breakfast. I remembered mother's porridge was a lot smoother when she used a double boiler and let it set over-night.

We retired extra early as we were tired from the day's exploring and we had run out of candles and for the moment we were tired of each other. The light we were using was also very smokey; we had made it out of a tomato can, some grease and a rag. By pinching the top of the can tight all around the protruding rag, so that grease would not take fire in the can, we managed to see somewhat, like in a dense fog.

It had to do until we could go to town again and buy a lantern and some coal oil. Bed looked very inviting that night and each took with him his dark thoughts that would dissipate with the morning light.

58

The next evening, just as I was preparing our supper with our limited supplies and my limited knowledge, there was a knock at the door. My first thought was, "Good Lord, NOT company."

When Roy opened the door there stood two men. I knew at once that he had not been kidding me about talking to them. He asked them to come in and there was hardly room for all of us to move in the small shack. They both looked rather dirty. The tallest lad was doing all the talking with Roy.

I was busy becoming more confused about the chore of having to prepare something for them to eat, and my language was foul and flustered. Finally, after considerable excuses and not too kindly I said, "Sit up and eat." It was a challenge on my part and they accepted.

It was then that the short lad took off his hat and I saw it was a girl! I really became flustered and thought of the language I had been using.

They were Joe Schmeler and his sister Pearl from Magnetewan, where their family operated a village hotel and took in tourists and hunters. They had traps set all the way from the Nippissing trail along what they called the poor man's road to the Miller Lawson settlement. They came in once a week to check the traps and usually spent two nights in their tent.

When they were leaving, Joe apparently, after eating my meal, decided he was sorry for us, as he went down to their canoe and came back with six lake herring.

He said, "We use a short gill net to catch fish for bait as well as food," and continued, "You know there are pickerel, perch and herring in your lake."

We felt rather foolish to think we had been camping within a few feet of excellent fishing for over a week and never even thought of fishing. In fact we had nothing to fish with.

I was to meet Joe and Pearl several times that winter and learned that Pearl could cuss better than I, so no need did I have to be embarrassed that first night.

We decided that I should go out for supplies the next day. I left early and got as far as Yerkies by noon. Charlie offered me his horse and a two-wheel cart to go to Commanda, as I could bring some things for him as well.

59

It started to snow before I returned from Commanda, and it continued all night. It was a heavy wet snow that clung to trees and brush. Next morning Charlie said, "Don't attempt to make that long trip back with that heavy load under these conditions." But not realizing what lay ahead of me I made up my mind to go. So Charlie said, "In that case I will take you as far as the north road turn, but you are making a big mistake, mark my word."

It was about five miles using a slupe sleigh, and there was at least 16 inches of snow. As we got beyond the clearing into the timber, I realized that Charlie was right. I should never have started. Young trees and limbs were broken off. I cut a pole and walked ahead of the horse, hitting the trees so they would spring up off the road. It was very slow going, and when we reached the north road turn, Charlie said again, "Walter, come back with me, you don't stand a chance."

By this time I had planned to spend the night at the Camp Glory Hunt Camp, which was just across the Little Pickerel River, three miles further. I could not make up my mind to turn back.

Those three miles were really hard and seemed like thirty. My pack became heavier with every step. When I got to the river bridge I sat down on my pack to rest. Suddenly I saw a team and sleigh coming.

It turned out to be Sank Whitehead, who was taking a stove and mattresses to Camp Glory, as the deer hunters were arriving the next day. Sank explained, "I've come across the hard scrabble road from Golden Valley, and it's been all day coming six miles." He said, "I was damn lucky I had a good team and was able to walk ahead with a pole and my horses followed."

I told Sank who I was and that I planned to spend the night at Camp Glory. He let me know who he was and warned me to be careful with the fire as I helped him put up the stove. I felt that I was lucky he came along with a stove, as I would have been very cold and uncomfortable without it.

Suddenly Sank said, "listen," then we heard men's voices hollering at horses. Sank said, "That must be the Hummel hunters going into their camp. If you hurry back down to the bridge, maybe they will take your pack as far as their camp." With this, I took off in a flash.

60

It was approximately five miles further on and that much closer to home. When I reached the bridge, I saw they had four wagons. They told me that they had left Trout Creek the day before and stayed at Commanda that night. They had started out with the wagons before the snow. Tom Hummel spoke up, "We met Charlie going home, and he told us it was you who had cleared the road ahead of us, and we are grateful. Put your pack on one of the wagons and help us break trail to our camp."

I was only too glad to help and have company. They had a party of twelve hunters from Buffalo, several of them were priests and most of them were too fat to walk or help, and were riding on top of the loads.

Two of the hunters and myself were breaking trail up ahead. When we got to what Hummel called Twisty Lake Hill, they had to unhitch one team and rig up a block and tackle line at the top of the hill and use that team to help pull the three wagons up the hill. A couple of times we had horses down. We had to unhook another team to get the fourth wagon up and over the hill.

By now we were travelling by moonlight and I was so tired I had trouble raising my pole. A few more times it was necessary to use the block and tackle to haul one wagon that must have been loaded heavier than the others. I was sure that night would never end.

It was 2:30 a.m. when we finally reached their camp. We could tell by his tracks that Roy had come that far looking for me. As tired as I was I thought to myself, "He already misses my cooking," and this added strength to my weary bones. He probably assumed I had not even started out from Charlie's, due to the storm, but I was pleased that he had come looking for me.

It took awhile to get fires going at Hummels and to warm up our cold, cold bodies. No help was coming from the hunters that rode the wagons; they had drank enough to put them to sleep; in fact, we had a hard time getting them into their bunks.

The teamsters had to take care of their horses; they were all frothed up and over-heated. One teamster was too drunk to do anything, except get in the way. Tom Hummel finally pushed him outside and slapped him around trying to straighten him up.

Daylight was breaking when we finally were able to get food into us. Tom poured a good portion of rum into my coffee and said, "Hesman, I am glad we met you and I also want to thank you for breaking trail before we caught up to you at the bridge." I was too tired to make a proper response.

After resting for a couple of hours, I decided to go to our shack. Before leaving, Tom told me the two hired teams were going back to Commanda, and if they could bring anything back for us he would be glad to do it, as they would return to pick up the hunters and their deer and could very well haul supplies for me. All I could think of at the time was a bag of potatoes, a few vegetables and some coal oil.

I followed the tracks Roy had made when he came looking for me the day before, and arrived at our shack just as he was starting out to look for me again. He had decided to keep coming until he met me.

When I related all I had gone through on this trip, Roy said, "And all this time I thought I was the strong one." Apparently, with all the exercise I had been getting out west, as well as here, had built up some endurance I had never had before.

The day I had left on my trip, Joe and Pearl came by in their canoe and gave Roy some fish hooks. They were even generous enough to tell him they were leaving a minnow trap in the pool below the shute, as they would not be back until the ice was on the lakes and ponds, and they were lifting their traps. They also left the herring taken in their net, keeping the pickerel for themselves.

They were expecting a large group of deer hunters at their Magnetawan Hunt camp they would have to take care of. They told Roy that we should have been prepared to trap and get acquainted with the area, at least a month earlier than we had, as racoon, fox, mink and muskrats were easier to take in open water, and once it starts to freeze up it is difficult to keep traps working properly and the water levels fluctuate.

Most of all we needed more experience and knowledge of the area. However, Roy had picked up three weasles from our traps and they were snow white.

The snow began to fall and melt off the trees by noon on Sunday. Roy went hunting early Monday morning, but I was still too stiff and sore from Saturday's trip, so I stayed home and nursed my aches.

62

I decided to make a small root cellar in a bank behind our shack to keep our supplies in. It was much too warm inside when I had a fire going.

About mid-afternoon I heard a hound baying and getting closer. I was standing in the doorway, when suddenly a big buck bounded out of the woods, intending apparently to cross the marsh and go around the end of the lake. When he either smelt me or the smoke from the stove, he stopped and gave me time to reach my gun and shoot.

I was surprised to see him go down kicking. By that time I was shaking so bad I couldn't fire another shot, but it wasn't necessary as he was finished.

By this time the hound arrived on the scene and I rushed over to beat him off, but all he did was sniff around a few times, then turned and went back in the direction he had come from.

Now I was all alone with my victory and my first thought was "Where the hell is Roy, now that I need him." I was still nervous and shaking and somewhat in a panic, as I had never gutted a deer. I did know enough to bleed it and open it up. The bleeding was not necessary as the bullet had hit in the neck and it bled out good, but I felt I had to do something besides just stand there in complete amazement at what I had done.

I was bursting with pride at making such a good shot, but the reason was, no doubt, it had happened so fast I had no time to get "buck fever," until after I shot.

I was still doing the best I could to get the deer dressed out when Roy came around the end of the lake. He burst out laughing at the way I looked and the way I tried to excitedly tell him all at once what had happened, with blood all over me. He said I looked like a raving maniac. I said, "I was never so glad to see someone in my life, and especially you!"

He finished dressing out the deer and we dragged it behind the shack and hung it in a cedar tree to drain and cool. We figured it was a hound from Hummel's that had brought us this good luck, so I was well paid for my night of labour.

We had a feast that night: Roy sliced part of the liver and with the onions I had just brought in we had a delicious liver and onion dinner, toped with strawberry jam and hot biscuits spread with butter, that I got from Charlie, instead of the lard we had

63

been using. In fact I considered we ate very well from that time on. Broiled steaks, etc.

That night it froze just enough to make a thin ice on the lake, and in the morning Roy skinned out the buck. He did it in such a way that he left the skin on the front part, so he was able to wrap the skin back around the carcass after he had cut off a quarter. This way it would prevent the birds and squirrels from getting too much. We also cut thick spruce bows and placed them around the carcass to add more protection to our valuable cache of food.

The rest of the week was spent in exploring our area until Thursday when we walked out to Charlie's place, then out to Commanda Friday. We needed to purchase everything we might need until Christmas, and take advantage of the teams and wagons coming Saturday for Hummel's hunters.

All along the road we met hunters and lost considerable time talking to those who were standing watching for deer to cross the road. Most of them had seen deer but only five said they had got one. We saw several hounds that appeared to be looking for their owners.

Besides purchasing the food we needed, we bought two pair of double wool blankets, heavy underwear, socks, insoles, sewing kit, towelling, wool and leather mitts, tobacco, swede saw, files, axe, a draw knife and a used toboggan that really came in handy many times. We also bought a two gallon can of coal oil for our lantern, as the daylight hours had been getting shorter steadily. On cloudy days it was dark by five o'clock. One of the teamsters, Cecil Ricker, agreed to pick it up at Schwartz's store Saturday morning and would meet us at Charlie's.

We rode part of the way back with Ricker, but it was so rough on the wagon we chose to walk ahead much of the way. The snow had all disappeared.

When we arrived at Hummel's camp they had a horse hitched to two poles, like the Indians used to move camp, and they were skidding deer out of their trails and hanging them on a pole. These poles would slide over logs and most anything along their trails.

Hummel's camp was appoximately 20 ft. x 30 ft. and built out of hemlock logs and the horse stable as well. The stable had room for four teams. The hunters had their count of deer, which included some fine big bucks and one doe that turned out to be the largest I was ever to see; it must have been better than 250 pounds.

We carried everything perishable back to our camp and left the rest to pick up later with the toboggan when it snowed again, which came two days later.

We continued to explore. We had no maps of the area and this was a bad mistake, although as far as I knew the only maps at that time were not very accurate of the lakes and streams. It was a good thing that Roy's sense of direction was exceptionally fine. We covered a large area in our travels but saw few signs of fur, except for fox and weasel tracks, and occasional mink along the creeks.

After the lake froze over, Roy shot a deer on the far side. To save a long rough trip carrying it around the end of the lake, we attempted to drag it across the ice.

About half way the ice became a bit rubbery, so we separated to avoid so much weight in one place. I took the guns and went ahead and Roy pulled the deer. When the ice began cracking, Roy yelled at me, "Get down on your hands and knees and crawl." As I did, I gave the guns a shove and they slid right into shore. I crawled gingerly around a weak spot, then turned to watch Roy.

He made two steps and broke through. Fortunately, a rock was two feet under the ice and he stood on that. He reached back and pulled the deer across the hole, then he climbed out and headed for shore.

While I was shocked as he broke through, and concerned, I could not stop laughing at his actions of trying to balance himself on that rock; and later when he asked me "What was so funny out there?" I doubled up laughing again and could not answer him, so he threw a book at me.

We hung Roy's deer in the cedar without skinning it. That ended the deer hunt for us and deer season closed two days later.

That night Roy said, "Walter, if we go back to the Little Pickerel bridge and head southeast or east, we should come to Pickerel Lake just above Raganooter." "Why not try it tomorrow and see what happens," I replied.

We left early in the morning and checked weasel traps along the way. The snow was about eight inches deep and this made walking a bit tough. We made a mink set under the bridge, then left the road and took one of the trails the camp Glory hunters had been using. They apparently had just gone out two days ago.

That trail led us around several old beaver ponds, and finally we came to a beaver dam where there was some fresh peeled beaver sticks. We walked the ice around a bend and came onto the largest beaver house I have ever in my life seen.

It was easy to see that it was active as the water close to the house was open. We had no beaver traps with us, and would not have had time to make sets if we had. But we were pleased with our find as there was no sign of anyone trapping there.

Roy took out his compass and headed in the direction he thought would bring us to Pickerel Lake.

We climbed through some very rough terrain, for it seemed to us a long while and then decided that was why no one had been to the beaver pond. We seemed to be going uphill steadily and I was beginning to have cramps in my legs from climbing and stepping over logs and brush.

It began to get dark and we still had not reached Pickerel Lake or even the river. Roy said, "I feel sure we will come to it if we keep in this direction." "If you say so," I replied, "we'll keep going."

Half an hour later we stumbled down a long hill onto the lake and discovered we were at the outlet where it emptied toward Raganooter. He said he had seen the remains of an old log shack above the log-driving dam. The men who had operated it probably stayed there, so we climbed up to it to eat our lunch that we had carried all day long.

The moon had come out by the time we finished our lunch, and it was almost as light as day but much colder.

According to his figuring we had more than two miles to go to our shack and the route along the river was a real obstacle course. In a number of places, below each rapid, we tried to travel on the shell of the ice along the shore. At times we crawled on our hands and knees. It was no picnic. When we came to open fast water we stumbled from tree to tree on the bank until we finally reached Raganooter and could again walk on ice.

66

We were both so pooped by then that we were moving at a snail's pace. When we reached the shack we fell in the door and just laid there on the floor, without starting a fire or taking off our wet clothes.

It was after trips like this that the old shack seemed like a palace to us. But after a day of resting Roy said, "Let's move over to Hummel's camp; if we are going to stay all winter, this small room will drive us both crazy." After letting me digest that, he continued, "Besides, most of the area we have our traps in are back that way."

I said, "It sounds good to me, and Joe and Pearl will soon be back here trapping, now that the hunt is over." I knew they would appreciate us leaving, as we were too close to their area.

That day we started to move using our toboggan and our packs. The stove in Hummel's was an 1865 or 95 Prince of Wales, with the oven on top and a three foot fire box. They had left most everything in camp, enough utensils for 20 men, oil lamps and lanterns and every kind of spices for tasty cooking, and enough reading material to last us a year. The main thing, which was important in the bush, we had room to get away from each other and breath. In fact that is important no matter where you live, and creates many problems where people cannot obtain it. Roy and I had the whole outdoors but we still needed space inside, especially during the winter.

That first night we were in our new home, I decided to make a big pot of trapper's stew now that we had so many pots to cook in. I cut all the meat I could off the heel of the hind quarter of venison we had cut our steaks from, and added potatoes, carrots and onions. When I felt they had cooked long enough I added a can of tomatoes. This turned out good and improved each time I warmed it up.

After seeing all the spices and extracts, I wrote to my mother asking for a cook book. I wanted to try some baking now that I had an oven and my new status as chef.

Roy was building a sleigh to haul wood on, as we knew we were going to need a great deal before winter was over. I decided to walk out to Charlie's.

Past the river bridge, I saw fresh horse tracks and soon met a man coming on horseback. He said he was Gene Boughner, owner of a fox farm on the old Whitehead homestead. I had heard Yerkies mention him the year before.

He asked, "Where did you come from?"

"I was born in Windsor," I replied.

"I was raised in Detroit, right across the river. Where are you heading now?"

"I am going to pick up our mail at Commanda."

"If you go out the hard scrabble road to Golden Valley, it would be a lot closer than Commanda is. You would save yourself 10 or 12 miles and they also have a post office."

I thanked him and said Roy's father had a small fox farm on Prince Edward Island.

"Nellie and I would be pleased to have you and Roy drop by anytime," As he was leaving he said, "And make it soon."

I went on to Charlie's and Commanda. I told Schwartz to foward my future mail to Golden Valley. I had gone through Golden Valley on Oliver Moore's stage the year before. That night I asked the boys at Charlie's why they had not told us of the closer location.

"Well, we thought you knew what you were doing."

That is where a map would have shown us how to save miles of walking as well as time.

I returned with four beaver traps on loan and left them at the Camp Glory trail, as we would be coming back that way. Roy had finished his sleigh and cut a couple loads of wood with the swede saw and hauled it to the stable.

We were anxious to get the beaver traps set so we wasted no time and left at daylight next morning. We had spent hours reading and re-reading our trapper book on how to set for the beaver and now came the test of our knowledge.

We made the cubby just like the book said; put the bait and the traps in place; scraped snow and ice in the hole so it would freeze. According to the book the traps should always be checked regular, but due to the distance we had to walk, we checked them every third day.

After making three trips and opening the sets each time without any results, we were sure someone must have shot those beaver during hunt season.

I had invited Charlie to come in and visit us; he had mentioned he would like to get two deer for the winter. He was a very poor man but a very kind and honest one, and he had been good to us when we needed it the most.

Charlie arrived one day while we were cutting more wood. He had come with his one horse jumper (a home-made sleigh). After we fed him and his horse he insisted that Roy and I keep cutting and he used the horse to draw our wood to the stable. We accomplished twice as much as we would have otherwise.

This was the first time Charlie had been to Hummel's Camp, and he was very impressed, not only with the camp but especially with all we had in it. The fact that I had slept several nights at his place, I knew we really were more comfortable in this hunt camp than at Charlie's home.

We sat up and talked fairly late, listening to all his experiences and his struggle to raise a large family on a homestead. Next morning he was up and fed and watered his horse early as usual. During breakfast he said he felt sure he could get the deer he wanted, if we would let him use one of our 30-30 rifles.

He said, "One of you come with me, the other wait two hours then bring my horse and jumper as far as Twisty Bridge, I should have my deer there by then."

Charlie and I started out. When we crossed the big swamp on the north road he stopped and said, "Walk until you come to a marsh, then turn left on a ridge; keep the marsh on your right and in sight until you see Twisty Lake." I digested that and he went on, "Continue to keep the lake on your right; follow on around the lake until you come to the outlet and I will meet you there."

I was to give him a half hour start and then off I went. When the marsh came in view I also noticed a well-travelled deer trail going in my direction. I followed it keeping the marsh in sight until I could see Twisty Lake. Working my way around the lake I realized I was going out on a blunt peninsula that jutted into the lake. There were deer tracks all over; some went across the lake, others around the bay and up the ridge.

As I reached the top of the ridge I heard two shots and suddenly saw three deer coming toward me. Before I had a chance to shoot they saw me and disappeared over the ridge.

When I came to the outlet of Twisty Lake I could see old Charlie with his coat off busy dressing out a deer. Coming closer, I was amazed to see he had his two deer. He was all smiles; and he had shot both in the head, not spoiling the meat. We only had to pull them 200 yards to the road and Roy soon arrived with the jumper. I had received a good lesson from Charlie on how to hunt, he had all my respect and admiration. He said deer usually yarded up in places like this once the snow came and lakes froze. He left us, heading on home with his winter supply of meat. All his life he had wanted a good trapping area farther north, but he never got the chance to leave where he was.

Roy and I returned to camp and picked up two more weasels on our way. Mrs. Yerkie had told me how to make a batch of bread and I decided to give it a try while Roy skinned the animals. That night we had a light fall of snow and next morning we saw fresh weasel tracks going in and out the dog kennels.

When we investigated we found seven deer hides that the hunters had thrown in for the hounds to lay on. I knew that Oliver's brother bought deer hides, so I hung the hides out on a pole, flesh side out, so the birds could pick off the remaining flesh. It wasn't long before they had them picked clean. The hunters apparently had eaten deer in camp and no doubt packed away some over their count to take home.

Concerned about our beaver sets we made another trip but still no luck. Coming back we noticed fresh animal tracks crossing ours and set out to follow. According to our book it looked like a fisher, and they were listed up to $200.00. However, it led us in a very erratic course and we had to give up.

Approaching the outlet on Twisty Lake we saw an otter, and he was fishing near the dam. While we were debating how to get it, it came sliding along the shore. We had been crouching behind a rock island and decided not to shoot it with our 30-30 as it would ruin the pelt. When it came opposite us, we made a rush for it and it took off into the woods, with Roy and I gaining on it, but each time we got close it could out manouver us by ducking under logs and windfalls. Before we realized it, the otter had led us in a large circle back to the hole where it had been fishing. Too late we learned that one of us should have stayed at the hole.

70

My first batch of bread turned out very good; in fact, every batch turned out well except one, that became chilled one sub zero night. Our biggest problem was our eating far too much warm bread. My oven was a big boon to my becoming a quality cook and I found you can do most anything if you just try (and there is no one else to do it).

Returning to camp one day, we found Henry had come in for a visit and brought a couple of bottles of his home brew made from cracked corn. I was a little afraid of it, but he assured us it had been well tested at home. To my surprise it turned out to be a very good liquor, and we gave it another unnecessary testing.

The next morning I wanted to go to Golden Valley to check our mail; we had sent weasel skins to Shubert's Fur House in Winnipeg and I thought we should be hearing from them.

Henry decided to come with me and we missed the hard scrabble road and wound up at the fox farm. I blamed Henry and his liquor. Nellie, Gene's wife, said he and Sank Whitehead had gone to look at traps at Irish Lake. She suggested I take Gene's saddle horse and bring back some groceries for her and Henry could wait there for me.

It sounded like a good idea, so she showed me where the saddle was. I put it on the horse, mounted and took off. I am sure that horse knew I was a greenhorn right from the start, as I had trouble making him go where I wanted. After I got him to the hard scrabble road though, he seemed to realize I was determined to go to Golden Valley. He settled down to a steady walk and I was almost enjoying the ride.

Suddenly, a partridge that had been under the snow, exploded from under his feet and that horse made one jump sideways, then backwards and I sailed right over his head, still hanging on to the reins. When he reared up I let go as I thought he would jump on me, but he wheeled and took off at a gallop.

The last I saw was the saddle had slipped down under his belly and I was afraid he would kill himself. However, there was nothing I could do, so I walked on to Golden Valley. I think we were both kind of glad to get rid of one another.

Hard scrabble road was well named, as it was just one steep hill after another. I learned at the post office that mail would not get there before 5:00 p.m. By the time I got the mail and walked

71

the four miles back, all the time worrying about the runaway horse, I was really pooped out.

A mile before I reached the fox farm, Gene came galloping up to me on his horse. It didn't take long for me to realize that Gene was quite drunk. He wouldn't listen to me and instead of relieving me of my load, he wheeled the horse around saying, "I'll, show you how to ride," and took off at a gallop. I had my own dark thoughts as I trudged on, the least of them was that the horse would throw him on a big rock.

Soon after I saw a light from a lantern coming, it was old Sank and Henry. It was quite apparent they too had been drinking from the same well as Gene. At the house I saw the well was a keg of wine that Sank had brought in. On the table with a spike stuck in the bung, Gene pulled the spike and filled a jar, then poured me a water glass to the brim, saying, "You and Henry had better stay here for the night." But Nellie said nothing and had not offered to get me anything to eat. This could have been due to all the drinking.

After a short rest Henry and I started back to camp. It was tough walking as the sun during the day had softened the snow, then formed a crust at night. We arrived at camp at 1:30 a.m. Fortunately, Roy had left the stew on the stove and Henry and I practically dove into it.

Roy said, "The reason your saddle slipped on the horse was the cinch not being tight enough."

"But I was afraid I would hurt the horse if I made it too tight."

"Walter, that is practically impossible to make it too tight." He went on, "That alone would make your horse nervous."

Anyway, I was happy to now have an excuse for falling off the horse and I had learned about cinches.

In our absence, Roy had been exploring north of our camp and discovered two lakes, Stanley and Whitehead (see map). He said he could see a building at the east end of Whitehead but it was too late for him to go any further.

Henry figured the lakes had to be near the fox farm. He said, "That might be your best route to the hard scrabble road and Golden Valley. You would have much better walking on the lakes."

72

After Henry left for home, Roy said, "Let's go and find out."

When we got to the building he had seen, it turned out to be a boat house where six canoes were stored. We followed a trail leading up a hill and in the distance we could see part of the fox pens.

We arrived at the farm just in time to see Sank leaving for his home in Golden Valley. Gene was still on his drinking spree, loud and boistrous. Nellie invited us in and called for Gene to join us.

After having some coffee, Gene seemed quite pleased to meet and talk to Roy about foxes. Nellie needed some wood to make lunch so we three men went out to get some.

I had noticed as we came in a pile of wood drags outside the kitchen door with a only a few blocks cut off. I gathered that Gene had no wood cut ahead, and it turned out I was right. Gene could not file a saw and they had been waiting for old Sank to do it. I split a couple of blocks and Nellie soon had our lunch ready.

After lunch we toured the fox pens; he had 50 pair at the time and they were a mixture of silver, cross and arctic blue, with a couple of wild red he was keeping to breed.

Roy suggested we give Gene a hand on his wood problem and I agreed. Nellie was so delighted to see the split wood piling up, she asked us to stay all night. We did stay for supper and had our first pie since leaving the west.

While Gene was feeding the foxes, Nellie told us about his drinking problem. He was an alcoholic and his parents were afraid he would kill himself in Detroit. Their solution was to put him in the semi-wilderness and hope it worked.

They bought this old Whitehead homestead from Sank. Sank and several other local settlers had moved to Golden Valley, where land was more suitable for farming. Gene showed some interest in fox ranching, so his parents set him up, thinking this would keep him occupied and away from booze and his former associates.

It was a very lonely life for Nellie during the winter when she and Gene stayed alone. In the summer his father, who had been a cattle buyer, would buy up cattle and sheep to pasture on the clearings made here by the settlers.

The closest neighbour was over four miles, and that was out the hard scrabble road. This did not encourage visiting.

During supper Gene said, "Henry tells me you are trying to catch some beaver, is that right?"

When he saw our concern he told us, "You know, Sank and I are trapping, too."

"Well, so far all we are doing is trying with no results."

When we told him how we made our sets, he said, "There is nothing wrong with that. Maybe you are distrubing them too often? We agreed we had checked frequently. Eager beavers.

"Change your sets and put fresh polar bait in, THEN STAY AWAY FOR A WEEK and see what happens. We agreed to give it a try.

It was late when we set out for camp but we could not afford to stay all night, as our things would freeze without a good fire going. Nellie had given us a dozen eggs, one of her raisin pies and they both invited us to come back often. Walking the lakes back was a great deal better than the road.

We returned to our beaver pond the next day anxious to reset the traps and wait for results. Somehow we managed to stay away for six days.

Our patience was well rewarded; we found three big beaver and carried them back to camp instead of skinning them there. Before we reached camp we were sliding or dragging two of them, as our load became heavier and heavier, but we didn't complain in view of our success.

For two days we were busy skinning and stretching the pelts. We followed the book in detail, even lacing them on hoops we made from alders.

On a trip to the Valley, we ordered snowshoes and a cheque for the weasel skins came in the mail. Some we were happy to learn had brought as much as $4.00. We sent off another 16 skins right away. I also received a long letter from mother, along with the cook book. Roy heard from his brother in Moose Jaw, advising him he could dispose of our beaver skins in that province.

We delivered Nellie's mail on the way back and Gene was happy to learn of our success with the beaver. "Sank sells his pelts to a local travelling buyer, but suit yourself," was Gene's advice.

Nellie regretted she couldn't have us for Christmas as they already had company coming in from Commanda for a few days. "Don't worry about it, we have accepted an invitation to be with the Yerkie family, so we couldn't come anyway."

The next few days Roy and I were both busy. He was checking traps at Twisty and Raganooter Lake and I was slaving over a hot stove. Actually, I could hardly wait to experiment with my new cook book. I went whole hog!

I didn't fool around. I made a coffee cake, some cookies, a raisin pie, and couldn't resist my favourite pie, when my mother made it, which was lemon. Everything else turned out O.K. including my crust for the lemon pie. I was assured and carried away with success as I began my filling. I could see Roy coming home and commending me on my culinary art. Drooling at the first taste of my lemon pie. Thumping me on my back in his ecstasy and bragging, "I knew all the time you'd be the greatest cook. If it hadn't been for me, you'd never know this great talent that lay submerged, begging to come out."

When he did come home, he could hardly wait until the dessert was served. It did smell heavenly. The whole cabin reeked of exotic flavours and he was ravenous.

After two bites of lemon pie, he just stared at me with a questioning look, "Hey, are you trying to fool me?"

I wasn't a bit surprised, because I had made the filling with lemon extract I had found in camp to give it a lemon flavour. I kept adding a little more as I was cooking it. But each time I tasted it I could not taste any lemon. I finally used all the extract in the large bottle, and it was mostly alcohol, that just steamed away.

He had picked up five more weasels and reported the latest bush news. "I saw a huge wolf track cross the road near Twisty Lake near where Charlie got his deer."

The next day we buried all the food and supplies that would freeze. By cleaning the snow off the side hill, we made a small cave and lined it with browse. We covered the supplies with a sheet of felt paper first, then roofing paper and more browse and finally a good layer of snow. Everything was in good shape when we returned after Christmas; in fact, we left our potatoes and vegetables there, taking small amounts as needed.

75

On our way to Charlies' next day, we saw three more wolf tracks out near the river bridge. Their tracks showed that when they came to our tracks, two of them had made a long leap across our tracks and bounded away. The other had turned back in the direction they had come from.

The Yerkie boys told us, "We have been hearing wolves for about two weeks just south of here. After the lakes and streams freeze over, it is usual, as they no longer have access to beaver and muskrats. Deer becomes their main food."

We stayed two days and enjoyed the change. The girls had decorated with wreaths made from stems of princess pine, wrapped on wire with a few red winter green berries added. Cedar and pine boughs around the room scented the house. They had strung yards of popcorn around the doors and windows as well as on the Christmas tree, with a good amount of tinsel, which had been carefully saved over the years, and made from foil wrappings.

They had made a quantity of maple sugar and taffy, which I particularly enjoyed, as I have always had a sweet tooth. Our contribution was two dozen oranges and some mixed nuts we had purchased at the Valley store. It was a great Christmas and good to be surrounded with a kind and loving family.

Theodore and Bill's two daughters talked Roy and I into taking a ride on their toboggan on a hill in Bill's field. We were directed to steer between two stumps at the bottom of the hill, then head out into the field.

We got aboard. I was to steer and Roy on his knees was behind me. With a big shove we were off. As we approached the stumps we were flying. I took careful aim and guided us through, then suddenly we were sailing over a ten foot drop. I went tumbling end over end. When I was able to look back for Roy, all that was visible were his legs sticking out of a snow drift below the drop off.

The kids were hilarious, but as funny as it may have looked to them it was dangerous as well, and it sure was a big shock to us.

On our way home we met a team and sleigh with the folks who had spent Christmas with Nellie and Gene. Some were still full of holiday cheer and willing to share.

We took a side trip to check our beaver sets. Two more beaver were waiting for us, but none of the bait had been touched in the other sets. It was too far to walk for nothing so we gathered up all the traps to take home along with the two we did get.

Returning to camp was like being home and we were content to be alone again. After skinning the beavers we nailed them to the door as we had observed the way Yerkies did theirs, and it proved to the best method and less trouble.

Our next problem was transporting the pelts to Moose Jaw. Sub zero weather arrived for a few weeks and trees would crack like gunfire. With two heavy snowfalls, we picked up our snowshoes and more checks for weasels plus sending out twelve more.

We settled in for the winter; at times cutting wood for Gene, in exchange for eggs, which I used in my baking as well enjoying them for breakfast. I had never got the habit of eating meat and potatoes for breakfast as so many country people often do. I had now mastered the art of baking bread and enjoyed doing it. I did a lot of reading and Roy spent his evenings whitling, encouraged by the fancy things he saw done at Yerkie's place.

With a tooth giving me a lot of trouble, it was necessary to see a dentist in Powassan. It was a good time to take the pelts with me. We used Roy's fiberboard suitcase, wrapped the skins in old clothes that had been left in camp, sprinkled them well with talcum powder then locked the suitcase. I shipped them from the Trout Creek station.

The dentist hesitated to pull my tooth because it was a badly infected wisdom tooth. When I explained where I came from and the difficulty in coming back, he pulled it, and I had no further trouble that winter.

I had to stay another night at the hotel in order to catch Oliver's stage back to the Valley. I told Oliver about the deer hides we had and he made arrangements for his brother to pick them up. He gave us $10.00 for all the hides.

Later we learned from Sank that Oliver had told around the Trout Creek Hotel that we had been shooting deer just for their hides! This got to the Hummel's who owned our camp and they tried to get the game warden to come in after us.

77

Apparently he wasn't too brave and may have thought we were a couple of outlaws, to be staying way back there by ourselves, so he never came in.

In mid-February we finally decided to leave our camp. Gene asked us stay at his place. He said we could not hope to make much on fur for the balance of winter.

The wolves became more active as the winter progressed and we saw five at a distance crossing Stanley Lake. By following their tracks we found where they had killed a deer just half a mile from our camp. During the real cold spells we had often heard deer walking around the camp at night. They would follow our snowshoe trails, as they were able to walk without breaking through. The snow had become too deep for them except on the thick hemlock ridges where the trees kept the heavy snow off. They had eaten all the browse off the hemlock and were forced to feed in other areas where they were at the mercy of the wolves.

More on the deer hides we sold. In 1944 when I raised the lodge roof, I had hired Charlie Hummel, who was the owner of the hunt camp we moved into in 1925. One night while we were reminiscing about my spending the winter in his camp, I asked Charlie if he remembered the deer hide epidsode, and if he ever knew where we had got those hides. When I told him we got them out of his dog kennels, he looked shocked and exclaimed, "I told my brother Tom not to leave those hides there. He also admitted they had tried to get the warden to come, and said they were lucky he didn't go in. Charlie was a barn framer, and he made a good job of raising the lodge roof.

CHAPTER 10

WORKING AT THE FOX FARM

Roy fixed us a crosscut saw and we cut a number of wood drags and used Gene's horses to skid them nearer to the house, where we cut them up and filled the wood box and his woodshed. Nellie was so pleased with all her wood, she said, "You know, Gene, just never liked to cut wood, I really do appreciate all you boys have done."

Sometime in March we received a check for $220.00 from Moose Jaw for our beaver skins. With all this money, Roy decided to go back to Prince Edward Island.

Gene asked me to stay and work for him. He needed me to help him build more fox pens in the spring, as well as all the chores that needed to be done daily.

His father, Joeb, owned two drug stores in Detroit; he had purchased them when his daughter married a pharmacist and he set them up in business. Joeb had been a farmer and a cattle buyer around St. Thomas, Ontario. As long as I knew him, I had never seen him read a newspaper or write. I assumed he coud not read or write.

When Gene was not drinking he was a wonderful guy to be around, but a holy terror when he was on a drinking bout. There were usually long periods between, and I got along fine with him. All the experience I had had as a taxi driver was a big help in this situation.

Joeb would come back to the fox farm during the summer and stay until December. He enjoyed the peace and quiet of the bush country and still thought of himself as a farmer and cattle buyer and he always dreaded going back to Detroit. He always put up enough hay to keep a few cattle and sheep on the 600 acres of clearings through the winter.

79

I did the chores around the barns and helped Gene feed the foxes, as they required more care during the period they were carrying their young. There were always repairs to be made around their pens. Occasionally they would chew holes through the partitions separating the pens.

We had a big thaw around the end of March and muskrats began to come out from under the ice. I decided to trap a few. There were several beaver ponds near by as well as Perch Lake and Clear Lake. I managed to catch enough to make it interesting, at the same time I was learning more about the country.

It was just as well, although at the time I never realized that I was only a few miles from the site of the lodge that I would eventually build. How little we know what guides us to our ultimate destiny.

The sheep started to wander away as soon as the snow was off the clearings. Once in awhile I would have to go after them and lock them in at night; otherwise, we were afraid the wolves or bears would get them first.

One night in the early part of April sixteen sheep never came in. Just before dark I went to look for them. Two of them had bells on and usually were not hard to find. That night I could not find or hear any trace of them and had to give up.

Next morning I was out at daybreak, anxiously covering every place I thought they could be. I had 600 acres with several swamps and timber to cover. They seemed to have vanished completely. We assumed they must have gone out the road when it was frozen at night and left no tracks.

The following day I had to cross the hard scrabble road with a team to meet Joeb, as he was coming in. I dreaded having to tell him about the lost sheep.

"Walter, I just don't understand why you can't find any sign of their tracks. Not even a dead one?"

"Joeb," I replied, "I have looked all over and I don't understand it myself."

Our nearest neighbour was at Golden Valley and there was really no place else they could go.

Joeb and I spent a couple of days looking together with no results; it appeared to be a mystery. He was finally convinced that I had done my best to find them, which relieved me a lot.

Two weeks later, with the ice off the lakes and ponds, Gene told me about a small muskeg lake surrounded by a thick cedar and spruce swamp, just off the south side of Perch Lake.

"If you want to catch muskrats, that is the place to go."

"I'll give it a try on Sunday and see what happens."

I walked into it, and while I was looking for a place to set traps I noticed white objects floating in the water on the opposite shore. It appeared to be white blobs of foam you sometimes see below a waterfall.

I decided to fire a 22 rifle into one of these blobs. I knew if it was foam I could tell when the bullet hit. It just made a dull plop. I decided to do some investigating and worked my way around the shore to have a better look.

It was difficult as the shore edge was like walking on an air mattress; very springy and full of holes.

Close up I could see it was a sheep, all bloated and floating in the water. I counted sixteen, all our sheep!

Eventually, I figured out they had been chased out there on the rotting ice by some animal, probably a wolf, or a bear, and the ice gave away and they could not climb out.

The fifteen ewes would have given birth to their lambs in a few weeks. It was quite a loss to old Joeb and I felt sick at the loss myself.

In circling the lake I found pieces of wool stuck on the brush and I traced it back to where they had been chased from the field, through the woods to this little lake and then onto the lake ice. I was quite sure then it must have been a bear. Wolves, I knew, would have made a kill right in the field before they had gone far. Besides, this was the time bears were coming out of their dens and ready for a gourmet meal.

Soon after that I was picking up my rat traps and saw where a bear had pulled a sheep out of the lake and eaten it. You could smell sheep from a distance by this time.

Joeb told me, "Sank has some bear traps I am sure he will be glad to loan you. Ask him, and see what you can do."

Sank was only too happy to demonstrate how to use them, so I became a bear trapper.

81

According to instructions, I made a logged-in brush pen, open at one end and put the dead sheep in the back. I then placed my trap at the entrance and fastened the chain to a heavy birch log.

The very next day Nellie's spaniel dog began to bark loudly and when I went outside to check on the disturbance I could hear the bear roaring almost a half a mile away.

Shaking and excited I ran with my 30-30 and Joeb brought up the rear, close on my heels.

It was a good size bear and he was really ripping things apart by the time I got there, but I managed to get a shot into him and thankfully he went down.

Before I stopped trapping, I had seven bears that spring; five of them were after the sheep, as the smell of them was so strong and kept so long in the cold water that they drew bear until berries and other food was available.

However, there was one extra clever bear that kept taking my bait without getting trapped. He would tear the pens apart and take the sheep out the back way. I tried placing the sheep on a log out in the lake; even concealing my trap in the water, where I felt the bears would have to step to reach the sheep. The first time he just swam out and took the bait from behind.

I thought, "I'll fix him," and I put logs together with the sheep wired solid, then pushed it a few feet out in the lake. Then I felled two thick spruce trees, with the limbs still on it in a V shape, on top of the bait. I even concealed two traps in the water, where I felt he would have to step in order to get at the sheep, then covered the traps with swamp moss to look like a moss-covered rock.

I told Joeb, "If that bear beats me this time, I quit," and I meant it.

When I checked, I could see where the bear had started to scratch with this paws, six feet in front of the traps and gradually kept scratching closer until his claws caught one of the trap's chains.

I found the log and trap about ten feet back over a log. So, I quit. He was smarter than I and deserved his freedom.

Later that summer, Joeb was sitting on a cliff overlooking Clear Lake watching for a deer when he saw a huge bear coming along the shore, where he had been feeding on blueberries. As soon as he came close to the cliff, Joeb shot it.

I went back to check if the pelt was worth saving and discovered three toes missing. I felt sure this was the old smartie that had out-smarted me. I was sorry he had become careless and allowed Joeb to do him in. That was the last time I tried trapping bear, but later I did have other experiences with bear.

An unusual number of things happened during my stay at the farm; one particular incident will prove how smart a fox really is. As well as foxes, the farm was a menagerie of animals like rabbits, which were used for fox feed during the hot summers when the young pups required fresh meat.

We had porcupine that Gene trapped, as they were very numerous at that time. They are also very easy to skin and were more fresh meat. Of course Nellie had her chickens, as well as cats and kittens.

On this particular occasion, some of the chickens were running loose around the yard and one morning we discovered a chicken in the yard with its head off; it lay in the path leading to the barn. It was unusual, as we didn't know what had killed it.

A few days later we found another chicken in the same condition. This went on until we lost four chickens. We still couldn't figure out how these chickens were losing their heads.

At that time, Gene used to cook up a meal, such as oatmeal, cornmeal, bran and add meat. He cooked this and made it into an animal cake. When fresh meat was scarce these cakes were fed to the foxes. Any crumbs dropped were quickly snatched up by the chickens that were always pecking around the yard.

The fox manure inside their pens made the grass very green along the wire enclosure. As I came out of the house, I noticed that he had just fed a particular pair of foxes, that were in a pen right next to the house. The foxes as a rule never liked the cake as well as the fresh meat, and this one fox just picked up his cake and took it over and layed it down along the outside edge of his enclosure.

At the same time I saw a hen pecking at the green grass as they often did before. When the hen came opposite the piece of cake it shoved its head through the wire; the fox all this time was crouching back about a foot away.

The moment that silly hen stuck her head through the wire that fox made one jump and he had her head off in no time.

We had chicken for dinner again that night, as we had for the last few days, but it solved the mystery at last.

That fox was smart enough to figure out a way to entice those chickens to put their heads where he could snap them off. I thought it was a very clever trick and could easily see how they got their reputation.

After the foxes had finished having their pups and all the orphan problem was taken care of, Gene and I started to build another group of fox pens. A hired man by the name of Dave came in to break up a couple of old hay fields, that Joeb wanted replanted with oats. There was always rocks to be removed from their fields, so we kept busy.

The early settlers who had cleared hundreds of acres of this homestead land had also destroyed much valuable timber. When they discovered it definitely was not suitable farm land, they only used the land a few years and they gradually left and resettled in valleys with more productive results.

It had been a mistake for the government of that period to promote homesteading in a district that proved to be less than 30 per cent suitable for farming. Also, much of this land had been taken up by settlers who had never intended to farm in the first place.

They mainly acquired the free land to get the timber; however, governments and people continue to make serious mistakes and always will.

Another serious mistake made during that early period was the leasing of land having very large tracts of timber to individual lumber companies, for periods of many years into the future.

As soon as the spring break-up was over and the water temperature became suitable for the lake fish to start up the streams to spawn on the Pickerel River Lake system, the first fish to come were the pickerel.

People from the surrounding area would come back here and camp beside the rapids to spear fish, as there were practically no enforcements of fish and game regulations at that time. Several of these spawning rapids were close to the fox farm on the channel connecting Dobbs Lake, Whitehead and Stanley Lake, then Charter Lake (see map).

Several nights I walked down to the outlet of Dobbs Lake where some people from Commanda had fires built along the shore and a few of them were wading in the stream, spearing until their legs were too cold. After a warm up by the fires back they went again.

They were using carbide headlights; the pickerel eyes would reflect like cat's eyes and those experienced seldom missed a fish when they struck with their spear. I was amazed to see them taking pickerel up to 15 lbs.

Fortunately this slaughter only lasted a few nights, and as soon as the pickerel came back to the lake, after spawning we could catch them with hook and line at the mouth of the rivers. Joeb and I went fishing evenings, which proved to be the best period for pickerel fishing.

I used a steel rod and reel that I had used in the Detroit River. Joeb used a pole cut from saplings out of the bush, with a length of heavy fish line wrapped on the end; he would unwind whichever length he required and whenever he hooked a fish he just heaved it into the boat.

When the fish were biting good, he would land three to my one. He would tease me about my modern rod and reel until he convinced me to change to a wooden pole. We also caught some nice small mouth bass as the water became warmer.

By the end of May the blackflies and mosquitos became unbearable. At certain times of day they just about drove me crazy sometimes. I would breathe them into my mouth and they would get into my ears. The fly dope in those years was so oily and strong I only used it when it was absolutely necessary. One thing that helped was to make a smoke smudge with chunky wood.

Sank told me, "When we first settled here, my mother would open the door and windows then take a pan of hot coals from the stove and some green grass on top; then she would walk through the house just before we went to bed. The smoke would drive mosquitoes and sandflies out. Rushing she would close everything up and put the light out."

The insects were never so bad in clear, bright days. By mid-June, when it became very hot during the days and the waterholes dried up, the insects tapered off. We only had mosquitoes at night or if we were in a shaded, wooded area. Wind was a helper, especially when fishing on the lakes.

About the time the pickerel finished spawning the suckers came up to spawn too. They were so thick at times that you could dip them up with a landing net. At this time, Gene needed a more balanced diet for the foxes, so he made two large fish traps out of wire, the same as a regular minnow trap but much larger.

We set these in narrow channels, and when I would go to inspect them I sometimes had to roll them into shallow water, as they were too heavy to lift clear of the water. The suckers made excellent fox feed when cooked in with cereals. At times we were lucky and got a few perch for ourselves.

I was to learn that all animals are individuals the same as humans. For a high price, Gene had purchased a western silver dog fox. This fox was big, mean, bold and a real glutton.

The first time I went in to feed him and his mate was after their pups had been weaned and removed from the pen.

Gene told me, "The female is very shy and seldom comes out of her box when anyone is around. Put her food inside the chute, so the dog fox can't get her food."

When I walked in the pen with a pail of food, he rushed over to climb into the pail to get her food. I had to beat him off with a stick. I gave him his portion, which he immediately took to a corner and buried and rushed back for more. I couldn't believe it. He tried to get her portion before I could get the slide door shut.

This side of his character remained that way until the following March when he mated with his mate. Gene always knew when that happened because "old meanie" suddenly became the perfect gentleman. We could go in the pen, put down as much food as we wanted and "old meanie" just picked it up and put it in the chute for his beloved. He only ate what she had left.

He would lie on top of the box or fox house regardless of the weather and give her the danger signal whenever anyone approached, after the pups were born. They always had three pups, and when they were old enough to tumble out of their box they would playfully tumble around "old meanie," biting his legs or tail and generally make a nuisance of themselves.

He proved to be the most tolerating father fox on the ranch. It was a different story if Gene neglected to separate them when it came time to wean them, because he would suddenly revert to his ugly old self again and would have gladly killed them if they hadn't been removed. According to him, "Kids are fine up to a point." And apparently he felt the same about females. He would remain selfish until next breeding season and then charm her all over again.

I could tell so many stories about these foxes alone, but I also have many other experiences to relate.

We finished building the new pens just in time to put the weaned pups in. We had to be careful and separate the weak pups from the stronger or they would kill each other. One thing for certain, if a knot in the partition fell out of the wooden sections and a fox could push his leg through the hole, the fox on the opposite side would be quick to grab it and either break it or chew it off.

It would take three of us to treat all the pups and parent fox for worms and fleas when they were weaned. I would catch a fox with a large net; Gene would apply the flea powder, then put a pair of holding tongs around its neck and pry open the mouth with a stick and pour a spoonful of castor oil in the throat. At the same time shove a worm pill down and hold the muzzle until he swallowed.

It took a lot of time and patience before we finished and we were all thankful when it was over for another year.

Gene did not specialize in silver fox; instead, he experimented by trapping wild fox and cross breeding. At times he had unusual results as the demand for silver fox gradually declined. He started to get orders for red and cross fox breeders, which brought higher prices than pelts.

He had also purchased two pairs of Arctic Blue Fox, but never had much success with them. They were apparently a freak of nature as they would not cross breed with other species of fox. But they were terrific breeders among themselves. Even though they were smaller than most foxes the females gave birth to as many as fifteen pups, but they seldom raised any, even when left four or five. Gene had to finally dispose of them.

Eventually Gene built seven groups of pens in locations surrounding the homestead, taking advantage as much as possible of the outcropping surface rock. This prevented the foxes digging out as they were prone to do. We had to dig at least three feet down making a trench and fill with rock when none existed.

Each group of pens consisted of from 10 to 16 individual pens about 30 ft. x 12 ft. with a solid wooden partition separating each pen lengthwise, with a 8 ft. high wire mesh surrounding the outside wall of each group. The roof of each group was also covered by wire mesh to prevent them from climbing out. Each pen had a special built insulated box with a shute-like entrance, to simulate the usual underground den or hollow log.

Cats nursing fox pups, 1928.

During the time I was involved trapping bear, Gene and Nellie were busy with the foxes as the pups were being born. At that time many problems came up. Some foxes would not have milk to nurse their pups and others would disown their pups.

For that reason Gene always had some female cats that had kittens around that period. Nellie would take the orphaned pups and give them to the cat to raise. Sometimes they would have to destroy some of the kittens to make room for the baby foxes. She kept a room up in the attic of the old log house for this occasion.

At this particular time, she had too many orphans for one cat to care for. So she placed two cardboard boxes in opposite corners and put three pups in each box for each cat. However, the cats became so attached to the pups, that when one cat went outside for exercise and potty, the other cat would steal her pups and carry them to her box.

Fox pen, 1928.

Walter snowshoeing down lakes
to trap camp on Hardscrabble Road,
east of Whitehead's Lake.

When that doting mother took her turn outside the procedure was reversed by the other cat. Nellie was afraid they would kill the orphans with all this carrying back and forth and their well-meaning T.L.C. (too much loving care). Her solution was to get a larger box and put them all in together; the cats then agreed among themselves to take turns at their profession. Between the two mother cats they did an excellent job of raising their joint family. I was able to get some good pictures of the nursing session to show to unbelievers.

On some occasions, if there was just a single pup, we'd leave the kittens with the cat. Of course the pup would grow much faster than the kittens. The cat was allowed to take her mixed brood and wander around the yard and as they became older off into the bush.

It was really funny to see the old cat heading for the bush with her tiny kittens and this oversize baby fox, bigger than the mother. They would be gone most of the day and come back proudly with a chipmunk or a mouse that the cat had killed for them. Then the fun began as they played and romped around with their prize.

Several times Nellie made pets of these orphans and she continued to keep one in the house after it grew up. It was very attached to her and behaved much like a little dog. When it was out in the yard and Nellie came out it would run up to her, lay on its back and squeal for her to scratch its tummy. It remained afraid of strangers, but didn't bother us men folk around the house. If it was outside and a stranger approached it would run and pull open the screen door and hide under Nellie's bed. It stayed there until the stranger left.

When it came time to mate the foxes in the fall this was a procedure that had to be done carefully because sometimes the foxes were not compatible. You had to observe them for awhile to see that one of them didn't turn on the other and attempt to kill it. It was either love at first sight or death! It was frequently death.

Nellie decided there was no point in keeping the little female pet, so she put her in a pen next to the house and carefully observed the reaction to her first male suitor. It was a good choice as they hit it off right from the start.

In due time, the following spring, she gave birth to her pups at the usual time, the last of May. The box she had her pups in was very well insulated and had a private chute, so that the fox thought she was in a den. But this little tame fox was a real show-off. She wanted to show everyone her family, and especially to Nellie, who the fox considered was now a grandmother, maybe?

She would carry her babies in her mouth, out of the box and over to the wire fence and whine for Nellie to come and look at them. She eventually killed one this way and we were forced to take them away from her. She may have thought that her real den was under Nellie's bed, where she had always found safety and now wanted this for her babies.

I had a run-in with Joeb that August, 1926, and Gene took up my cause, which resulted in him having a bad falling out with his dad. So I decided to go home to Windsor.

90

A day before I left I had gone to Twisty Lake to pick up some bear traps. Crossing Twisty Creek I heard a fox give the danger call. It was a call I was very accustomed to hearing at the farm, so I began looking around and saw two pups ducking into a hole. When I went over to look, the female walked out onto a fallen log and tried to drive me away by barking at me.

I gathered up rocks from the creek bed and covered all the holes I could find and built a small fire next to the creek to keep her from digging them out while I was away.

I ran almost all the way back to the ranch and Gene got several small no.-o traps and we wrapped the jaws with rags. I had intended to get a shovel and dig the pups out. Gene said, "Walter, that would be hopeless because of the tree roots."

He went back with me and we set the traps at the holes. I returned in the afternoon and we had three pups. Unfortunately, one had broken its leg. The other two were fine and at the weaning stage.

I felt badly about the broken leg so I fixed up a box and took the pup to Toronto with me and to a vet. The vet. didn't think the leg would take and he amputated. The pup survived the ordeal and soon became a fat chubby fox.

It created a lot of interest as I walked him on the Windsor streets on a leash. I soon realized he would have to be tied all the time, so for his sake I gave him to a chap that had fox pens near Essex.

Gene Boughner's Fox Farm in the winter of 1929.

91

CHAPTER 11

CITY LIGHTS AGAIN

I took a job again at Rivard's dry cleaners pressing pants. Things had been very slow for some time and jobs were scarce. My dad was still working in the tool department at Ford Motor Company and he learned they were re-hiring men they had previously laid off.

I went down to the employment office at 7:00 a.m. the very next morning and stood outside with about 1,000 other men. (Now in 1980 history is repeating itself with plants closing and all the layoffs.)

Mr. Moore, the employment manager, who I used to sell a paper to at the gate, came out on a balcony and started calling out jobs that were available. I hadn't held up my hand, but each time his eyes turned my way he hesitated.

Finally he pointed to me and said, ''Go inside.''

I got in line with the others and when my turn came, the man asked what previous department I had worked in.

I said, ''This is my first time.''

''I'm sorry, but we are only taking on former employees.''

This same thing happened three mornings in a row, but I told my mother, ''I am going to get a job at Ford's.''

I changed my clothes and went back to the main office building where I knew Mr. Moore's office was located. Just inside the door was an information desk and girl. She asked me who I wanted to see.

I said, ''Mr. Moore.''

''Do you have an appointment?''

''Yes, I do.'' I lied.

Picking up the phone she asked him if he would see me. Apparently he wasn't sure if he had another appointment or not, but she told me where his office was. There was a sign on his door saying, "BE SEATED."

After awhile a man left his office and Mr. Moore asked me to come in. He looked me over and asked what he could do for me. I said I wanted a job. He looked up and asked if I had an appointment with him.

I said, "No, but you have picked me out three mornings in a row and yet when I get inside I am told only former employees are being hired."

He said, "Where have I seen you before?"

I told him I had handed him his paper for two years at the new plant gate.

He looked at me for a moment then said, "Walter, you don't want to work here."

"Well, I wouldn't have gone to all this trouble if I hadn't."

"What can you do?"

"I can do anything anyone else can do if shown how."

Finally he said, "How would you like to wind armatures?"

I wasn't sure what an armature was, but I said, "That would be fine."

He then wrote on a card and told me, "Be at the employment office at 7:00 a.m. in the morning."

I thanked him and left.

The next day I got in line and when I came to the man inside, he said, "Not YOU again!"

I handed him the card and it said, "See Moore."

He reached for the phone and spoke to someone, then told me to go for my physical. When I finished, the next man asked again if I had seen Moore. He got Moore on the phone and then handed it to me. Mr. Moore asked me why I had not reported to him at 7:00 a.m. as the card said.

"I got in line at 6:45 a.m. and was pushed through my physical."

He seemed satisfied with that and I was told to report to the timekeeper.

The foreman of the armature department, Mr. Hillman, also wanted to know why I looked so familiar. The same thing happened again with Jack Ward the bench boss. It was he who taught me to wind the Model "A" generator armature.

Jack spent a lot of time showing me how to wind, but he mainly wanted me to discuss my trip out west and all my experiences in the trapping camps with Roy, and the fox farm. He would shake his head and repeated a number of times, "Why did you ever come back to this rat race."

I was soon winding armatures as well as the old timers, and they were turning out 30 to 35 a shift. One day Jack said, "Walter, I am going to tell you something, and I could lose my job if the super ever finds out. Old Hank has been winding armatures here for 14 years, and now that you know how, I would suggest that for the next few weeks, you only turn in about 25 a shift, then gradually increase your production until you are even with Hank in about two weeks, then never try to pass his production."

"Also," he said, "It is my duty to come by and ask all you fellows to try and increase your production; however, just ignore me."

Everything went along fine for a few weeks, then demand for the Model "A" Ford increased and they had to hire a group of Technical School graduates, 14 in all. This increased the number of men to 21 on the bench. Seven on each 8 hour shift.

These students were working for less money as learners, and as they progressed they naturally caught up to Hank, and easily passed him; the rat race was on.

Every time they turned in more than Hank, he had to beat them. Finally, we were turning out 65 each shift. By then burned-out generators were coming back to the factory by the barrel full and the super spent hours trying to find the cause. They blamed it on faulty insulation on the winding wire. It was decided we would have to place a piece of fiber insulation on the top and bottom of each 23 coils, that wound onto each armature.

Production was immediately cut to 25 per man, until they became used to the procedure, then the race was on again.

Believe it or not, we finally reached as much as 85 of those armatures per man, and more were coming back as rejects. The old timers knew what the trouble was but the super never thought of asking them for advice.

With all the racing going on, the metal bench where the winding machines were was vibrating so badly that the wire guides were damaging the insulated wire as we wound it on the armature.

We reached over production and then the lay-offs began and the men who had the greatest number of rejects were the first to go.

Finally, they gave an Oshawa firm the Armature Contract and closed the Armature Department, except for the occasional Model "T" generator order and Hank could do that.

Everyone on the bench had been layed off except old Hank and myself. We were only working two days a week when they informed us we could take a transfer, as they were completely closing that department.

I was sent to the Automatic Coldheader Department, where they made all sizes of bolts. My job was to watch when and if the tolerance of bolts size changed. I would then change the die.

We were only working three days a week. The first week I operated one machine, the next two machines, the third the foreman had me looking after four machines.

All during that period I was also driving a Checker cab for Bill Mechanic on my time off. I decided to quit Ford's and drive steady for Bill. My time card had never been taken from Hillman's department.

When I told him I was quitting, he informed me I was supposed to give a week's notice. But he marked my time card as if I had given notice. This would keep me in good standing with Fords if I ever decided to come back.

In the meantime, Gene wrote and asked me to come back north to the fox farm; by then I had been driving steady for Bill for several weeks. I hated to tell Bill that I was going back to the bush country, but I felt that was where I really belonged. Besides it was all I ever talked about.

95

The very next day Bill asked me to break in a new man. I objected, because I had been asked to make a special long trip to Chatham that a friend had arranged and I wanted no stranger with me. Bill insisted. I couldn't understand this, he had always given me a free hand, so I had to take the man along.

I drove to the address to pick up my pasenger. A lady answered my knock on the door and invited me in, as they were not quite ready.

A moment later someone else knocked on the apartment door and inquired if cab 118 was there. As I stepped out the door a blanket was thrown over my head and I was hogtied by several men. I put up a terrific struggle but I was way out numbered. I thought I would smother under that blanket.

They carried me bodily out of that building and placed me on the floor of a car. The men were talking in low voices and I heard one say, "Down to the river."

Many thoughts raced through my mind, wondering what I had done to bring this on. I really was scared.

They drove for sometime and finally stopped. As they lifted me out, I tried to ask what this was all about. I got no answer.

I was carried a short distance up some steps and into a building. They laid me on the floor.

When the blanket was removed, I found myself in my own home, with a group of friends who had arranged a surprise farewell party. Bill Mechanic had been in on this all the time. The next day there was an item in the Windsor paper about the cab driver being kidnapped and taken for a ride in his own car.

They had this all arranged with mother also. When I got over the shock I got her alone in the kitchen and said, "We have to get some refreshments, beer and so on, as I know they would expect it." I had never brought liquor or beer home as she would never approve of it.

She looked like she was about to object, then said, "Go look in the basement, Walter." More shock as I found two washtubs full of ice and beer.

The gang presented me with a Kodak camera and told me "Now you can take pictures of all those fantastic stories you've been telling us of the north. We want proof.'' I will never forget that day or my friends.

A few days later my cousin Orval drove me as far as Chatham where I hitch hiked north from there. I made it to Trout Creek in four rides. Two of the people went out of their way to make sure I was in a good spot to be picked up again. This was in 1929 or 1930.

I was happy to be back at the fox farm and soon picked up where I had left off two years before.

Author back home in his beloved North again.

97

CHAPTER 12

FOXES AGAIN

That fall, Nellie had four deer hunters staying there, and Sank came in to act as guide with me. Sank and I had done considerable hunting together. He knew every inch of the country and had taught me a great deal.

Sank was a bachelor and lived with his brother in the Valley. They, like all local people at the time, were related to everyone else in the area. Sank's five sisters had all married local men.

Gene never wanted to kill anything himself and he never went deer hunting. Nellie was a different matter. She was a rather small person but the best woman hunter I ever knew. For deer, she carried a heavy long-barrel 38/55 Winchester rifle. I always wondered how she managed to hold it up.

Sank decided to make the chase between the ranch house and Whitehead Lake, rather an easy section to cover with only a few hunters on the watches.

Nellie came along that morning and Sank took her cocker spaniel down by the boat house. He turned him loose so he could chase through to us. The dog was not long in picking up the deer scent and I heard two shots from the hunters, then suddenly on the ridge next to me I heard Nellie fire four fast shots and I heard her calling the dog.

When I got over to her she was jumping mad. She said, "A beautiful buck came through on the side hill opposite me and I missed him." She cussed and continued, "He was running but I had good clear shooting."

When we reached the place where the buck had gone through I followed his jumps in the leaves for two hundred yards and found him with his horns jammed between two trees.

Later when I dressed him out I could see where she had hit him in the heart area. All four shots in a small group. It was apparent the buck travelled so fast downgrade that his momentum had carried him on, as any one of her shots would have killed him. All of us were impressed.

During that same hunt we had gone to the burn by Irish Lake. The 1915 fire had gone through that area, starting at Georgian Bay and it burned for 60 miles. That fire had been mainly a tree top fire and killing the trees. Sank said, "In 1918 one came through again and burned everything almost to the bare rock the second time."

It was now producing vegetation again; blueberries, bracken ferns, as well as poplar and white birch. The deer liked the burn before the snow came. I placed the hunters on watch, then circled with Sank to chase through. I heard Sank shoot a few times.

When we all met later Sank said, "I missed each time. But I found a hole in a knoll under a windfall and it sure has me puzzled. It's not big enough for a bear and too big for a wolf, with fresh earth pulled out in front."

Right away I said, "Let's go back and check it out."

"No, we won't have time, it is getting late leave it until tomorrow."

One of the hunters spoke up, "But we are leaving tomorrow."

The hunters were slow walkers, so I convinced Sank that at least he and I should go take a look. We put them and Nellie back on the trail to home and Sank and I took off.

It still amazes me how he could find it again. I got down on my knees to look in the hole. I said, "It's got to be a bear," as I pulled bear hair off roots.

He agreed but said, "It will be dark soon and will take time to get him out, wait until tomorrow."

I was too excited and wanted to do it now. Sank said, "O.K. if we are going to do it we must decide who will do the shooting, as one of us might get hurt."

I knew he did not want to chance what I might do, so I said, "I'll poke the bear out and you do the shooting."

We found a ten foot balsam pole and broke some of the limbs off, leaving some six inch prongs sticking out. Sank stood in front with his gun, an old 32/40. Down on my knees I began poking into the trash that blocked the hole and pulled it away. Reversing ends I poked it until I could feel the soft hide of the bear. Apparently in a state of sleep I had to poke it a number of times before I heard him grunt. I turned and asked Sank if he was ready and he said he was.

After much more poking and snorting the bear started out. Instead of waiting until the bear got his head out, Sank fired as soon as he saw fur. That happened to be the bear's front paw.

I had swung myself off to one side and I yelled, "You only hit his foot!"

The bear let out a roar and tried to push his head out as Sank fired again. The bullet went through his nose and quite scared I yelled again, "Hit him again." He made a lunge to get out and as the bear's head came into view, I heard Sank shoot, but the hammer of his gun slammed on an empty barrel.

I never saw anyone move as fast as old Sank, as he rammed his hand in his pocket for another shell. Luckily the third shot hit just above the eyes and he was dying. Sank had forgot to re-load after shooting two shots earlier that afternoon.

He was really upset with himself. "To think I was worrying about you getting excited and I almost got us killed."

We pulled the bear out the rest of the way, but it was a tight fit. He was about a two year old and we didn't stop to clean him; just tied him to two poles and carried him straddle our shoulders all the way home and right into the kitchen. The hunters were pleased that they would have a bear to take home and we had a big celebration that night. Sank and I were lucky that we had managed to get back to the good trail before it became too dark.

Joeb had gone back to Detroit early as he wasn't well. Sank came back several times for a hunt and just before Christmas we talked Gene into taking the dog down to the boathouse to start him on a deer drive. After Gene turned the dog loose he returned to feed his foxes.

I soon heard the dog yipping and saw a doe and a buck coming. I managed to get both, then I heard Nellie and Sank shooting. When we got together, we found we had four deer and discovered the tracks of sixteen coming out of that swamp. They had yarded up there.

There were several other homesteads that had been abandoned adjacent to the Whitehead homestead, with a few hundred acres cleared. These old stumpy fields were an excellent place to trap fox.

Gene had me clean up his traps and boil them; then we set fire to some of the old stumps. They burned down to the roots and went out. Most had mouse nests in them in the roots. After the fire burned out, there was still a smell of burnt mouse nests which attracted the foxes, and Gene said this was a good place to set the traps. He then gave me a lesson on how to set the traps.

He put all his equipment in a basket and carried a 12 ft. piece of canvas two feet wide. When he approached the stump to set

Walter's Red Fox catch being admired by Frances Kelly.

101

the fox set, he stopped and unrolled the canvas and he only walked on this. With a pair of gloves and a trowel, dug out a shallow
place usually in the ashes, to place his trap that he already had
secured to a stake.

He would drive the stake out of sight then place his trap on top
and cover the pan of the trap with a piece of boiled cloth. Using a
can with holes in the bottom, he sifted ashes or fine earth over the
trap until it was concealed.

Barn chaff that mice had worked in was scattered inside the
stump, ahead of his trap, carefully he would back away from the
set on his canvas and leave no scent.

Gene said, "This set always works better after a rain but
sometimes I catch a fox the very first night. I have also caught a
skunk and a coon," he laughed. "If you can kill the skunk and
remove it without leaving your own scent and reset your trap, it
will catch the first fox to come along, as they will try and in-
vestigate why the skunk had been there."

All I could think of was "Good Lord, do I smell stronger than
a skunk?" And believe me there were many times when we ran
neck and neck!

Gene also had a water set, as he called it. There were several
springs in and around these old clearings and he had prepared
most of these a few years before and they looked natural now, but
to teach me he prepared a new one.

With a shovel he dug out a spring hole, making a round basin
about four feet in diameter, so the overflow of the spring water
could runaway. He cut a large piece of sod and placed it in the
center of the basin so it would protrude above the water line.
Placing prepared fox scent or bait on top of this sod, then another
piece of sod or flat rock about eight inches from the rim of the
basin and UNDER water, just enough to permit him to set his
trap on top, with the trap pan level with the surface.

Previously he had cut some round pieces of moss five or six
inches in diameter off an old log. Placing the moss on top of the
trap pan to make it appear to be a nice moss-covered stone that
the fox could step on, in order to reach and smell the bait or scent
that was on the center moss, without wetting his paws.

The chain of the trap was fastened to a short piece of hardwood
drag, concealed under water, so that when he stepped on the trap

he could get some distance away from the spring before the drag would get stuck and hold him there; in this way the spring hole was ready to use again.

Gene always used rubbers and approached these sets by walking in the overflow water, to not leave any human scent.

I was now a fox trapper who was anxious to get started. While he took care of the sets close to home, I branched out to the surrounding old clearings and farther down the lakes. Some of the traps were checked every morning, others every two days. The foxes were always taken alive.

I would approach them with a crotched limb of a tree and place it over their neck and hold them while I released the trap; then put the fox in a sack to take him back to the ranch.

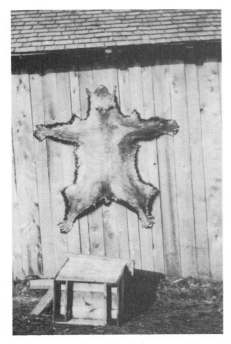

Bear hide, one of 7 taken at the fox farm in spring, 1926.

Beaver pelts at the fox farm in 1929.

Nellie applied disinfectant or iodine to any injured paw before we turned them loose in an empty pen. In a few days they would settle down and come out of the box and eat the food we left them.

The odor and barking of the ranch fox seemed to attract more wild fox all the time; that first fall we caught 27.

I pelted 22 in November, when the pelts were prime. Gene used the others to mate with ranch fox.

Speaking of pelting, Gene disliked killing and pelting his own fox, he said, ''You do a much better job of it anyway.'' He just didn't want to admit he was such an old softie at heart, and would avoid killing anything when he could.

As I mentioned, Joeb liked to hunt and so did Dave. Occasionally they would go out in the evening and watch for deer at some of the salt licks that Joeb had planted; this way they kept the larder stocked with venison.

On a few occasions they left themselves open to ridicule. Joeb would hire Sank to take him around the area farms and lumber camps in the fall to buy up old horses and cattle for fox feed. Dave had to bring them in.

We would put them out to pasture until the weather was cold enough to keep the meat for winter. The first time I killed a horse I got sick to my stomach. However, it had to be done and eventually I got used to it, but I never liked it.

One fall evening Joeb and Dave went back to the stumpy field; Dave said he could jacklight a deer. Sometime later they returned with a story about seeing several deer with their jacklight, but the deer became frightened and ran away.

According to Dave, ''Suddenly, I saw a pair of eyes in my light and downed it with my first shot.''

It turned out to be one of Gene's fox meat horses.

Nellie told me that two years previous Joeb and Dave pulled another boner and shot one of Joeb's sheep the same way.

I was a witness to the best one. One night Dave and I were returning from Charter Lake where we had been fishing. Charter Lake was ten feet lower than Stanley Lake, so we were walking the mile portage back into Stanley.

As usual, Dave hoped to jacklight a deer on the marsh. He was walking ahead with his headlight on. He stopped and whispered, "There's a deer!" He fired a shot then quickly fired a second and third time.

All this time I was trying to see the deer, and with no light on I couldn't see anything. Finally I said, "Dave, what in hell are you shooting at?"

He said, "The damn thing won't fall."

I got behind him and followed his beam of light. I could then see what he was shooting at. It was a six inch balsam tree that was right in line with Dave and a quarter moon that had just come up. The tips of the moon were showing on each side of the tree. It did look like a pair of eyes.

Many of the settlers jacklighted a deer in those days. Every so often we would hear of someone shooting a horse or a cow by mistake. In all my years here I only shot one summer deer and not with a light.

After the pelting was done in the fall, Gene and I began to trap. Gene quit as soon as the walking became tough. With maps he had given me I covered a large area and managed to get beaver, otter and raccoons before Christmas.

Pat, Gene's horse, knew where every porcupine trap was set; I could ride him out and he would take me to every trap that Gene had set. Gene used his saddle horse whenever he could. He said animals paid no attention to him on horseback.

On one occasion he was able to ride up to a deer and he once kicked an old sow bear as she jumped at his horse when he rode between her and her cubs. Three wolves just stood and watched him ride by.

Gene and Nellie suddenly decided to go to Detroit for Christmas, so we had to get busy and butcher all the old horses. We had to pile them up among the thick spruce to help keep the snow off. They left on their holiday and left me to care for the foxes.

Until March, the foxes only had to be fed once a day. Gene had hired Dave to look after the saddle horses and cattle, but it was mainly to keep me company. Dave decided to go to his home in Commanda for Christmas, so I was left alone.

I didn't mind it a bit — until Christmas morning. Then a real case of home sickness and the blues came over me and I just sat down and had a good cry.

Afterwards, I got busy and fed the foxes and took care of the cattle. I struck out on snowshoes for Golden Valley as fast as those snowshoes would travel.

I met some of the Murphy family skiing on Jack's Hill as I came out into the Valley. They kindly invited me home for dinner and I almost cried again with joy, and I sure felt a lot better.

After dinner the boys hooked up a team and sleigh and we visited their relatives around the Valley. Returning we all played cards until midnight. In the moonlight, I started for the fox farm and invited them to come the next week-end.

Dave never showed up until after New Year's day. The Murphy group, along with old Sank and the Golden Valley school teacher, came in on skis and snowshoes, that made six of them. I had made a cake that turned out fine and they all enjoyed my dinner. I was glad I had learned how to cook.

Winter really set in strong and the snow became very deep, so I picked up the few traps I still had out. I had plenty to keep me busy as Dave had left again. Sank came in a few times to keep me company. One of the things that kept me occupied was to try and mark the date each female fox came into heat, or if I happened to see them mate. Gene needed to know when the pups could be expected to be born.

One pair of foxes had gone three years without producing pups, even though he had seen them mate. I noticed the female was in heat, so I switched mates with her. "Old Meanie," the silver fox, had already mated with his mate, so I used him.

Sank and I went into the stable to watch; I was ready with the catching net in case things turned out bad. When I released "Old Meanie" the female acted shy and cowed in one end of the pen. The male put his nose in the air and strutted over to her. She arched her back and snarled and he jumped back and went to the opposite end.

This performance took place about three times. Each time he backed off, then suddenly he rushed over, grabbed her by the neck and gave her a couple of shakes. Sank yelled, "He's going to kill her!"

106

By that time I was already on my way with the net. By the time I got around the end of the barn "Old Meanie" had put an end to all her fooling around. Sank and I had a good laugh as it appeared Meanie had said, "Young lady, I'll show you what this is all about."

They were stuck in the mating position. The final result was she had five pups in the spring. We learned when we pelted her mate he only had one testicle.

I had been telling Gene to use one dog-fox with several females, and he hesitated to try until after that test. Also a crippled female with a broken hind leg from a trap; she had not primed out properly to pelt, so Gene had kept her over the winter.

I put her in with another pair of trapped foxes that he had kept. In the spring she became so heavy with pup she would fall over on her side. However, she raised three pups and was an excellent mother. Her children adored her. I felt I had helped her fulfil her mission in life.

Nellie and Gene came back home near the end of March. Gene had been off the wagon most of the time in Detroit. He looked very bad, but eventually he took over his duties.

The snow had drifted so deep the foxes were able to reach the top wire of their pens. One got out, and was walking the top frame. We managed to catch it before it got away. I don't think it really wanted to leave all its friends behind. It was a lot tougher on the outside and no assurance of daily meals.

On another occasion, two of them got out during the summer and killed two geese and several chickens. Before we caught them, they were so full of chicken it was hilarious. They would run a few feet, then sit down while trying to catch another chicken.

Everyone was feeling the pressure of the depression, which had developed in that period; it hit luxury things like furs that people could easily do without. It also became obvious that promoters of fur farming had over done it. The only persons that had made money out of foxes were those who sold breeders at fabulous prices to those beginning a fox farm.

For me it became moving day again. I stayed with Gene until the end of March. I moved down to the Jordan Hunt camp at the west end of Stanley Lake, intending to trap rats in the marshes.

On a trip to Golden Valley I stayed overnight with Sank. While discussing what I could do to make a dollar, Sank said "Why don't you try making maple syrup? There is a good maple ridge across the river from my trap camp."

"What will I use for equipment."

"Do like my father did when he homesteaded here. Make it yourself."

Sank then gave me the details on how to do it.

Relaxing in the livingroom at the Fox Farm.

CHAPTER 13

A TRIP TO REMEMBER

The year was 1930. I was staying at Gene Boughner's fox farm, helping with the foxes and trapping during the season. (This was before I started the maple syrup project.) I would also like to relate here that 46 years later in 1977, seven years after I had retired, this true story was read on the Canadian AM CBC Radio Station, Toronto, Ontario.

Gene had an arrangement with Josh Wilson, who had a homestead on the old Nipissing trail near Magnetawan, to collect old cattle and horses for fox feed. When the animals were collected, it was necessary for his sons to deliver them approximately half way, which was about 20 miles to the village of Commanda.

They were paid one dollar a head for doing this. Then I would meet them and bring the animals the balance of the trip to the fox farm. This was another 15 to 20 miles via the bush road.

On this occasion Josh had advised us by mail that he was acting foreman on a relief road job, and had all his sons working with him.

Josh said in his letter, "I've eight horses to deliver and could you pick them up at my place? Sorry, I can't afford to have my sons lose the time."

I walked out and phoned Josh from Golden Valley. I inquired, "How do I get to your place?"

During our conversation he asked, "Do you know where Pickerel Lake is?"

I told him, "I have been to it several times" (see map).

With confidence he replied, "I am sure you can make it to my place in one day, if you walk south after you cross the lake." Then he continued, "it will bring you to the Nipissing Trail."

to Trout Creek

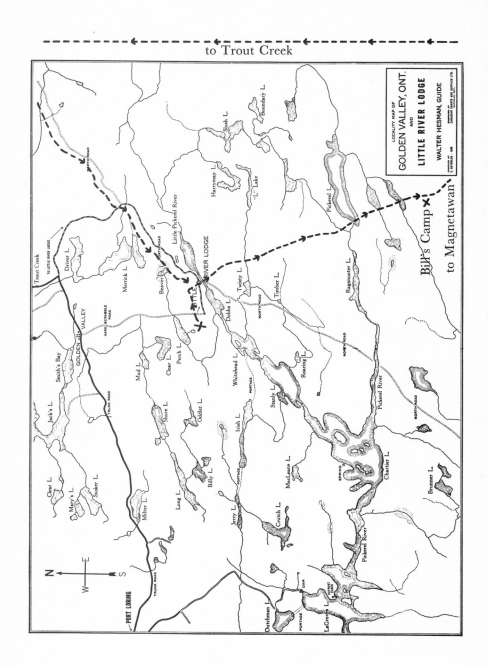

LOCALITY MAP OF
GOLDEN VALLEY, ONT.
AND
LITTLE RIVER LODGE
WALTER HESMAN, GUIDE

Bill's Camp

to Magnetawan

Trip To Remember

110

The morning of February 5th I packed a lunch and rolled a tobacco can full of cigarettes. At daybreak I started out.

There was about 10 inches of snow on the ground and hanging on the trees. Shortly after I had crossed the Little Pickerel River it started to snow mixed with rain (unusual at this time of year). I made good time until I reached Pickerel Lake at noon. I found it deep with slush on the ice. Deciding not to eat I crossed the lake and headed south.

Walking became more difficult and my makinaw pants and jacket were soaked with the rain and wet snow. I continued to walk until 3 o'clock. Trying to keep a straight compass course in strange territory made walking much more difficult, some of it being very rough.

After climbing a very high hill and not seeing any sign of a settlement, I decided to back track myself to Pickerel Lake. I had heard there were a couple of men from St. Thomas staying in their hunt camp at the east end of the lake. They were trying to make a few dollars trapping.

Happily in my thoughts I figured I would be able to spend the night with them. However, before I reached there, again I came across a man's track that had crossed my track within the last half hour and he was heading east. I was sure he must be one of the fellows from the hunt camp. I decided to follow his tracks instead of travelling the whole length of the lake in the deep slush.

Just before dusk his tracks led me to a small lake and out onto the ice, where his tracks disappeared in the slush. By circling the lake I picked up his tracks again and followed another short distance onto another small lake or beaver pond. After crossing this I found it difficult to tell his tracks from the blobs of wet snow falling off the trees. It was also too dark to see properly.

Stumbling along over several fallen trees I made up my mind I would have to spend the night in the bush. I began looking for a dead dry stub to build a fire. I did find a suitable cedar with enough dry material inside the hollow to start a fire, but when I tried to light my matches I discovered they were too damp. I found one among my rolled cigarettes, that I managed to light.

After I was certain my fire going to go, I began to look around for enough wood to last out the night. It was then that I noticed that the glow from a lighted cigarette enabled me to see the man's tracks again. I had made up my mind whoever he was must not be far from me, as his track had crossed mine in mid-afternoon. When I considered the condition my makinaws were in, I thought it best to keep on lighting one cigarette after another until I found his camp, rather than stay in the bush all night.

I knew also that he was a trapper, as I had seen where he had checked several of his traps where the beaver were. My progress was very slow and frequently I stumbled and fell. I was so weary by this time all I wanted to do was just lie down and go to sleep. Only my better sense kept me going and the farther I went the more weary I became. My legs were cramping bad. On several occasions I had trouble forcing myself to get up and go on. My tongue was burning and seemed red hot from all the cigarettes, as I was forced to chain smoke by lighting each cigarette from the last.

After what seemed a long time to me, I came out into an open hard wood bush and onto a well-travelled path. This really gave me courage and raised my spirits as I knew I must be getting somewhere. Any place was welcome compared to the bush.

However, my problems were far from over; I came to a fork in the trail and faced a monumental decision. "Which one to take?" I couldn't afford to make a mistake.

I did know that any settlement had to be east of me, so I took the left trail and continued to stumble along. It appeared to be following a very high ridge. After an hour and a number of falls and a terrible desperation to reach some warm haven, I suddenly saw a bright light down in the valley. I wanted to fling my body at that light.

Right then I must have really lost my head; instead of staying on the trail, I headed straight for the light!

Between falling and sliding, I went straight down over a cliff and into a frozen creek behind the cabin. Due to the racket I made, a hound dog started to raise the devil at the cabin. The bright light blinded me and I couldn't see where I was going or where the door was located.

I heard a man call from the far side of the cabin and ask, "Who's there?"

With breath I reserected from somewhere, I replied, "Where in the hell is the door?"

112

"Come around to the front," he shouted in response.

I must have been an awful looking character as he just stood in the doorway and never said, "Come in". I wasn't about to be left out in the cold and my first remark just came bubbling out, "AM I EVER GLAD TO SEE YOU." And I meant it from the bottom of my heart to my soaking mackinaws. I went on, "I have been following you ALL AFTERNOON until now."

Slowly, questionably he said, "You have not been following me."

With unconcerned relief, I said, "I don't care who I was following, I am just damn glad I am here."

"I am Walter Hesman, and I have come across country from Golden Valley."

He then said "Man, you're crazy."

"I will agree with that."

Finally, he stepped aside and said, "Come on in."

When I got in, I could see that the dye from my blue mackinaw had run out and was all over me. I was really a mess. I looked like someone from outerspace, and I felt like I had circled the globe more than once.

Briefly, I related why I had come across country and he said, "I have heard of the fox farm and I know that Josh Wilson has been collecting horses for it. Well, Walter, you sit yourself down on this bunk and let me get these clothes off of you, and some trapper's stew into you."

He took my clothes off and rang the water out. My hands and feet were wrinkled as if I had been in a laundry tub all day. The trapper's stew on the back of the stove really gave me a lift as I had not eaten all day.

After my meal I tried to explain why I had attempted this trip. Bill said, "Josh Wilson should have never told you to travel south from Pickerel Lake. You should have travelled almost straight east."

As it was, I had been travelling parallel with the Nippissing trail and would have eventually crossed the Magnetawan River.

This camp was Bill's trapping and hunting camp, and his wife usually spent the trapping season here with him. However, she

113

was presently out to Magnetawan helping her brother at Smeller's Hotel. So Bill and I talked rather late swapping our many varied experiences.

It was after nine o'clock when I reached his camp. This meant I had travelled over four hours by the light from my cigarettes. Bill assured me he would put me on a well-marked trail in the morning. It would take me to his father's homestead on the Nipissing trail called the Bummers Roost by the lumber Jacks. I could get to Josh Wilson's from there.

Before daylight the following morning Bill woke me and said quietly, "You are one lucky man that you made it to my place last night." Shaking his head he went on, "You would never have survived the night. It was 15 below zero and there is a real blizzard blowing right now."

I wanted to see for myself and attempted to get out of the bunk. I found I couldn't straighten my legs, the muscles and tendons had contracted. Bill massaged and worked on me until I was able to get up on my feet. He suggested that I not attempt to go on that day. However, I felt that I should as Josh was expecting me and I knew it would take me two days to get the horses back to the fox farm by the road.

By noon I made it to the Russel homestead and had lunch with Bill's brother, then on to Josh's place for supper. He was a very poor man with a large family. Several windows in his old house were covered with cardboard. I put in one miserable night and was anxious to start back with the horses, as I felt I was going to be ill from the effects of my trip.

It was still snowing and blowing hard when I got the horses out and tied them like a team, two abreast and head and tail together, then drove them up the trail ahead of me so they were breaking a trail for me. As difficult as it was I did manage to get back to Bummers Roost by noon and fed the horses. That night I reached Commanda and put the weary horses in Oliver Watt's barn. He arranged to accompany me through the old north road and back to the farm the next day.

I fell into bed as soon as I could and stayed there for over a week. I am sure I had a touch of pneumonia. I was so feverish and weak.

The trip had taken me four days, one day of rain, two days of blizzard and the fourth wading in deep snow. I recall reading many stories of people who became lost or stranded in the woods and how they became so fatigued they lay down and sleep anywhere. A number of times I had an overwhelming desire to do this also, but luckily I fought it off. I often think back to what I endured to earn a measly eight dollars plus risking my life to do it. During that depression period there were many people who did things that seem almost unbelievable today.

The local map will show the location and route I took on "The Trip To Remember." Had I had such a map in 1930 it would have helped a great deal.

Snow plow used in the 20's and 30's to plow bush roads.

CHAPTER 14

MAPLE SYRUP PROJECT

I stayed with Gene until the end of March, then moved down to the Jordan Hunt Camp at the west end of Stanley Lake intending to trap rats in the marshes. On a trip to Golden Valley I stayed overnight with Sank. While discussing what I could do to make a dollar, Sank said "Why don't you try making maple syrup? There is a good maple ridge across the river from my trap camp."

"What will I use for equipment." I asked.

"Do like my father did when he homesteaded here. Make it yourself," was his sharp reply. This made me face the facts of life real quick and then he gave me the details of how to do it. Old timers don't drop a hot potato in your lap and leave it there, they tell you how to get rid of it!

I remembered seeing a boiling pan at Ed Yerkie's when I worked there a couple of years before. He had made it in his blacksmith shop. I phoned his Loring home before I left the Valley. He agreed to sell it for $4.00. I walked the thirteen miles to Charlie Yerkie's and stayed all night. In the morning Henry decided to come back to camp with me. I borrowed the kid's toboggan and tied the pan and Henry's 10 gallon brew can on it. We pulled that toboggan approximately fourteen miles to the trap camp on snowshoes.

Charlie loaned me a crosscut saw he had filed and it was in good shape and an axe which he said had been made especially for making that kind of troughs I planned to make. He also agreed with everything that Sank had told me.

With our tools we crossed the river the next day and we found some good basswood trees among the maples. I picked out several likely looking trees, felled them and cut them into 20 inch long blocks, then split them in half, chopping the center out to

116

make them look like a long wooden bowl. The axe was designed and shaped to smooth out the inside.

Henry was handicapped wtih his crippled hand. He could handle one end of the saw but unable to use two on an axe. He willingly helped as much as he possibly could, and he was able to use the axe to smooth out the troughs.

Basswood is easy to work with and I managed to make 40 troughs the first day and before long had made 300. Sank came in while I was busy making them. He laughed and said, "Walter, all you need is a paddle and then you could use some of your troughs for a canoe." I had cut large trees; some of the troughs would hold five gallons!

Sank made a few spiles before he left by cutting small soft maple about one inch in diameter and cutting them into six inch lengths, then boring a one-quarter inch hole at one end about two inches into the core. He then made a cut half through and split the remaining four inches off. He put a three-quarter inch tapping drill in the brace and bored a hole in the block of wood to show me how to taper the spiles into it. I made the spiles I needed at night at camp.

We had felled a large basswood tree about two and one-half feet in diameter, and before I cut the log off the tree I made a number of saw cuts six inches deep and six inches apart in the log. I split these cuts-off, leaving a little more than half the log. I chopped the center out the same as I had done with the short troughs. When finished I had made a twelve foot long trough that would hold about three barrels of sap to use as a storage trough.

Next to a rock cliff I made a rock foundation for the sap pan. By using flat rocks I made a short chimney to direct the smoke and sparks away from the boiling sap.

Henry had carried most of the troughs around and placed them against trees we planned to tap. After placing the sap pan, I started to bore the holes and tap in my wooden spiles. The troughs were in place to catch the sap. Henry was busy gathering dry poles to start our boiling.

The first day or two the sap just ran enough to wet the troughs and I took advantage of this time for gathering more wood. The best wood was small dead trees that had been smothered and still standing.

The sky was clear one day and the sun really got the sap runing. With a yoke on my shoulders I gathered with two pails. I worked like an ox and felt happy as a lark. The dollar signs were dancing in my eyes, as I envisioned the money.

Henry, with his feet planted firmly on earth, was busy getting the fire going and cleaning the pan by boiling a couple of pails of sap and then dumping it out.

Everything went well that first run, or so we thought, as we managed to have two full water pails of partially finished syrup to carry down to camp that night and finish up on the stove. I strained the syrup through a wool cloth before I put it in a large pot to finish on the stove.

When it reached the right thickness I dropped egg whites into it while it was boiling. Sank had told me the foreign matter would adhere to the egg whites and it really did leave the syrup clear.

Due to the sky clearing it froze hard that night. In the morning I noticed that the troughs I had emptied the day before had partially filled with sap before it froze and stopped running. The sun had melted the snow at one end of the trough, and it was tipped enough to permit the sap to go to one end, and it had frozen hard enough to crack the end of the trough. This permitted the sap to run out. I could have cried and I DID!

It stayed too cold for the sap to run, so I hiked all the way to Sank's, about eight miles. I need to work off this disappointment. I asked him, "Why did my troughs crack?"

Well, Sank felt terrible and he said, "It's all my fault, Walter. I forgot to tell you to char the inside of the trough over a hot bed of coals before you used them."

Sank insisted on coming back with me to see what he could save. When he looked the situation over he said, "Now you are lucky you made your troughs so big. The good end will still be able to hold enough sap."

Encouraged we got busy and made three big fires around the area I had tapped, then gathered up the troughs and placed them upside down on red hot coals until the inside was charred like charcoal, then they were replaced at the trees.

The outcome of our effort was worthwhile, as I made approximately 75 gallons of syrup before I had finished. I bottled much

118

of it in quart beer bottles. The hunters had left cases of them around the camp and I put them to good use.

Sank told me later that his dad made his troughs out of ash and maple, and charred them before he used them and they had lasted for years.

While the basswood was more easy to work with it was more porous and split easier. You can see that was just more proof that experience is a very dear teacher.

Before I finished making the syrup the ice was getting bad on the lakes, so I brought one of the hunter's canoes from the boathouse down to the camp on the ice. This assured me of getting out when the water opened up. Henry left me before the ice went out. I never bothered to pick up my sap troughs; I just left them there at the trees and years later hunters would come across some and ask about them. I did take the boiling pan out and sold it for $3.00, which meant my syrup outfit only cost me $1.00.

I trapped muskrat when they started to move in open water. When the pickerel came up on the rapids to spawn right in front of the camp I lived high. At night I would pick out the size of fish I wanted for the next day. Preferably I would pick the smaller males. If I did get a female by mistake I would strip her eggs into the eddy in the rocks; fertilize the eggs with a male and flush them out into the rapids.

One afternoon Sank and Joeb paddled down the lake asking for a feed of fish. Sank said, ''You know, when I was a young fellow settlers would bring oxcarts to the Big Pickerel River above the Kimakong River (which was just above Chartier Lake) and the men would get out on the rapids with dung forks and fork the fish out into their wagons.''

''I would like to see if the fish are still that numerous,'' I said, ''let's go take a look.''

Sank was a good canoe man but Joeb was more suitable for a scow. So we made Joeb sit in the bottom of the canoe and I took the bow so I could spear and Sank handled the stern.

Paddling down the Little Pickerel River to Chartier Lake I saw many pickerel's eyes darting out of our way, but I had no intention of trying to spear them there. Once we got to the Big Pickerel River, and just about the point where Kimakong River, emptied into the Pickerel, I put my paddle down and I started to go into action.

119

I did manage to take a few fish before we got to the first rapids, but they were not as plentiful as Sank had predicted. Sank was having trouble holding the canoe against the fast water so I decided we would both paddle upstream over several rapids, then float back down. This we did, but instead of me staying in the canoe we would pull the canoe close into the bank where Sank and Joeb could take hold of the alders or brush and hold the canoe while I waded downstream after the fish. This worked okay on the first rapids, but when we got to the next rapids and they were holding the canoe, the alder Sank had hold of came loose by the roots. The stern began to swing out into fast water.

Sank yelled, "Joeb hang on to that alder." But Joeb got up and jumped on the bank flipping the canoe over with Sank and everything in it.

I was downstream wading and looked back in time to see Sank get back on his feet and shout at Joeb, "Damn it Joeb, what a damn fool thing to do, you stupid ass." Sank continued to rant and rave at Joeb for everything. He was wet and furious. The canoe had filled with water and was rolling sideways under water, dumping our fish as it came along.

Sank's flashlight was caught under the seat with the light on. With some difficulty I managed to catch the canoe and a few of our fish. I pulled the canoe over and up on the bank. With a fire going Sank wrang the water out of his clothes, casting dirty looks at Joeb and muttering under his breath. Joeb was wise enough to keep his mouth shut and eyes on the fire.

After warming up as much as we could we headed back to the camp fast, as Sank was still wet and there was frost in the air. Although I am sure as far as his blood was concerned, it was boiling! He told Joeb, "This is the last time I will ever get in a canoe with you again." By the tone of his voice you could tell he meant it.

They took off for home when Sank had dried out. I was able to catch enough fish near the camp so they didn't go home empty handed.

I continued to catch a few rats. The porcupines began their usual trips to the camp, for they would chew on the salty or greasy wood. Gene had asked me to bring him as many porkies as I could. I kept a club at the door and when I heard them chewing at night I would step out and knock them on the head. My final count was 36 porcupines.

CHAPTER 15

$1.00 A DAY AND ROOM AND BOARD

As the weather warmed up the insects started to get bad. The camp was not a good place to be. The next week-end I took my rat skins and paddled down the lake and went to Sank's. He had just bought a used car, a Chrysler. He had never driven a gear shift before and he wanted me to take him to Port Loring. Also Julie Murphy, who had cooked me that Christmas dinner a couple of years ago, was now cooking at the Port Loring Hotel. I was pleased to have a chance to see Julie again.

Sank and I had dinner at the hotel and I learned Oscar Clapperton operated three hunting and fishing camps as well as the hotel. Port Loring was a very active village at that time. It was considered to be the headwaters of the Pickerel River, as Dollar Dam, just 40 miles down the river, backed the water up to Port Loring. It made that river navigable for lumbermen and tourists.

There was a steam tug that plied the waters, towing logs and log rafts and scows up and down the river. I was impressed with what I saw that day and asked Mr. Clapperton, "I like it around here and I understand you have some fishing camps, I would like to apply for a job."

He informed me, "Walter, I am sorry, but you are just a few days late. I have already sent for a man to manage one of the camps. But I certainly will keep you in mind."

Reluctantly, I left Sank's Monday morning and returned to camp at the end of Stanley Lake. I stayed and did some half-hearted cleaning up. I seriously considered packing up and returning to Windsor, although mother in her letters mentioned that things were in a terrible state down there.

People, especially from Detroit, were seen scrounging in garbage cans for food. I was in a quandry as to what to do. But

Wednesday morning I decided to pack anyway, as Sank had told me I could help around his place for my board.

As I carried things down to the canoe I saw a canoe coming up the lake. It turned out to be Sank, with a message for me from Mr. Clapperton. Sank yelled to me, "Walter, you have a job. Mr. Clapperton wants you to come to work." Sank was so happy for me and I was really thrilled the way everything was working out at the last minute.

The first two weeks my work consisted of cleaning and painting boats with Mr. Clapperton's father-in-law, old Alf Gordon. I only learned after the first week that my wages were $1.00 a day and board.

June 15th Oscar informed me, "I want you to take two of the girls to Camp Caribou and open and clean up the camp. There are nine cottages, a very large lodge and dining room."

The location was on an island close to the mainland. It was a beautiful spring-fed lake that drained into the lower Wolf and Pickerel Rivers. It required a three to four mile trip from the east end of the lake. Both girls had worked there the year before and knew what was required to be cleaned. My first job was learning to operate the boat and transporting our various supplies. I also repaired the forestry phone line on the mainland that was connected to the hotel in Port Loring.

It was a single wire ground circuit system connected to the forestry tower and Clapperton's camps. It helped the rangers keep in touch with these outlying areas. Fallen trees during the winter had knocked the line down in several places. It was almost necessary for me to bathe in fly repellent, as the insects were at their worst.

Eighteen boats had to be cleaned from the previous season's dirt before I could paint them. It was hard for me to believe they had been stored away without being washed. I had just finished doing a number of boats at the hotel and this was another big job. Bedding had to be handled from storage on the dining room tables; the legs were sitting in tin cans to keep mice from climbing up and bedding down.

Prior to June 29th Oscar phoned to advise us he was sending the first party of tourists in on the 29th and wondering if we could handle them. We were not nearly finished but we had no choice — they came.

We managed to keep them happy, but it slowed our efforts as far as getting our work done. There were extra boat trips to the landing; ice delivered daily from the ice house; boats and motors to fuel up; minnows to catch at Loon Lake, which was one-quarter of a mile from Caribou; gas lights to light at night and shut off at sometimes 1:00 and 2:00 a.m. However, we kept them happy and gradually the camp filled up.

There is one episode I will not relate the details because it would require names and personalities of folks that were are still living. It will be enough to say I wound up being the manager and host of the camp instead of the usual hostess.

Most of the guests were from Buffalo and Pittsburg and a few from Ohio. They were all grand people and co-operated with me whenever I was in a bind. All of Oscar's camps and the hotel in particular were busy at that time, so we saw very little of our boss.

There were several times when I would have to have a guest drive me to Port Loring to get supplies and to take in money that I had collected. I was putting in such long hours I was beginning to fall asleep while walking.

Walter the guide (right) with some lake trout taken in 1932.

123

Kidd's store in Port Loring, on Wilson Lake.

When I complained to Oscar he sent me a chore boy, Freddie Stillar. Most nights I went to bed at 1:00 or 2:00 a.m. after I turned the gas light off. I set an alarm for Freddie to get up at 5:00 a.m. His job was to take care of those fishermen who thought the only time to catch fish was before the sun arose. When the continuous ringing of his alarm would waken me, I would have to pick him up, stand him on his feet, shake him and then when I let go he would fall back to sleep on the bed. I really would be better off without him.

Oscar gave me a 100 per cent raise in my pay. I was now getting $2.00 a day. However, I was meeting and associating with such nice people and it turned out by the time we closed Camp Caribou in late September, that I had made twice as much in tips as in wages. The best part was, I had no place or time to spend it.

A great deal of credit for my success at the camp was due to my being able to handle my liquor. It was no place for an alcoholic. It did not take me long to see it was getting to Oscar. Everyone wanted him to join them for a drink. Sometimes it was just a matter of courtesy, but if you didn't know when to say no, you were licked. I had learned that when I drove a taxi cab for Bill Mechanic.

124

After Caribou was closed I worked around the hotel. There was always maintenance work around the cottages, docks and roofs. In October I would go back to Sagamesing Lake, to the camp there to prepare for the deer hunt, with some guides. A group from the Buffalo Trap and Field Club, who were more or less dominant, took over that camp.

During the three years I worked for Oscar, I believe a book could be written on all the stunts and practical jokes they pulled off during the deer hunt back there. One of the big shots in the group owned a couple of breweries in Buffalo and one in Welland. They were all huge beer drinking men and in most cases very wealthy.

The deer hunting back then was something we would not likely ever see again. Even as plentiful as deer were, the Buffalo group would not tolerate anyone shooting a deer without horns, except the first day when they wanted deer for camp meat.

A 1933 deer hunt where 19 bucks were taken.

Sagamesing Camp was six miles from Port Loring on the Wagon Road. The head of the lake was a jumping-off place by boat for several hunt camps down the lake, as well as Stinking Lake Camp on the road beyond Sagamesing. The teamsters that brought hunters in usually used our stable to feed their horses after unloading into boats at the dock.

125

The Buffalo group always had a bar set up in their log house. One of their stunts was to invite some of the hunters going to other camps, and the teamsters, to come in for a drink. They would ply them with beer and liquor until some were too drunk to walk. This naturally caused a great deal of confusion for their fellow hunters to get them loaded into boats for the lake trip. Several times we had to tie teamsters onto their wagons and head the horses homeward.

On one occasion they got a deputy game warden drunk for three days. However, it was a different story when it came to their own group; they would not tolerate anyone drinking more than they could handle.

One year they had a guy, who turned out to be one of those "know it all boys," especially when he'd had too much to drink. They cured him quickly by plying him with so much booze until he passed out; they undressed him and put him to bed and painted iodine spots all over him, then doused him with cold water and covered him up. When he eventually came to, he packed up and had the team take him out. I often wonder what kind of story he told his wife.

On another occasion they had brought Fred Heinsman, President of the Buffalo Trap and Field Club. Fred was really a fine old fellow. He weighed close to 300 pounds and was hard of hearing. They gambled quite heavily at cards and Fred used to worry that they would get into a fight, because they were so boisterous.

One day they asked the guides to save some blood when we dressed a deer. That night when the card game was going strong they arranged for two of their members to get into an argument and stage a big fight. We had placed a pan of deer blood on the windowsill of the porch. As the "fixed" fight showed signs of turning into something dangerous, Fred tried to be a peacemaker. He was really worried now that one of them would get hurt.

The two men really put on a good act. It looked so real that Fred got between them, trying to stop them while the rest of us were doing all we could to get them out on the porch. They finally did, and upset the blood and got it well smeared on themselves. Poor Fred almost had a heart attack and we had to get Dr. Pinkerton to administer to him.

When Fred later realized they had tricked him he said, "I don't care if you S.B.'s kill each other, I'll never lift a hand to stop you again!'' There was no end to what they would go to pull a joke and get a laugh. If laughter is the best medicine, this group had some of the best.

One of the guides, "Jack," was responsible for keeping their fireplaces going and tidying up around the camp. He came in one night to gather up the empties. Suddenly, one of the men yelled, ''Who in the hell left a god-damned dog in here?'' He was pointing to a huge pile of dog dirt on the floor. Poor Jack was conscientious about keeping the place clean and he was so apologetic. One of the men yelled, ''Well, get the damn stuff picked up and out of here.''

Jack got his dustpan and broom; dipped a pan full of ashes from the fireplace and sprinkled ashes all over the dung; then carefully pushed it into the pan and started out the door. But just then one of the hunters reached over and quickly grabbed the dung and put it in his pocket.

I'll never forget the look on Jack's face. Of course we all had a good laugh and the dung really looked like the real thing. There was never a dull moment in that hunt camp.

One of their members, Charlie Hoffman, who was a big "butter and egg man" in Buffalo, stopped in Loring on one trip to hire a medium size pony to ride back to camp. The owner refused to rent it to him, but Charlie kept raising his offer and promised to take good care of the pony. The owner finally gave in, but I don't know if Hoffman rode the pony all the way in or not, but when he came into view of the camp he was in the saddle with his feet almost touching the ground. With a straight face he rode the pony up the steps and right into hunt camp.

Then he hired the chore boy for $2.00 a day to take care of the pony for a week. Part of the chore was to bring the pony down to camp from the stable once a day for Hoffman to thoroughly inspect, even to the teeth.

The last year I worked for Oscar the depression was at its peak. The government was issuing relief vouchers, which were distributed by the local party favourites. Oscar was handling them in this area. It was a paper voucher worth $3.50 in the grocery stores. To earn it you were supposed to work three days a week doing road work.

When I came out of Sagamesing that fall I asked Oscar, "Can you use me around the hotel through the winter?"

His reply was, "Walter, I can hire all the men I need right now here in town for 75 cents a day, and they board at home. So if you want to do that, okay."

I knew what was going on as they were all doing it. You worked steady for Oscar for 75 cents a days and got the voucher for $3.50, without doing any road work.

I went back to Sank's and we cut hard maple firewood and he delivered it around Golden Valley for 90 cents a cord! In 1979 it was $30.00 plus; in 1980 and 1981, just out of sight.

I decided then to make an attempt to try and do something for myself.

Through November and December, 1933 and January 1934, Walter helped Sank Whitehead cut good maple firewood, split it and deliver it around Golden Valley for 90 cents a cord, for which Walter got free room and board.

128

CHAPTER 16

APPLYING FOR CROWN LANDS
AND VISIONS OF MY OWN LODGE

During my three seasons at Camp Caribou I met George
Wade. He had retired as head of the Canton Provision Company
of Ohio and he had several other interests. He came to camp
Caribou that summer and spent the entire summer at the camp.
He had taken one of the housekeeping cottages with his wife.
George took me to town a number of times when Oscar's son
neglected to get supplies to me. He also helped me a great deal at
entertaining guests.

After his wife returned to Canton in August, George stayed on
until after Labor Day. I took him on a fishing trip to Chatier
Lake and the fox farm as well. We spent a couple of days in the
hunt camp where I trapped. George was quite impressed with
the waterway and the fishing. He mentioned several times that I
should consider starting a camp there myself.

He indicated to me he might even be willing to help, if I found
a location. However, when we returned to camp he had very bad
news awaiting him. Word from his wife informed him that three
banks he had stocks in had collapsed.

Afterwards he was telling me, "You know, I thought I had
security for life," he sighed and continued, "now I must go back
and salvage what I can." I had nothing to lose at this point in my
life, only my vision of my future and my youth, but my heart
went out to George Wade. Being at the bottom of the ladder I
could only look and hope to climb up.

I mentioned my plans to Sank and together we discussed locations. It was Sank that came up with a solution. There was a
parcel of property on a peninsula approximately fourteen acres at
the narrows of Stanley and Whitehead Lakes that was purchased
in 1904 by a surveyor named Ben Carr.

Sank had gone to school with Ben and he knew that Ben had been running a boarding house in Morrisburg, Ontario. A Dr. Lock, who was curing people from all over the U.S. and Canada by foot manipulation, lived in Morrisburg. So people were staying at Carr's Hotel. Sank felt that Ben might sell the property to him, as he had done nothing with it in all these years. Sank wrote to him.

In the meantime, I made application to the Crown Lands Department to purchase five acres at the east end of Dobbs Lake, which was the logical approach to the waterway. In due time my application was accepted by the Crown Lands, but I would first have to get consent from the Pine Lake Lumber Company. They had a timber lease on this area but they were no longer operating or cutting logs. They were also sub-leasing their cutting rights to small operators. It was still necessary to have their timber manager inspect my location. If he decided the timber on it had no value, I could then go ahead with the purchase.

I wrote to Mr. Boucher, their timber manager. In the meantime, Sank received word from Ben Carr and he was able to purchase the narrows property for $200.00. Sank gave me an option to purchase the narrows property within three years.

The time was almost mid-January of 1934. Sank was through with the wood cutting and I asked Oscar about allowing me to work three days a week on the wagon road leading into Dobbs Lake. I told him, "If I could do that, I could trap the balance of the week as that is in my trapping area, and I need that $3.50 a week voucher." Oscar agreed.

About four miles in on that road was a hunt shack. It was only built with one ply of lumber and the outside covered with one layer of tar paper. This was going to be my headquarters, and I planned to spend the three days a week in cutting and clearing trees along the road, about twenty-five feet on each side to allow the sun in to dry the road. It was just a wagon road and instead of trapping the balance of the week I would cut logs for MY lodge and prepare to build that summer.

Although I still had not heard from the Pine Lake Lumber Company, I could see no reason for them to prevent me from securing that location.

I had gathered together everything I needed to go back to the shack. Melvin Smith, the fire ranger's son, agreed to work with

130

me and also get the voucher. Arrangements were made for Wendall Moore to pick up my things with his team and sleigh. Not having received a reply from Mr. Boucher I wrote him again.

The morning Wendall picked me up at Sank's was the 3rd of February, and that morning was extremely cold. We could hear the trees snapping like fire crackers during the night. Even without a thermometer we knew it was damn cold! Sank went out to the barn and when he came back he said, "I am sure that Wendall won't come, because it is too cold for the horses." I was disappointed as I was anxious to get going, and yet I knew it was terribly cold.

About 8:30 a.m. Sank yelled to me, "Here he comes, Walter!" Then I saw him coming up the lane, running beside the sleigh. I had no choice but to load my things on the sleigh and go. We put hay on a padded horse blanket and piled my food stuff in, covering it with more hay and blankets and took off for the store, where more groceries waited to be picked up. On the way I called for Melvin Smith.

When we got to the store at Golden Valley, loggers came out to the sleigh and told us, "Are you crazy or something, don't you know it is 65 degrees below zero? You and the horses will freeze to death let alone the food. We weren't about to go to work this morning."

Melvin's dad was there also, and he had us wait until he went out to the shop and cut a pipe hole in a 20 gallon grease drum. He said, "This will act as a box stove for you, that tin camp stove that you have just won't be enough in this weather." I also picked up a few rolls of felt building paper and we went on until we passed Wendall's home.

From there on we had no tracks on the road, as there had been no traffic since hunting season in November. Finding the snow too deep for the horses to lift their feet over, I said, "Melvin, you and I will have to walk ahead of the horses and break the snow down for them."

It wasn't long before our bodies were perspiring heavily, but our faces were freezing. When the shack finally loomed into sight Melvin said, "It may be just a shack but it sure looks good to me." Even to me its woefull appearance had improved remarkably since I last saw it.

131

Wendall decided not to stop. He said, "Walter, these horses are steaming too badly and I am afraid they will freeze, so I had better head on home." At least on his way home he would have tracks to follow and would be able to make much better time and we waved him off.

Melvin and I busied ourselves clearing a hole in the snow and dumped everything we had on some hay and covered it up with felt paper and more snow, using our snowshoes like shovels. Everthing we had of course was frozen solid. The food would have to be thawed as we needed it.

It was now past noon and the temperature had gone up a little. We set up our stoves and with a fire going we thawed out some. I had spied what appeared to be a dead pine stump across the road. I said to Melvin, "Let's snowshoe over there and cut it."

The stump was a dried tamarack. We cut it into blocks and carried them back to the shack and split enough to last us the night. The early loggers used tamarack on their forge before they had blacksmith coal. It was an excellent wood for a hot fire, and that was what we were interested in. Our two stoves were soon red hot.

For further warmth, we went out and banked the snow as high as the eaves on the shack, using our snowshoes again. We took in what food we needed for the night and thawed it out. While I prepared something to eat, Melvin lined our bunks and the walls with felt paper. By this time the little shack was just like a steam bath; even the frost was coming out of the ground under our floor.

George Wade had given me a homemade radio when I was at Camp Caribou. I put a piece of aerial wire out through a crack in the window and tied a horseshoe on a ground wire and put it in a pail of melted snow. Melvin grinned broadly when music came floating into our wilderness camp.

We never took our clothes off for three nights, as we had to keep firing up our small stoves. It was so cold the trees were cracking like gunfire from the frost all night.

During our first night we got a news flash at midnight that Mayor Cermak of Chicago had been assassinated. A few days later we broke a snow trail across Merrick Lake, cutting the distance to the post office in half. On that trip I shot a deer so we could have some meat to get us through the winter. The balance

132

of winter we did our three days a week of road work and the balance of the week I cut logs needed to build the lodge.

I had a load of cheap lumber brought in to build a shack on the location at Dobbs Lake; also a boat I had purchased on credit and a load of saw dust to keep ice. Later on Ralph Dobbs skidded my logs to the location I had chosen for the lodge. All he charged me for doing this work was $5.00. This is hard to believe in 1981. We didn't have much in those days but a few dollars went a long way.

By this time word had travelled to Oscar Clapperton as to what I actually was doing and immediately our relief vouchers were cut off. He wanted no competition in the tourist business.

I built a 12 x 14 foot cabin on the location as soon as the snow left the clearing, and I moved in there. Then began the clearing of the underbrush and the alders from the property.

In May I began pealing my logs. On the 24th of May I had some surprise visitors. Sank walked across the Hard Scrabble Road with Sally Bain and a girl friend. I had met Sally when her parents had left her at Camp Caribou for two months of the summer while they were in Europe.

Sally was their only child and to most Caribou camp guests she appeared a very delicate girl. However, she was not in camp long before we all changed our minds. She took part in all the outdoor activities and outdid most of the other guests. She was good at all water sports, as well as an accomplished horsewoman. She was much in demand to ride jump horses at the Royal Winter Fair in Toronto and owned a jumper of her own.

The day she and her friend arrived with Sank they had walked the four miles across the Hard Scrabble Road. The black flies were so bad they had rubbed black swamp muck on their neck and faces to keep the flies and mosquitoes from biting them. You can imagine what they looked like. You couldn't tell one from the other. I gladly took them fishing and we got enough nice pickerel for a fish fry. I really enjoyed their company as I had been alone for several weeks.

Sank was worried about his $200.00 investment on the Ben Carr property as the 65 degree below zero weather had split a great deal of trees and all the conifers near the lake were all turning brown. This was the first time he had known of evergreen

133

needles to be winter killed. Sank was very happy when the new buds came out in June and the trees recovered.

By the time this happened I had changed my mind about locating my camp on that property. I decided instead to locate at the head of the lakes, where it could be reached by car when the road was passable, as it would save transporting guests and equipment down the lakes. Also they would be free to come and go when they liked. I should have thought of this sooner after the experience I had when I worked at Camp Caribou, and realized all the trouble we had meeting guests by boat at all hours when they arrived and having to transfer all their luggage from car to boat, and from boat to cottage, and back again when they leave.

I told Sank, "I still intend to take up my option on the Ben Carr property and will double your investment." My friend and I shook hands on that. The property was located at the narrows between Stanly and Whitehead Lake, with approximately ten acres on the south side and four acres on the north side, both sides well timbered. I knew that the timber alone was worth more than Sank paid for it. In 1936 I sold north side four acres for enough to pay Sank for both sides, then took 800 logs off the south side and had them sawed at the mill. Believe it or not, I delivered and loaded it on box cars at Trout Creek, 40 miles from here, and received $18.00 per thousand board feet. Today it sells for $180.00 to $200.00 per 1000 ft.

In 1976 I sold the south side ten acres for $15,000.00. Old Sank would turn in his grave if he knew his $200.00 investment would bring such a return.

The Lodge staff at Camp Caribou.

134

CHAPTER 17

THE LODGE SITE AND MY FIRST GUEST

I wanted to locate my lodge on a knoll beside the Little Pickerel River, facing a small pool created by logs tumbling down the rapids end over end during the log drive.

All the pine logs taken out up to 1915 were floated right to Georgian Bay through a series of log dams that backed up a good head of water. The dams, when they were suddenly opened, flushed the logs down the different water levels right to the Bay. From there they floated to Lake Head Mills or shipped to Europe.

The area between the pool and the lake was actually a portion of the lake that over a period of many log drives had been filled by silt and debris gouged out of the banks of the stream by the logs.

When river drives ended the river cut a widening channel through the silt to get to the lake. In time trees and alders grew on this flat. The alders on the bank of this channel were gradually bent by heavy snow until they tangled with those from the opposite bank, acting as a catch-all for the floating debris each spring. At this time the flood waters were over the banks.

When the flood waters had receded, I cut all of the alders along the bank and to the lake and piled them back. That year when the water flooded several times, I took a pair of ice tongs and a pike pole and pulled everything out and over the bank. Pulling the heavier logs as far as I could I would saw them off and pull again. Gradually I was able to float the rest out to the lake. I was then able to bring my boat up the channel right to the pool.

All this required many, many hours of back-breaking work. I often look back now and think what I could have done with power saws and bulldozers that are available today. Alders grow very much like tropical mangroves. I had to constantly keep cut-

135

ting them down year after year until finally the roots died out. Once I started to run my boat and motor up and down the channel, it gradually deepened and widened.

Dr. Yant was another guest from Camp Caribou I had met while there. He was Superintendent of the Western Reserve University Dental Clinic of Cleveland, Ohio. Doc was a very devoted and accomplished outdoorsman. We had made several trips out of Caribou Lake together and one had been to visit the fox farm.

I wrote to him of my plans to build a camp, and as we had been corresponding frequently, it was finally agreed that he would make a trip up with his brother, Bill, their dad and a nephew in June.

They arrived at Golden Valley on June 4th, 1934. I had hired a pack horse to bring their duffle for the six mile hike from the Valley to my cabin. They had to walk in as the bush road was still too soft for cars.

Walter's first guest, Dr. Yant of Cleveland, Ohio, was brought in by pack horse to the tar paper shack in 1934.

With five of us in my cabin it was a tight squeeze. However, we spent most of our time outside, so it really didn't matter. I had brought two of the hunter's canoes from the boathouse to use as we had a short hundred yards of portage around the rapids between Dobbs Lake and Whitehead Lake; also another three hundred yard portage from the Deep Bay at the end of Stanley Lake, to the marsh where we could float our canoes down into Chartier Lake.

One particular day it was overcast, the kind of day the insects were out in force with back-up troops and a bomb squadron to boot. The general idea was to eat us alive. Doc and I, unaware of their planned strategy, went down to the river to clean some fish.

I did not have the alders cleared at that time and with the leaves on them it made it worse. The blackflies and the mosquitos became so bad I had to cut a handful of brush with leaves still on so Doc, could keep flailing around me in a futile attempt to keep them off.

Finally Doc said, "Walter, I can't take this anymore. The mosquitos are so thick on your back I can't see the colour of your shirt, let's get out of here now."

This is the shack Walter built to live in while he was building the lodge. It was also used for paying guests until the lodge was built. In 1934, Walter's mother and sister Ferne came to see him from Windsor.

We dropped everything but our pants and took off like a couple of crazy men, which we actually were, mean-while flailing ourselves madly with the brush. With a smoke smudge going in a pail we were finally able to finish the fish-cleaning job.

On the good side, they had excellent fishing during the visit of ten days. Doc's father, who was all of 84 years old, was really beside himself with excitement. He had never enjoyed fishing like we had. With the insect season at its peak, he would forget to put repellent on, and at times the blackflies would get inside his clothes, but as long as the fish were biting he never once complained.

Several times when he undressed for bed we would see his underwear all bloody from insect bites. Doc would glance at me and just shake his head, but I knew he was so proud of his father just the same.

We were catching so many fish we bent the barbs on the hooks. When we brought a fish to the surface if it wasn't just what we wanted, we shook it off, secure in our knowledge a larger one would be next.

When Doc and his party bid me goodbye, they thanked me profusely for the grand time they had had. I learned later they stopped at the Trout Creek Hotel for a beer. A chap by the name of Cecil Clapp, who owned Skinner's Sport Shop in the Arcade in Toronto, was there also.

Cecil usually had a column in the Toronto newspapers, telling about the hot fishing and hunting spots. He was known to all the fishermen and hunters all over Canada and the United States. He was a terrific promoter.

Clapp noticed that Doc's party were fishermen, so he asked, "Where have you guys been, had any luck?"

According to Clapp they all started talking at once, each one embellishing on the previous story. And they had the pictures to prove it.

When Clapp returned to Toronto he mentioned all this in his column and graciously sent me a copy. In doing that it reaped him many thousands of dollars over the years that I operated my lodge. I made a point of purchasing all my baits and tackle from him, besides the millions of worms that we eventually used.

Due to his frequent mention of my Little River Lodge in his column, and the prize fish that I sent down to be displayed in his

138

window, I was soon well known. I could credit Clapp with a large percentage of my business, so we both benefited.

I can name a number of very prominent professional men from Toronto who became regular guests of mine, due to his directing them to my lodge. I always insisted that they report back to him on whether they had enjoyed their stay at Little River Lodge or not.

Between Doc Yant and Cecil Clapp, I earned enough money that summer with just a small shack to work from to carry me through the winter.

The first of August Dr. Yant and another professor from the University, Dr. Fernus, came back with their wives, and stayed a full month. They were able to drive their cars all the way in as the bush road was dry, but to be on the safe side we took the cars out again in case it did happen to rain.

Dr. Yant had brought two silk tents with him and we set these up outside the cabin for storage, and I slept in one to give them privacy in the cabin. It is without a doubt the most enjoyable period I ever put in. They did not permit me to do anything but the chores, guiding and cleaning the fish. Dr. Fernus and Mrs. Yant did most of the cooking and believe me it was the best of everything.

My sister, Ferne, and two friends came in for a week from Detroit while my party were there, and they also stayed in a tent. We were becoming a bit tired of our daily fish diet so Dr. Fernus said, "Walter, if you get us a deer I will show you how to can the meat."

"That sounds like a good deal to me," I replied, "you can start preparing now."

The detective from Detroit came with me and we had only walked one and one-half miles into Twisty Lake when I spotted a deer. It was across the bay feeding on lily pads out in the water. By crossing a swale we were able to get to a small island, approximately 200-300 yards from the deer. I had an old war surplus German Lugar 6.5 mm rifle.

Sitting down I levelled the gun on the deer with my elbows resting on my knees, raising the gun site about six inches above its back and fired. I saw the deer go down. I don't think I was ever able to make a better shot in my life. The detective remarked, "I just don't believe it."

"Well, neither do I, but I guess it happened." As I jumped down off the island, in my exuberance to get around the bay to the deer, one foot landed on a round beaver stick and I sprained my ankle. It was so painful I picked up a stick to use as a cane and hobbled on.

Then I heard the detective yell out, "Now, I have twisted my knee." He had stepped into a muskrat hole, so we were both cripples. We managed to get around to the deer and pull it up on the bank and dress it out. I hung it up in a tree to drain and we headed back the one and one-half miles to camp. It was a slow and painful trip for both of us.

When our party saw us coming down the hill they were sure we had shot ourselves and they came running to help. Mrs. Yant was a nurse and she soon had us all taped up professionally.

With a map I made, Dr. Yant and my sister set out to find our deer. After locating it he skinned it and cut it up and they put it in two pillow cases. With two pack sacks they were able to pack it back to camp. So I managed to get out of that job also. Dr. Yant said, "I am sure you did it on purpose."

My excuse was, "I only promised you a deer; you and Ferne are damn lucky it wasn't five miles away." They agreed to that.

We dined on steaks that night and had a big meat celebration. The remainder we buried under a big block of ice. The next day was canning time; Dr. Fernus cut all the meat off the bones and packed it in quart jars. He left a space at the top and then seasoned it with salt then placed the jars in a copper clothes boiler with water about three-quarters up the jars. He boiled this slowly for a couple of hours, then tightened the tops. The meat kept well until I had used it all.

Now you can believe this or not, but I never did shoot another summer deer in my sixty years in this country. At that time I needed all the help I could get to survive.

When Dr. Yant left he gave me his outboard motor. Occasionally he would take it home after a deer hunt and bring it back to me in the spring, completely overhauled. I finally paid the duty on it about fifteen years later and kept it.

During the time he was up here Doc helped me clear the area for the lodge. There were two large pine stumps in the way, so he said, "If you can get a couple of sticks of dynamite, I will blow them for you." And he did. He was quite a man.

In September, my cousin Dick came in. He had written me asking if I could use a helping hand. I needed all the hands I could get. Sally Bain and her friend Betty came in for a week, with what turned out to be their future husbands. I left them pretty much on their own, as I was anxious to get the lodge up before November.

I had already peeled the bark off the logs in May and June when they were easy to peel. Now they were dry and easy to handle.

A photo of the site being cleared for cabins.

CHAPTER 18

LITTLE RIVER LODGE BEGINS

Once Dick and I had all the foundation posts in place and the first round of cedar logs placed I arranged with Sank and Alex Smith, the ranger, Henry Knapp and Cecil Driver to come in and notch the corners. Ralph Dobbs with a horse decked the logs up the wall on skids. I offered to pay them $1.00 per day, but I told them, "I can't pay you now, you would have to wait until I can spare the money?" They all agreed. Can you imagine anyone doing that today?

We were only three days putting up the walls. I would have liked to have added one more round of logs higher, but Alex seemed reluctant to spend more time, so they went home and Dick and I were left to finish.

I purchased what was considered at that time number three hemlock lumber from a local mill, at the cost of the sawbill only, which was $7.50 per thousand. I took it to another man who had a planer that vibrated badly, causing the dressed lumber to have permanent waves. He charged me $5.00 a thousand. These people also agreed to wait for their pay. I had credit unlimited!

Ralph hauled the lumber in for $15.00, as well as the $12.00 for tarred felt roofing paper I would use for the roof. Dick and I worked like mad. He did all the cooking and inside work. Dick was just out of the U.S. Navy and really trained to do laundry properly and keep things clean.

Soon the rafters were up and the sheating on the roof. Sank and the other axemen had notched in the dining room ceiling beams as they worked the walls up. Just before we had finished the sheating we had company.

Sally, Betty and their mothers, as well as Mrs. Bain's maid, Stella, a polish girl, came in. It turned out they were a big help to us. Stella was a gem. She wanted to do everything. Besides, she

The lodge during construction in September-October, 1934.

Lodge, 1934.

fed us like she was our mother. Mrs. Bain (Effy) was a very small person, but she apparently was raised to be well acquainted with work.

Every day Effy was at the building pounding nails right along with us; we couldn't even keep her off the roof. Like a busy little ant she was everywhere and accomplishing a great deal. I admired her ambition and it was gratifying to me when I had time to contemplate about all the kind and thoughtful people who had given to me their time and hard labour, so that I could realize and complete my dream of my own lodge. Being almost a pauper at the time, it was a humbling thought.

When we finished my $12.00 roof, the next job was to put in a floor, which was known as a floating floor. In other words, we made a separate foundation for the floor inside the wall foundation. The idea was to keep the floor as low as possible, and if the outside walls were to shift, due to frost, it would never interfere with the inside floor.

Now to the shape and size of the lodge. The main section was 18 ft. x 36 ft. (this was the dining room and lounge), with the kitchen added on the back 12 ft x 24 ft., so the dining room floor and the kitchen floors were on their own foundation. The dining room section was one and one-half stories and the kitchen one storey (see picture).

Once the floors were in, we tackled cutting out the doors and windows. This would have been a simple job with a chainsaw, but all we had was a crosscut saw and a swede saw. In fact, a lot of the door and window work was done with an axe. It is laughable when you think about it, but that is the "way it was."

I was anxious to get all the chinking of the cracks between the logs and plaster done before the frost came. I had slacked some rock lime during the summer, and got what I felt was fair mortar sand from the creek. With a bunch of horse tails from the fox farm, I cut the hair up into my mortar to help bind it. The fox farm was only one and one-half miles from the lodge.

Even though I had peeled and dried the logs all summer, I knew they would crack and shrink some more. This would require replastering later. Eventually, after a few years, I only had to go over it four times. Finally, it was finished enough to move in, but I decided not to build a porch until spring.

144

Mrs. Bain and the girls left about ten days before deer season began. I had no idea how many hunters I would have — if any. Building the lodge was a full-time job; it left me no time to make any arrangements for guests (the reason it had been built). My dream was now a reality, but whether it would be productive remained to be seen — and soon.

Before the girls bid me adieu, they offered to come back to help, if I needed them. Betty was a good cook; Sally's specialty was riding jumpers at the horse show. She was also proficient at any outdoor activity. She had been an only child and her mother hadn't delegated much housework to her.

I continued to work as though my guest book was filled to overflowing. I tried to finish the inside. I had no furniture, so I improvised EVERYTHING, with the exception of the two bedsprings and mattresses, which I brought from my cabin. Our beds were just bunks filled with beaver hay, covered with canvas. I graciously put one bedspring at the end of the kitchen for the girls and brought the cookstove from the cabin.

For tables, I built them from whatever I happened to have on hand. I outdid myself, I think, when it came to making an ice box. With tung and groove flooring left over, I lined it with galvanized sheets and insulated it with sawdust, of which I had a plentiful supply. For "central" heating I had a forty-five gallon oil drum made into a stove for heating my dining room. Now, all I needed were some hunters, to share this exquisite decor, that I had fashioned with such ingenuity from scraps and the sweat of my brow.

I would like to tell a fairy tale of guests having to be turned away in droves, but the bare facts were my deer hunt turned out to be a big disappointment. I only had one paying guest, and a staff of four. At least I was prepared to give excellent service, but how much service can you lavish on one lone guest? It was difficult not to spoil him, in case he returned and expected the same ultra service.

In trying my damndest to get my hunter a shot at a buck, I failed miserably. He refused to shoot at does or fawns and he also insisted on shooting his very own deer. This I admired as I knew many hunters, who year after year took home deer that someone else had shot. One day I had taken him on a very hard trip into what I called the "Pines."

I had always enjoyed sneaking around still hunting on the moss-covered rocks and ridges in the "Pines." It was always a good area for smart old bucks. That same day we returned to the lodge really tired, only to find my help had "tied one on."

One of the hunters from the Jordon Hunt Club had stopped by and opened a bottle of liquor, and besides that had left them a gallon of Jordon Wine. With far too much time on their hands, you can imagine what developed.

Dick had his laundry tubs in the middle of the dining room floor and had stumbled into it. Feeling no pain, he was quite happy about the whole situation. And he WAS clean.

Comrade, Sally's cousin, was just sleepy. Sally had a crying jag on and was in no condition to do anything. Betty finally got us something to eat, as she giggled and spilled stuff around, before she too pased out into oblivion. We were too tired to really care but it was an embarrassment to me in front of my very first paying guest in my brand new lodge.

Ralph Dobbs was to come in with team and wagon to take my hunter out. When Ralph arrived I suggested we make a short drive or chase between the first lake and the clearing, as it was easy to cover. I placed Ralph next to the lake, my hunter in the center and I stood next to the clearing. Dick and Comrade, now recovered, were to chase for us. I could hear them coming for a long distance, and suddenly I heard a deer running at the edge of the clearing. Seeing flashes of it, I yelled hoping it would turn toward my hunter, but instead it ran past me and to my disgust stopped. I had to shoot it if we wanted to take it. It was a beautiful six point buck.

I hoped that Joe would agree to take it home with him. However, when he saw the deer he refused to take it as he said, "I didn't shoot it myself." And that was that. This proved to me that he was a true sportsman, as most of my American hunters were, they insisted on shooting bucks only.

With no guest in camp, the girls and Comrade left after a couple of days. Dick and I were alone again, with much work to accomplish before winter set in.

During that September two men had come in and introduced themselves as Mr. Empy and his cousin, Mr. Ruppert. They wanted to hire me with my boat to take them down the lakes to

146

look at timber. Mr. Empy informed me, "Mr. Hesman, I plan to move in a sawmill." My first thought was elation as they would have to improve the road.

Later I learned how wrong I was. However, they did start to move equipment in during the month of October. They began setting up camp at the Irish Lake portage. At first they just hung long poles between trees, then placed lighter poles across the top, about two feet apart then covered it all with canvas tarps; then leaned poles around the outside to form the walls. To break the wind, spruce and balsam boughs were piled against the poles. To complete this, a large cookstove was set in one corner.

Men were already walking the nine miles from Golden Valley to their camp looking for work. They hired a few but turned many away. The men slept on browse or hay beds on the ground until they built their sleep camp. Their rate of pay was between $20.00 to $35.00 per month.

Dick and I kept busy cutting more wood for the big stove in the dining room. To keep out the cold we closed in the foundation with split cedar blocks and banked it well. I had to keep the snow cleared off the pool where we wanted to make our ice. Christmas week we were able to cut and put the ice up, then hauled in two loads of sawduts to cover it.

By this time I decided I should try and get a job at the logging camp to enable us to survive through the winter. They had built two huge log camps and one was used as a cookery and the other the sleeping area. For eight teams of horses they had a large log stable. All these buildings had been built with huge logs (see pictures).

Dick and I were put on the payroll for $20.00 a month. They were having trouble with foremen; two had quit already, due to the lack of having proper equipment. There was continuous friction between the owners, Mr. Empy and his brother-in-law, George Sills. Most of the time they would not talk to each other, making it difficult for the men to know who to take orders from.

Due to my owning a hammer and a saw, the only one in camp, I was given a promotion from trail cutting to camp carpenter. This lucky break gave me an increase in pay of $10.00.

In those days a blacksmith shop was a real necessity in a logging camp, so my first assignment was to build one, so they could

147

The 1934-35 logging camp. Men slept on brush until these camps were built. Walter built the blacksmith shop and got a raise to $30 a month instead of $20.

The dollar a day gang at the logging camp in winter, 1934-35.

get the forge under cover. The blacksmith had to make his own hammer on the forge so he could help me drive nails. I know it is hard to believe for conditions to get so bad.

One reason for this was Empy moving in there before he had finished another operation at Long Lake, especially when he did not have enough for both places. Also, they started too late to set up camp; besides everything was going wrong. The men were complaining about the last cook and he left. I suggested they put Dick in as a replacement and actually they had no other choice.

Dick really cleaned the place up and the men were especially pleased with his pies. That was understandable, as he made two-inch pie fillings instead of the half inch ones we had had before. He won them over and the complaints were nil.

The month of October turned out to be the coldest I can recall. We had many days below freezing and all these men still sleeping outside until the new camp was built. It was only very desperate men who stayed on the job. Local men who brought their team of horses in were paid $1.00 a day, plus feed for the team, and they were glad to get that.

Dick wrote a poem about the camp as being run by hay-wire and prunes. It was an inspiration, and so close to the truth that everyone found it hilarious.

About this time they had brought in the fifth foreman of the winter. He in turn brought his cousin, Bob, and his wife and another woman to help run the cookery.

To bring the logs out onto the lake the sleigh haul was started. The sun was becoming stronger during the day and this caused the runners to cut deeper into the ice log roads, so they quit hauling in the afternoon and began as early as 3:00 a.m. No one enjoyed this shift in the darkness and the early morning cold.

The foreman asked me one day, "Walter, do you have any idea where the sawmill is to be located?"

I replied, "No one has told me where it should go, but I know the only feasible place it could be located."

"Okay, at 8:00 in the morning I will give you eight men and I want you to prepare a place to put the mill machinery, and make a ramp so the sleighs can take their loads up off the ice." He continued, "I expect them to bring the machinery and the boiler sometime next week, before the lake ice becomes bad."

149

The snow on the mill site was close to three feet deep. It was lucky that I happened to make the place to get up, off the lake first; then we all trampled the snow down for the boiler.

All of a sudden one of the men shouted, "Look!"

I couldn't believe what I saw. Coming across the lake was four log sleighs with the boiler and the machinery, barely three hours after we had been sent to clear the place. To no one in particular I said, "This is one crazy outfit."

Later I learned they had torn down the mill at Long Lake to move it here, when they still had 25,000 logs laying on Long Lake to put through the mill; now it would be necessary to move another mill into Long Lake to replace the one they had just taken out. It was inevitable that they were going to go broke. To add to this, the foreman, trying to make a record for himself, was overloading the log sleighs. One load of ninety-six logs broke down three times before making it to the lake; finally breaking the sleigh bunk and dumping the logs and blocking the road for the rest of the day.

I could not refrain from saying what I thought of the situation. The next morning I was met by the foreman and fired. To add insult to injury my paycheck bounced. It took two months to have it honoured by the company who financed Mr. Empy.

The winter swamp road was built to Golden Valley and kept frozen by watering with a tank on sleighs. This cut the distance to the Valley in half.

I arranged to take advantage of this winter road by having two teamsters on Sunday haul two large loads of lumber to the lodge. With no hills to contend with and using sleighs they were able to haul four times the amount they could on a wagon road.

All winter long men kept walking in looking for work, regardless of a "no help" sign out at the highway. As each individual or company who were financing the operation for Mr. Empy gave up and quit, somehow he managed to find another to get the mill built in a "half-ass" way, until finally he ran out of backers in 1939.

During the next ten years the mill changed hands four times and I am sure none ever came out with a profit, unless it was one of the backers who made a re-sale of the lumber, which was much in demand. The mill was finally torn down and the saleable machinery was moved out. It seems a shame that our forest managers permitted companies to make such a shameful slash of our forests. It makes any of us, who have seen these forests before these operations, really sick to see the mess that they leave behind. One would think they would learn something from the experience in Europe. I believe our politicians are mainly to be blamed, as they grant long term timber leases to irresponsible friends of the government and permit them to sublet their cutting rights to individuals like Mr. Empy even after their companies had discontinued their operation for years.

It is only recently that some of these old leases have been cancelled, but not before they had exploited one of our main resources. Before the mill operated a month, the first summer in 1935, they discovered they needed a dam at the outlet of Stanley Lake in order to maintain the water level, so they could float their logs into the jackladder at the mill. So they had to build a two foot dam out of logs and lumber. This was the only thing the mill ever did that benefited me, as it maintained the water level between Stanly, Whitehead and Dobbs Lakes. This permitted me to navigate the first three lakes without a portage. However, our navigation was often blocked by huge booms of logs. And

Cabin No. 3 built in 1935.

151

there was always floating logs and debris. I began early in 1939 to campaign to have the rotted-out Reserve Dam on Legrou Lake rebuilt. It would not only permit navigation on the five lakes without a portage, but would also be a blessing in the event of another severe forest fire. I finally was successful in having it built in 1942. It made this chain of five lakes a very scenic water-way, that was seldom too rough to navigate with small fishing boats. LITTLE RIVER LODGE was to become very popular.

The front of the Little River Lodge in the late thirties.

Rear view of exterior of lodge.

CHAPTER 19

COTTAGES, MARRIAGE AND EARTHQUAKE AND TRAGEDY

I continued clearing around the area of the lodge by hand and prepared to build my first cottage. But first, as soon as the snow was gone, I built a porch the full width of the lodge with Dick still helping me.

Before the fishing season opened the 20th of May, the fire ranger's wife, Susan Smith, agreed to come in and cook for me. I partitioned the kitchen, so she had a small bedroom at one end. I purchased a double folding cot from a used furniture store for her room. Later one of her daughters came in to help.

Doc Yant was the first guest to arrive (as he was for many years to come) when the spring fishing season opened. He usually spent more time helping me than he did fishing.

I was building a couple of flat bottom boats at the time and with so many other things to do, any assistance was most welcome. A friend of George Wade, named John, had come up with Doc. John was just recovering from a physical breakdown and he stayed all summer. Another guest was Harry Holton. He was a lumber scaler and he began coming in on week-ends. Harry was a bachelor who was a licensed lumber grader and he worked all over the district, wherever his services were needed. He enjoyed puttering around and grubbing out rocks and stumps around the lodge. He only went fishing when he was tired. Harry continued to spend his free time with me for many years until he retired and passed away shortly after.

By the end of June I had partially finished the first of my cottages. I had no siding on it, just tar paper with slats every two feet apart. As it was the only cottage I had that season I partitioned it into four sections. When it was necessary I had to crowd mixed parties into it. This just seemed to add to their fun and enjoyment.

153

Considering it was the first season for the lodge, plus our limited facilities and equipment, Dick and I had periods we had to give up our room in the lodge and we gladly stayed in our first cabin in the field to sleep. We had named it not to grandly "The Guide Shack." Regardless, everyone said they had a marvelous time, and they must have as they continued to come back. We were far from being formal and small enough so that everyone got to know each other. Our cleanliness, I think, also made up for other things we lacked.

Early in September I had a surprise guest. It was Lottie, the girl across the street from my home in Windsor; I used to ride her on the cross bar of my bicycle. She was on it the night a tire blew and made such a terrible stink.

Lottie arrived with a group of friends who were on their way to Parry Sound. I had a brilliant suggestion. "Lottie, you could stay here and have your friends pick you up on their way back, couldn't you?"

She didn't hesitate very long and asked her friends to do just that. I was beside myself with her decision and it was a pleasant change to have someone from home to talk with, after the guests were all bedded down. We had almost grown up together and had much to talk about since I had left Windsor for good.

When the time grew near for her to leave, Lottie had decided to stay, and we were going to be married.

It wasn't that easy when her family learned of our intentions. In fact they strenuously objected, due mainly to their religion, as they were devout Catholics. Lottie herself had spent some time in a convent with the full intention of becoming a nun. I believe she was close to the point of taking her final vows when she left.

We were both 27 years of age, so Lottie didn't require her parents' consent. However, she did call her priest in Windsor for his consent.

He advised her to call on Father Reshea, in Trout Creek. After a few visits, I finally convinced Father Reshea I was not religious and I had no intention of changing. He agreed to marry us anyway. He may have appreciated me not making a lot of false promises.

We were married in late September. I had purchased an old Dodge touring car that seemed suitable for navigating our six mile bush road, under pretty bad conditions.

The day we were to be married it was raining hard and the road was a mess. I had to go out in my work clothes and hip rubber boots. My friend, John Odorizzi, had offered to loan us his car for the trip from the Valley to Trout Creek. We were able to change clothes at his place then drove on, where two of Lottie's sisters met us at the parish residence, as well as my sister, Ferne, and my favourite aunt and uncle.

After the wedding, Lottie's sisters returned to Windsor. The rest of the wedding party came home with us. It was quite a trip as the rain never let up. Several times everyone, including the bride, had to get out and push, in order to make the steep hills on our bush road.

We were all a bedraggled sorry looking wedding party by the time we reached the lodge. But a few "spirits" raised our spirits and we were able to laugh at the wet and muddy mess we were.

It was a drastic change for Lottie, and a sacrifice, as she could not always get out to mass when she wanted to. However, she made the best of it and together we worked darn hard for the next ten years. We both made many sacrifices to help make Little River Lodge a success.

I will never forget it was October 31st that Dick made himself a costume and went to a Hallowe'en Dance at Golden Valley. As if it was planned, about midnight I was awakened by the rattling of dishes and the kettle on the stove. My first thought was that it was a Hallowe'en prank, probably dreamed up by Dick. Then I felt the bed shaking and I heard a rumble.

It was hard to believe but I knew it had to be an earth tremor. It soon passed.

When Dick returned the next morning he said, "Those of us in the hall dancing never noticed a thing. Of course we were making more racket than the earthquake, and square dancing is enough to shake the whole Valley."

That was the first and the last time we ever had a tremor in this area. Very strange indeed. The amazing thing is that this country is practically solid granite rock and it was amazing to know it could shake like it did.

I managed to build my second cottage before the deer hunt. It was built from spruce logs standing upright. We had ten deer hunters in that first week and eight the second week. I managed

155

to see they got their deer quite easily. This was a big change from my first year with only one lone guest.

The second week the group wanted me to guarantee them our accommodations and services for the next five years.

After thinking it over I told them, "The only way I could possibly agree to that would be on a flat rate for the hunt season, regardless of how many days you stay." They agreed at the time, so it was a deal.

Dick decided to return to his home in Coldwater, Michigan, after the hunt was over. He had been with me through some of the toughest parts and I was sorry to see him go. We had shared many funny and unforgetable experiences.

The year I left the fox farm, Gene hired Mike O'Connor to assist him. Mike was married and had two small children. His wife, I would say, had a mental problem. Mike built a small shack a short distance from the fox farm in which to house his family in.

A short time later his house burned down and they moved in with Gene and Nellie. This particular winter Gene and Nellie left Mike to care for the foxes while they spent the winter in Detroit.

Mike's wife was going through one of her bad spells and Mike had to hire a young girl to come in and look after her and the children.

At the time of the tragedy, Mike was hauling sawdust for my ice from the sawmill. The girl, Audrey Smith, was washing a bedroom floor. Mike's ten year old son was annoying her. He had found Joeb's 22 rifle in Joeb's closet and he had removed the shell magazine.

Thinking the gun was empty, Audrey, in trying to scare Johnny out of the bedroom, picked it off the bed, where he had laid it, and pointing it at him she touched the trigger.

The bullet went through his heart and out his back. He managed to get out of the room and died in his mother's lap.

I was walking a short distance behind Mike and the sleigh. We were about a mile from the lodge when I hear Audrey calling. "WALTER, WALTER — Walter!" I turned to see her running towards us. Mike had not heard her as his hearing was bad.

156

When she came up to me she was hysterical and out of breath and barely able to say, "I shot Johnny, he's dead!"

I calmed her down the best I could and sent her back. It was zero weather and she was only dressed in a thin dress.

Thankfully, I had to run to catch Mike and the sleigh, as he was unaware what had taken place behind him. In shock myself and the adrenalin flowing, the running helped to calm me enough to relay the dreadful message in a calmer manner than I had received it.

I said, "Mike, I will take the team and you should go home as your son has been shot." I went to the lodge and dumped the sawdust as fast as I could, picked up Lottie and we rushed to the fox farm, knowing it was too late to save little Johnny.

It was a very depressing and pitiful tragedy. Mike seemed entranced. I left Lotite there to look after things while I went to the lumber camp on snowshoes to get a car. The winter road from the camp to Golden Valley was plowed.

When I reached the Valley, I called the doctor and the coroner as well. He had to come in by taxi from Powassan, forty miles away, then walk over three-quarters of a mile from the winter road to the fox farm. Because of this he did not arrive until the next morning.

I returned from the Valley and fed the foxes, then it was necessary that I go back to the lodge and fire up our wood stoves so things would not freeze while we were away. The next afternoon, after the coroner had left, I wrapped Johnny in a blanket and carried him over my shoulder for three-quarters of a mile to the winter road.

By the time I got back with the car, Johnny was drifted over with snow. I took him out to the undertaker in Powassan, then I phoned Royal Oak, Michigan, to relate the sad happening to Gene and Nellie.

Nellie advised me "Walter, Gene has been taken to the hospital a week ago and he is in critical condition." She asked me, "Can you look after things until we are able to return?" I assured her I would. Unfortunately, Gene passed away before he could be released from the hospital.

Nellie and Joeb returned as soon as they could after Gene's funeral, to the unhappy situation awaiting them at the fox farm.

After the accident, Mike's wife, understandably, was in a terrible condition. Mike finally rented a house in Golden Valley and took her away hoping to save her sanity.

Nellie decided to carry on with the fox until pelting time. She "asked if I would do it for her." I agreed to do the pelting after I finished with my deer hunters in November, as there was over 300 fox including the years young. And they were really too fat, which made the fleshing job much harder. Some of the older breeders had beautiful pelts. Nellie sold them on the Canadian Fur Auction in Montreal. She did not receive a good price, as fox furs had taken a severe price drop. That was the end of the fox farm. Joeb finally sold the land and timber to the Empy Lumber Company. Fox pens and buildings have since fallen down, and all the cleared land has grown up with second growth.

Thelma Yant of Cleveland, Ohio
with her catch, 1934.

CHAPTER 20

PHONE COMES THROUGH BUSH TO LODGE;
SECOND MAPLE SYRUP PROJECT

I had prepared everything for the winter coming and had set a few traps. Earlier that fall I was held up by a phone crew on Highway No. 11 just north of the town of Trout Creek, as I was on my way to North Bay.

They were in the process of pulling down the main lines which were being replaced by closed cable. There were twenty-three strands of wire on the crossbars; it was apparent to me that they were just rolling the wire up for scrap, after removing the insulators.

I approached the foreman and asked, "Would it be possible for me to purchase this wire?" I also explained, "I could use it to run a phone line into my lodge."

He hesitated for a moment, then replied, "Look lad, if you promise to remove the wire before dark," and then he emphasized, "and leave nothing on the highway, you're welcome to it."

I could hardly believe my good luck. Making a very fast trip the two miles to Powassan, I hired a truck to pick up the wire and insulators and to deliver it to Golden Valley.

At that time there was a local phone company operating between Powassan, Restoule, Golden Valley, Arnstein and Port Loring. Their switchboard was located at Golden Valley and Powassan. They agreed to mount my phone beside the switchboard so I could have messages relayed to and from my lodge.

I was able to purchase two crank phones from the Pine Lumber Company's warehouse. They operated with three dry cell batteries, so after the hunt season I started to build my own phone line. I contacted the local Lands and Forests Office and mentioned how they could benefit by my having a phone at my lodge during an outbreak of forest fires. They readily agreed and let me have two men to run the line.

Our biggest problem was to untangle the four miles of wire that had been rolled up in twenty-three strands at one time. Some of the wire was like new, while other strands were rusty. We unrolled them about half a mile into a side road ditch and pulled out the strands we required, then started to mount our insulation on trees behind the Golden Valley Schoolhouse. We followed adjacent to the Hard Scrabble Road most of the way, which was through the bush, cutting off when we got close to the lodge. We only used a single wire, which was grounded at both the switchboard and the lodge. The entire line was mounted on trees except for using three poles on the highway near the schoolhouse.

It was like having a brand new toy and we really had a big celebration when we finished and put our first call into the switchboard. This single wire line worked fine in good weather and even during the winter months, but it was poor during a thunderstorm or real hot weather. However, the main benefit was I could now advise guests to call before starting in on my road just in case they had trouble.

To be able to communicate this way meant a great deal to me as well as my guests; in fact, it proved to be a blessing to everyone around the sawmill as well. I would deliver many messages that were important to them. More than once it was worth a lot when they had an accident or when they had a breakdown at the mill.

On several occasions lumber jacks who quit working at the logging camp cut the phone line down as they walked back to Golden Valley. They were mad at the camp foreman and had the mistaken idea that the phone line belonged to the lumber company. Deer hunters also cut it to use for hanging up deer. It was like a mountain that entices some people, like a magnet to climb it. The line "was there" and a temptation to cut it.

A little earlier in the season two young fellows came in to see me, Roy and George Sloat, from Southern Ontario. They were looking for a place to trap and the local warden had told them I might direct them to an open area in this district. Everything north of this district of Parry Sound was zoned and registered to individual trappers.

160

I tried to discourage them as I was quite certain they would not make enough to live on, as the best part of the trapping season was over, but they still wanted to give it a try. So I directed them where to go and told them, "I know where I can find you some work if you decide to give up." They thanked me and said, "We'll keep that in mind."

In May, Henry Knapp, who was one of the men who helped me put up the walls of the lodge in 1934, had injured himself while pushing a boom of logs with a pikepole. It had slipped hitting him in the stomach causing internal bleeding. Henry was known as a bleeder. He died before he could receive the proper attention.

His homestead was about five miles out our road. He had just purchased a Grimm maple syrup evaporator and had just finished making maple syrup before his accident. Henry's closest relative was his sister who lived in Saskatchewan.

When she came to settle Henry's affairs I told her I would like to purchase the syrup outfit. However, I could not give her any cash. Instead, I would leave the outfit on her property and operate it there until it was paid for. Each year I would give her half the produce of the plant until it was paid off.

She had not accepted, so I was very surprised to find a letter from her at the end of February saying, "All of the relatives around Golden Valley have been after the syrup outfit, but I have decided to let you have it on your terms. I would rather deal with you than relatives."

I was glad to learn I could have the evaporator but I was sorry it took her so long to let me know. It meant I would have a lot to do in a short time before the sap would be running.

As I expected, the Sloat Brothers came out from camp one week-end prepared to work for me. Roy, the older one, decided to stay and work, while the younger one, George, returned home to help his dad.

Roy and I went out to the Knapp place to inspect the outfit. We found Knapp had had less than a thousand buckets and no covers. Besides he had used a wooden barrel on a sloop to gather the sap in.

I wrote to the London Soap Works and ordered four empty one hundred gallon drums. The soap company had imported

161

coconut oil in them and some of them were priced at $8.00 each. I converted two of them into fast-emptying gathering tanks. We decided we could make sap bucket lids from sheets of galvanized metal for much less than the patent ones in the Grimm catalogue. We made a die on a hard maple block to form the hinge for the cover. By cutting each 30 in. x 96 in. sheet into twenty-seven lids, we kept the cost to 10 cents a lid.

After experimenting with the first galvanized sheet we were able to turn out lids in a production line style.

At that time all the lumbermen used horses for their winter logging and there was always a slack period during the spring break-up and before they could use horses on the land. Because of this I received several offers to have the use of good teams, just for their feed. The owners said, ''The horses will be much better off getting the little exercise that you will give them rather than standing idle in the barn. We would prefer that you use our teamster to handle the horses.''

This really worked out fine for me. We moved out to the Knapp homestead about the middle of March and prepared for the sap to run. The house on the homestead was just meant for a bachelor, but we partitioned one room for two separate bedrooms.

There was a good stable for the horses and a well-built sugar shanty to house the syrup evaporator, with the five hundred gallon sap storage tanks inside under cover. I had the teamsters haul slab wood from the mill, while Roy and I fired up the evaporator and boiled all the buckets, pans and spiles.

The snow was still very deep in the sugar bush making it necessary to use snow shoes. I had the teamster drive all around the gathering trails several times with the sloop to break a trail and spread buckets in proper proportion for tapping.

I had noticed during my earlier experience of making syrup at Chartier Lake that many old maple trees were scarred and faulty around the base of the tree. I soon learned the cause of this. As I mentioned before, porcupines were very numerous at that time, and while they appeared very slow and stupid they were smart enough to know how to get their sweets. As soon as it was warm enough for the sap to run, I noticed the porcupine trails in the snow going from one maple tree to another. They were chewing a patch of bark off the south base of each tree. The sap would ooze out of these girdled patches and be thickened by the sun in a day or so. Later, I would see the porcupines at some of these trees, standing on their hind feet, like kids in an ice cream parlour, licking the sweet sticky sap as though it was a favorite ice cream cone.

A great many maple trees were ruined after years of this girdling. Another time when I was tapping the trees I frequently felt sap falling from above and going right down my neck. This did not appeal to me at all and I decided to study the uncomfortable situation. I eventually discovered the reason and the culprits behind "the leaky faucet." A number of red squirrels were always active in the branches of trees I was tapping! They were also tapping, to their "sweet tooth," in the crotches of large branch limbs, where the sap would ooze out and thicken in small pockets of the crotch, creating a soda fountain for squirrels.

The competition got so bad we even had to put muzzles on the horses, to stop them from trying their damndest to drink the sweet sap out of the buckets while we were busy gathering it. It was funny, the squirrels in the top; we were in the middle; porcupines at the base and the horses in our buckets; all of us trying to outdo "the other guy."

We began tapping the last week in March and had a couple of small sap runs before it came on strong. It was enough to get the evaporator started and gave me a chance to experiment on the best method to fire the evaporator. When I had the right kind of fire and maintained the proper level and flow of sap coming into the main pan, I could have a small steady trickle of finished syrup coming out of the finishing pans.

Our first heavy run of sap came at the end of March. I fired up early that morning and had the men start to gather as soon as there was a couple of cups of sap in the buckets. I had 1200 buckets on trees. Before they gathered half of them, some were running over. By the time they had completed one round, the first buckets were running over again. Considerable sap had run onto the ground before it slacked off that evening. To put it bluntly, it was as though the maple trees had suddenly contracted "diarrhea of the sap."

I was firing the arch and boiling at full capacity, from early morning until breakfast time the next morning, until I emptied the storage tank as well as the spare drums.

Lottie was serving my meals at the evaporator, and I was lucky to find time to eat even then. I was on a perpetual treadmill and I was so hyped up I didn't want to get off.

When the fire died down, I changed finishing pans for clean ones, putting the used ones in a running stream of water behind the shanty. The running cold water flowing through the pans would remove the mineral coating that accumulates while you are boiling.

I soon learned that the felts used to strain and clean the syrup could be kept in better shape while soaking in cold water, better than hot water!

From that first run I canned thirty-two gallons of syrup. Contrary to what many people think, maple syrup should never be bottled or sealed in cans — until it is cold. Otherwise, the heat or steam will condense on the top and cause mold to form. We found that our home-made bucket covers worked fine and also prevented dirt, snow and rain from spoiling the sap.

Storms were frequent during the syrup season. We had several good runs of sap with a couple of slack periods in between. This was caused by freeze-ups. However, by gathering the sap as the run started, and not leaving the sap to accumulate, we finished the season with close to three hundred gallons of good quality syrup.

By carefully following the instructions in the Grimm Manufacturing Catalogue on syrup making most of my syrup was top grade; and due to the fact that it was my first try on the evaporator, I did not have ready-made customers for all my syrup.

I did manage to sell all but ninety gallons for $1.50 to $2.00 per gallon. I stored the other ninety gallons at Golden Valley until I would have the time to find sales for it. I never got the chance! Oliver Moore, who operated the stage, sold it to a buyer for 90 cents a gallon, thinking he was doing me a favour.

The 1976 price per gallon is $15.00 per gallon! $18.00 in 1977 — $20.00 in 1979 — $26.00 in 1982.

Roy stayed with me until the following winter, then he decided to go to Sudbury and work in the mines. He had gotten along fine as a guide for my guests that season and I hated to see him go. He was a fine lad and he helped me put up another two log cottages.

164

I continued to move out to the Knapp place for the next three seasons; however, it did interfere with my lodge operation. The month of April and May is the time I should have been preparing everything around the lodge before guests arrived.

One year the weather changed and everything was all frozen for the month of April, after we had moved to the sugar bush. I did travel back and forth to the lodge with a team of sleigh dogs I had purchased, but it was very evident I would have to give up syrup making if I was to operate the lodge properly. I had paid off the syrup evaporator and was free to remove it from the Knapp place any time I chose.

I decided to take a truck load of syrup to Windsor in my second year where I could get a better price. To cut down on the cost per gallon to truck it, I bought four hundred gallons from other producers in the area, to add to my two hundred and twenty-five gallons.

A gallon of maple syrup weighs approximately fourteen lbs. including the can. I had a weight of over four tons.

After placing my syrup on the truck first I picked up two hundred gallons at Restoule from Mr. Ratz. As we were loading I noticed some of the half gallon cans made a cracking sound as I picked them up. I asked him, ''Mr. Ratz, I would like to have a large kettle so I can empty some of the cans. I want to find out how much syrup has turned to hard candy.''

He obliged, and after I had emptied the first gallon and weighed the empty can it still weighed over five pounds. This proved how much had turned to solid sugar. I told him, ''Mr. Ratz I can't handle syrup of this quality. We will have to unload all we have already put on.''

After considerable discussion he said, ''Take it and do the best you can with it, also deduct my cost per gallon for trucking it.'' Then just as I was leaving, he said, ''If something should happen to you, I have nothing to show that you have my syrup. I very foolishly signed a note showing I had received two hundred gallons from him.

We proceeded to pick up the balance of our load at Trout Creek and headed south on Highway No. 11. Too late we learned that ''half load'' was in effect on the highway and we would be checked at the first weigh station, which was near Orillia. We were almost two tons overweight, although you could not tell by looking at the load as it did not take up much space.

Before we came to the weigh station we pulled off the highway into a roadside cabin to stay overnight. We told the proprietor our problem and he said, "Well, I can direct you to a by-pass of the weigh station but you will have to take a gamble you won't be stopped south of Toronto."

We decided to leave about 4:30 the next morning and get far enough south where no "half loads" were in effect.

The final disaster hit us that morning as the truck driver was attempting to turn around at the cabins. His back wheels broke through a rotten wooden septic tank cover. We had to unload most of the syrup before I managed to flag down a transport and have him put a chain on us and pull us out.

We made it from there to Windsor with only two flat tires to trouble us. The trucker stayed overnight while I rounded up a load of seed oats to make a pay load for him to go back with.

I had no trouble disposing of the good quality syrup. Mr. Ratz's syrup presented a problem. I managed to get a chain store to take a hundred gallons. I refused to lie about the balance which seemed to be getting more solid during the trip. I stored it in my mother-in-law's cellar until I could find out what Mr. Ratz wanted to do with it.

With the money from my syrup sales I bought a used Model "A" Ford and returned to the lodge. I had much to do before the guests arrived. I took the time to see Mr. Ratz, "who it turned out was properly named."

I had paid him for what I had received for the hundred gallons, less 10 cents a gallon for trucking. I told him, "As for the rest I cannot and will not attempt to sell it. If you wish, my father-in-law will crate it and ship it back, or to wherever you want it."

Mr. Ratz pulled out the note I had signed and informed me, "This note proves the syrup belonged to me and I will sue you for payment."

To conclude this briefly, I will only relate what I finally had to do.

The manager of the National Grocery Store or Warehouse in North Bay gave me a letter stating that he would accept the hundred gallons of syrup in payment of my account with him, if the producer of the syrup would guarantee it to be 100 per cent pure.

When I showed this to Mr. Ratz he refused and proceeded to sue me. I arranged to have six cans of the syrup sent to Ottawa to be tested by the Pure Food Department.

Their findings or report was not returned to me until the day we were in court. We received a telegram just one hour before the case came up. It stated, "The syrup in question has been adulterated and Mr. Ratz is subject to prosecution if marketed as pure."

His suit against me was dismissed and he was assessed the costs. I was told to have the syrup shipped back to him collect. Mr. Ratz really acted like one, and still forty some years later holds a grudge.

My final year of making syrup had an incident worth mentioning. The sap run was good and by now I had orders for all the syrup I could make. Then I received a letter from the Ontario Trading Company in Toronto. On an elaborate letterhead it said: "Importers and Exporters of Fish, Food and Nuts."

Dear Mr. Hesman:
I have been advised by your C.N.R. Station Agent at Trout Creek that you are a shipper of maple products, and as we have an outlet for quantities of this item, we would appreciate if you would quote us your price on a hundred gallon lots.

Signed,

Mr. So and So
Manager.

I replied by return mail quoting a price that would permit me to buy syrup to fill an order. I received a reply by telegram saying, "Ship at once fifty gallons of maple syrup. Express collect. Will remit by mail."

I phoned another syrup maker at Arnstein, who I had bought syrup from before, and instructed him to ship direct from his place in cartons, the fifty gallons to them. I was to pay him as soon as I collected from Toronto.

167

After sufficient time had elapsed and I had not received confirmation from the Ontario Trading Company, I tried to phone the man and was advised the phone was no longer in service.

I immediately called one of my hunters, who was President of the Queen City Glass Company, and asked him to check the trading company out. As soon as I mentioned the address he said, "Walter, I am sure you may have been taken in by a schiester; however, stay where you are and I will call you right back."

He called back and told me, "The man who signed as the manager has a record with the Better Business Bureau of specifically cheating farmers out of poultry, butter and eggs in the amount of less than $50.00 and his present place of business is a third floor apartment in a slum area. Walter, I doubt if it would pay you to come down." I decided to give it a try, just for my own satisfaction.

I phoned my friend Harry Holden, the lumber grader. He loaned me his car and I left for Toronto without going back to the lodge.

Arriving early next morning, I contacted Charles at the Glass Company as soon as I arrived in Toronto. He had contacted a detective, another hunter, and they had gone to the apartment house and with the aid of the janitor they learned where the schiester had my syrup stored — in an old barn on a side street near the apartment.

The janitor also informed them, "There is a regular parade of farmers trying to get ahold of this guy. He apparently knows all the loopholes in the law."

By this time I was ready to charge in and break the lock and get my syrup out of that old barn. I could even see it through a high window.

Detective Kennedy informed me the scheister could have me arrested for breaking and entering, even though it was my syrup, as 30 days had not lapsed since he received it. He had not as yet refused to pay for it.

Kennedy took me to see his inspector at the police station.

They decided there might be a chance we could bluff him and scare him enough into unlocking the barn. Then if I quickly got the syrup out onto the street, there wouldn't be a thing he could

168

do. The inspector said, "I will permit Detective Kennedy to try this, only if you promise to get out of the man's apartment the minute he might tell you to do so."

After checking with the janitor to make sure the man was in, we went to his apartment. When he opened the door Detective Kennedy pushed our way in showing his badge. He demanded to see his business license.

Naturally he couldn't show one. Also, he appeared to be half drunk on wine. Kennedy told him, "Get downstairs and unlock that barn door." As he was bringing the man down the hall, the man kept repeating, "I don't think you can do this." Kennedy just kept him moving and the minute he unlocked the door, I began hauling my syrup out onto the street.

Kennedy had warned me earlier, "Keep your mouth shut until all the syrup is out." While I am busy removing the syrup the man kept saying, "I am going to call my lawyer." As soon as I had finished I immediately sat on top of the syrup cartons. Charles and Kennedy went for a pick-up truck to haul the syrup to the Glass warehouse.

I won't repeat what I actually said to the schiester other than, "We had open season for his kind of people where I came from."

The old barn was cluttered with poultry crates and eggs. The Better Business Bureau told us they were very surprised he had tried to take me for so much, as most of his deals were for less than $50.00. This amount didn't pay the farmer to take action. But we all learned a lesson from him.

There were two gallons missing, so I was lucky. Without the help of my friends I would have lost everything. It is still hard for me to understand our laws that protect the guilty like him, but it was proved to me again a few years later and we see a lot of it today. The last time I was able to catch it in time. Experience is a good teacher but sometimes very costly.

To end up my maple syrup experience: One of the girls who worked for me at the lodge told me her father, Tony, had a good sugar bush. I went out to look it over. When I felt it was suitable for my outfit I made him the same offer as I had to Mr. Knapp's sister.

I would move it out there and ask for no money down. I agreed to help operate it the first year and take half the syrup each year until it was paid for. Tony wanted my outfit as his was outdated. The way he operated it was actually more work to make ten gallons than a hundred with the evaporator. Tony was getting old, so he first wanted to be sure his two sons would promise to be around to help. Naturally the boys were all for having a modern evaporator, so the deal was made.

I asked them to build a suitable shanty for the evaporator and to gather enough wood to fire the plant before the snow came. The shanty they built was not what I had asked for, but that fall I moved the plant in and set it up.

In the spring at syrup time I showed them how to operate it. First of all, they only had half the amount of fire wood needed. It had not been covered so it was too wet to burn properly.

After a couple of small sap runs the boys decided to go to an Easter dance, which was more important to them than making maple syrup. As I expected, that week-end was our best sap run. Old Tony tried to gather as much sap as he could and I gathered some dried hardwood.

I boiled steady for three days and two nights. My meals were bread with eggs boiled in the evaporator with syrup for dessert. Much of that sap ran over the buckets onto the ground. We struggled through the rest of the season.

Tony finally suggested I find another place for it as he could not depend on the boys to help.

On Adolph Fry's farm I did find a better location at the head of Commanda Lake in time for the 1942 spring run. Mr. Fry and his family were wonderful people to deal with. I stayed with them for part of two syrup seasons.

Many times I have said, "It was the best home I ever stayed, apart from my own home."

Mr. Fry insisted I take all the syrup except twenty-five gallons that they required for their family and friends, instead of each taking half as our contract called for. They operated the evaporator until it required replacement. Mr. Fry passed away in 1959. His son Rodney replaced the evaporator with a complete new modern plant, using plastic tubing instead of buckets, eliminating gathering, and fired the evaporator with propane gas.

Before closing this chapter I would like to mention a special event that happened on May 28th, 1934. It was world-wide news and it continued for several years. The famous Dionne quintuplets were born in Callander, Ontario, about sixty miles from here. This event was responsible for a sudden increase of tourists to this Area. They came to Callander by the thousands — by car, train and air. The Ontario Government took charge of the babies, when it was learned the parents, with the consent of the local priest, had signed a contract with Chicago World Fair promoters, to show them at the fair alive or dead, if necessary. It was one of few smart decisions made by government.

For several years after I started Little River Lodge practically every guest made it a point to go and see the quints. On a number of occasions I accompanied them as guide, and found it very amusing to sit in the car and observe men and women while they waited in line. They would sidle up to large boxes filled with rocks, and slip some into their pockets. The stones, taken from the Dionne farm, were supposed to make them fertile and assure them of having a child. However, it did accomplish one thing, it cleared tons of rock from the surrounding area, but it increased my rock problem, as they frequently left them for me.

Young people pitch in and help clean fish, 1931.

171

CHAPTER 21

THE LODGE IN 1939

In 1939, Little River Lodge was well established. We had built five cottages and a new bridge across the river to the boathouse. This permitted us to drive up to the dock with our cars to unload motors and equipment and saved us a lot of back-breaking hauling.

I was employing two regular guides by now, Bill and Walter Driver, both born and raised in Golden Valley and well acquainted with the territory. We had built screen porches on the lodge and the cabins, which made it more comfortable during the fly and mosquito season. Once you have these luxuries, you wonder how you managed without them.

We also added an overnight outpost cabin on an island in Chartier Lake. At the lodge, I installed a Delco thirty-two volt light plant with batteries, so it was not necessary to have the engine running steady. We had the cabins wired, but still had to cut ice for the cabins.

I purchased a kerosene-burning refrigerator for the lodge. We were becoming modern in our semi-wilderness and these conveniences, taken for granted in the city, were held in esteem by us. They helped lessen our busy workload.

The road, however, was a continuous problem, especially during wet weather. The lumber company contracted the hauling of their lumber and slash wood. The truckers would try to haul regardless of the condition of the road, and most of the time they were overloaded. Almost every trucker would go broke or his truck would break down. There were always other truckers ready and willing to give it a try.

So many truckers were buying trucks on time. They were desperate to make their payments. Seldom did they stop to use good judgment, so our road suffered from their abuse. Several

172

Lodge and shower house after re-modelling in 1939.

times I saw trucks buried right up to their frame in mudholes. They would have to go back sometimes two or three miles to get to the mill, walking, to get a couple of teams to come and pull them out.

Our fishing was standing up good. Bill Driver and myself were guiding steady. Guests could afford the low wages of the times. They used guides during their entire stay and therefore got more satisfaction and enjoyment out of their vacation.

When Bill and I returned from a guiding trip, our guests usually were talking and telling other guests how much they enjoyed the trip. It soon developed that Bill and I could not fulfill all the requests for guides. To bring in unexperienced guides who could not or would not extend themselves for the guests like Bill and I did, would only harm the business, which was being built up by satisfied guests and good management. I discovered that "word of mouth" travels fastest and loudest.

This was the year that World War II began. The terrible waste of human life and resources, reviving and increasing all the hatred of World I all over again. It is not the solution to world problems, but will our leaders NEVER learn?

173

I was concerned as to what would happen to my project if I was conscripted into the services, as my wife Lottie could definitely not carry on alone. Thankfully, the problem was solved for us. All those who were in my type of business were asked to register our camps and resorts as recreational accommodations for the thousands of foreign army and airforce recruits when on leave, or who were trained in Canada or recovering from injuries.

We did entertain several English and Polish pilots at different times; in fact, after the war was over a couple of the English pilots came back from England several times. They were flying for World Airways at that time.

RATES:

Comfortable beds and good meals—$3.50 per day.

Housekeeping cabins fully equipped—$15 to $25 per week.

Guides, including their meals, apportioned pro-rata among party—$4.50 per day.

Boats and canoes—$1.00 to $1.50 per day.

Outboard motors—$2.50 per day.

Reductions are made according to the length of stay.

Write for rates and details of our hunting season.

Guests requiring guides will receive better satisfaction if they mention the fact when making reservations. A deposit of $10.00 is required when booking.

Reprint of an original Rate Sheet of 1939.

The captain of our Canadian group of hunters, Howard Parsons, and his entire group were made up of survivors of the First World War fighter pilots. Howard had married an English woman whose family was connected with the producers of fine English china. Howard became a manufacturer's agent and the distributor for several English china companies — Royal Doulton among them.

Howard was entertaining two of the Johnson Brothers in our lodge during the 1939 crisis in England. At that time we were using the standard heavy restaurant china in our dining room.

174

A fine group of hunters.

A fine group of hunters.

The way we carried them out.

During dinner one evening, Howard jokingly suggested to the Johnson Brothers that they should present Little River Lodge with some of their fine English china. "A good way for you to promote your china," he told them.

By jove we will," one of them answered.

The next day the brothers received word they were to return to England at once, as they were reserve pilots.

Howard told us later they had informed him, when they got back to England, they were sent up with their fighter planes with mounted guns but no ammunition to use. That was the sorry state of England's readiness for the war.

After a year of more had passed and we had completely forgotten the incident of the china, I received a notice from our station agent at Trout Creek. It said that they had several barrels of china at the station and he was afraid to send it in with the transport for fear of breakage.

When I unpacked the barrels there was over 400 pieces of fine English china in an English bouquet pattern. What a surprise!!

I got in touch with Howard and asked him, "What can we do to show our appreciation?"

He told me, "The Johnson's mother was a former American and due to the shortage of sugar in England, they would surely appreciate some of your good maple syrup." I was doubtful it could be shipped overseas at that time due to the U-boat blockade; however, I shipped two cases of our best quality syrup. Eventually, months later, I received confirmation and thanks. I was also thankful that it had arrived safely.

Actually over the years we received many compliments on our extra fine china; also, due to considerable breakage by careless staff, we were always able to replace through Howard's warehouse in Toronto.

English china was very much in demand due to the shipping problem and most dealers were in short supply. In spite of this Howard supplied us with a variety of Royal Doulton figurines to put on display at our gift counter. I was amazed at the amount we sold, especially to our American guests. We learned later that some were resold for 100 per cent profit in the States. Howard Parsons passed away on a buying trip in England in 1961.

CHAPTER 22

GASOLINE RATIONING, First Vacation to Florida

In the spring of 1940 I remodelled the lodge by removing the roof completely, then added another one and one-half feet height to the main section and a second storey over the kitchen. This gave us more room upstairs, plus an extra bedroom and office over kitchen, where I could take care of my mail (which was becoming a problem), without interference. Also I put a good rock face roofing over all, and increased the height of the fire place chimney.

This remodelling included installing a toilet and bath and improved the appearance as well.

While our business was progressing each year, so was our problems with staff, mainly due to the fact that we were so isolated, the extra female summer help found it difficult for their dates to come in to get them and bring them back. They would apply for a summer job before school was out, and promise to stay until after September 1st. However, they seldom did. In fact, many times they would leave without giving any notice, even when we were very busy. There were times our guests would pitch in and help, by looking after their cabins themselves, even going shopping for us.

Student help would leave us, in particular during the busy season. This problem increased as time went on and I spent considerable time looking for help, as Lottie did not drive.

Another problem was guiding. So many guests felt that I should act as their guide personally. They felt I could provide more fish for them. This resulted in many extra long hours for me, and trying to handle the other camp duties as well.

Bill Driver was working for us from 1940 to 1951 and he relieved me from the guiding a great deal. He enjoyed guiding so much and had no trouble pleasing the guests. Unfortunately, Bill

177

was killed in the spring of 1952 by a gravel truck while doing some road work. I missed Bill a great deal.

Walter Driver, his brother, was a good guide. However, he never had Bill's ability to entertain the guests with conversation. He was a very thoughtful and quiet man.

We struggled through the early years with all the restrictions until 1942. That was the year I convinced the Public Works Department to build a LeGrous Lake Dam. Up to the fall of 1942 it required over a mile portage to get into Chartier Lake to fish, except during high water, when we could navigate about half this distance by canoe through a marsh (see map).

After the dam was in - fishing down the chimney.

I had built a small overnight log cabin on an island and kept a couple of boats on the lake. Many interesting and successful fishing trips were made to Chartier Lake, but once the water level of Chartier and LeGrous Lake was raised to our level by the dam, we could travel from the lodge through five lakes to the dam without a portage. This made a beautiful scenic trip, as well as many miles of shoreline to fish from. Also, these waters really never became too rough to navigate with small fishing boats at any time.

During the years of gasoline rationing and European travel was restricted, the number of guests coming to Little River Lodge increased greatly. Many came by train to Trout Creek where we would pick them up.

We only had outdoor privies, up to that period, for the cottages. Due to only having Delco power, the only way I could overcome this was to build a central toilet and showerhouse. I built it with two showers and four toilets, installing oil heat and hot water tank and a pump in the center compartment. This improvement was much appreciated by everyone.

About this time I also made an addition to the camp with a purchase of an island, situated in Whitehead Lake.

Jack Graham, who considered himself a writer (his pen name was Eugene Condie), had built a house on the island in 1937. He was employed as a bookkeeper at the lumber company. During the few years he lived on the island, he strived to make it a self-sustaining one, by gardening, raising rabbits and chickens.

After I purchased the island it became a very desirable place for guests, who craved seclusion and for families in particular with children and pets. It became their paradise.

From the time I started Little River Lodge, up to 1947, we had never taken a vacation. Lottie had been after me to give up the lodge for several years. I realized it was rough on her to handle the lodge with the staff problems we encountered season after season.

However, I could not think of giving up our resort just when we were becoming well established, especially with our improved waterway.

But that year we did close up the lodge in January and made our first trip to Florida. We spent some time on the Florida Keys with my sister. We returned to the lodge at the end of March, just before the spring break-up.

I had purchased my first NEW car for our trip to Florida. It was a Hudson, which was the only car available at that time. When we returned home I found I could not drive in on our road with the Hudson, so I bought myself my first Jeep. It turned out to be my best investment, not only for the business but for my trapping as well.

179

CHAPTER 23

DISPLACED PERSONS: FISHING TRIPS;
HELP PROBLEMS; HOW WE GOT THE HYDRO; MARY

In 1946 I had placed an ad in the Windsor papers "Help Wanted" section for a married couple. We were tired of our help leaving us because they couldn't get out enough with their dates.

We received the usual replies and tried several couples all with the same result: the wife would be fine, but the husband no good. Sometimes neither were any good.

We had times when our staff would leave without notice and our guests would have to pitch in and help. I spent a great deal of time during our busy season looking for help.

It was several months after I had run the ad in the Windsor paper that I received a lengthy letter from the British zone of occupied Germany. A displaced Latvian couple, Arthur and Vena Mietins, wrote and begged me to sponsor them.

Vena had a pen pal in Detroit who had sent her my ad. She said, "We can both speak English." In fact, they spoke several languages.

I was impressed with her letter and I contacted the refugee organization and made application for them to come. Immigration immediately phoned me saying they had several suitable couples already here in Canada and would gladly send them to me at once. They assured me I would not have to keep them if they proved unsatisfactory.

When I told them I wanted the Mietins couple, they said it would take some time and insisted in the meantime that I take ones that were here.

Over a period of the next two years, they sent me three different couples. All were too old and could not speak English. Each time I had to take them back. The last couple they sent were Lithuanians; their son and daughter had already been in Canada three years.

The woman told me they had been known as Lithuanian Kulacks and had been large land owners, employing 25 workers. They had bribed people in the refugee organization to get them to Canada with money they had previously sent here.

When I sent for their son and daughter to come and get them, as they were absolutely no use to me, they refused to come! They said, "We cannot be responsible for them." So I took the parents and left them at the children's apartment door in Sudbury.

In the meantime I had several letters from the Mietins asking, "Why aren't we permitted to come? You have assured us that you have made necessary application and you have promised to pay our transportation."

Finally, I went to see the area District Manager of Manpower at North Bay to ask, "Why?" I told him all the trouble I had been put to with the refugees they had been sending me.

He immediately called Ottawa, and in three weeks I got a telegram notifying me to forward their transportation money to Halifax.

The Mietins arrived in North Bay June 15, 1949, with two suitcases and not even enough money for lunch.

They turned out to be a wonderful couple. Vena could speak better English than most Canadians; she could read and write seven languages.

Her husband, Arthur, had a strong accent but he had no trouble conversing with guests. He was 27 and Vena 29 years old. They had escaped from Latvia, when the Russians came the second time. Arthur never did learn what happened to his family. Vena did manage a few years later to locate her mother and even eventually brought her to Canada.

Arthur and Vena were the best help we ever had, except for Mary, who was to become my second wife.

We had hired Mary a few weeks after Art and Vena arrived. Art and Vena stayed with me for over two years. Fortunately for me Mary was to stay for the rest of my life.

Shortly after they arrived here Arthur told me, "It is common knowledge in occupied Germany that refugees who have the means for bribing the refugee officials in charge are the first to obtain visas to come to Canada." The bribe rate at the time they left was 40,000 marks. He explained, "The elderly people that were sent to you over that three-year period were no doubt those who had managed to somehow have money and valuables transferred out of their country before they were occupied."

Two years later they approached me and said, "Walter, we are very grateful that you sponsored us; however, we desire to see more of Canada. We have to think of our future and we hope you understand." I did and told them. "You are free to go but I suggest you visit your friends in Toronto and Sudbury; if you can't find employment that suits you, then you are welcome to come back here."

After spending two weeks in Toronto they did come back. Art, speaking for both of them said, "We discovered that this north country has spoiled us, Toronto is not for us." They stayed with me for the rest of the season.

Their next venture was to Sudbury, where Art was accepted by the Nickel Mines and Vena, due to her vast knowledge of languages, could choose a number of positions. They had saved several thousands of dollars during their stay with me and after a few years in Sudbury they were well on their way to security, as they were excellent managers.

They never bought a car until after they had purchased a couple of lots and put houses on them, then sold them at a good profit. One of Art's favourite pastimes was hunting and fishing. He had learned everything he could while with me even to trapping, so I let him trap on my trap zone the winters we spent in Florida.

At this time our Postmaster, Mr. Cameron, had moved a saw mill into the pond just behind the lodge. Arthur put in two winters working for him at logging while we were away. Mr. Cameron said to me, "I have never known an immigrant who learned to do things as fast as Art has." I heartily agreed with him. "Yes, Art, is exceptional."

Unfortunately his great energy caused him to overdo his work in the mines and his heart gave out in 1971. They kept him alive for three years; he was in and out of the hospital until he died in 1974.

We visited them shortly before his final attack and while we were there he said, ''Walter, if I had stayed with you, I might have had less money, but I would not be in the shape I am now.'' He added. ''Money is not as important as I used to think it was.'' Canada could use more immigrants like Art and Vena.

Arthur and Vena Mietins shortly after their arrival from the British Zone of Occupied Germany in 1949.

CHAPTER 24

SEPARATION

For sometime my wife Lottie and I were having strained relations. She continually pressed me to sell out and leave the area. This was something I could not bring myself to do under any circumstances. I had gone through too much to establish Little River Lodge. Also the business had just reached the stage where it was really repaying me for all the years of effort and difficulties and problems I encountered with our road and waterway to give it up now.

The strained relations between us reached a climax in the winter of 1950. I could not possibly continue to operate the lodge unless there was some harmony between us. There seemed to be no prospect of a change, so I forced a legal separation and I agreed to a substantial cash settlement. I had to mortgage the lodge, as Lottie insisted on cash. My only regrets were the fact we were unable to settle our differences without giving our hard-earned money to attorneys.

That period was a particularly rough season for me, so much so that I developed ulcers. I was grateful for the help of Art and Vena and especially Mary, who had not only cooked for us but she also assisted in every phase of the lodge operation. Mary and Vena worked together like a perfect team until Art and Vena left for Sudbury in the fall of 1951.

1950 was an important year in many respects at Little River Lodge, besides the separation and my physical ailments, we had cause for celebration. The hydro came through the bush and lighted up our lives and lightened them as well in five months.

Mr. Dillon, the Regional Manager for the Hydro, while he was treating his staff to one of Mary's fine dinners, asked, "How would you like to have the hydro, Walter, brought into Little River Lodge?" Just like that!

It was such an electrifying question that I felt it had already arrived. I could almost see the lights blinking all over the place in
my imagination. As I would be the only user, I had never dreamed the hydro would come way back in here in the semi-
wilderness. Still, I thought miracles do happen.

At a cost of over $25,000.00 the right of way was cut through
heavy timber for four miles and they had to drill and blast
through solid granite, for over sixty of their poles.

The power was turned on in July, 1951! It was like a beacon in
the vast darkness of the bush, as we lit up all our lights.

I was then able to equip the entire camp with refrigerators and
freezers. Of course it meant I had to re-wire and change the electric motors from 32 volts to 115. I purchased a Beatty commer-
cial washing machine and heavy duty dryer. This was a blessing
for Mary, as she was doing laundry three times a week.

An artist's rendition of the lodge taken from a 1950's brochure.

Mary would amaze some of our guests. We served two
breakfasts: one at 6:00 a.m. and the second at 8:00 a.m. She
would start her first wash load in the machine while she was making the first breakfast and would be hanging it on the line before
the 8:00 a.m. guests came in, besides making up the lunches and
shore dinners for the early fishermen. Now that took super planning.

I am still amazed the way Mary gets through her housework
and still has time for her flower gardening, sewing, knitting, baking and taking care of me. Her meals are still prepared with the
same care and attention as they were for the lodge guests. Their
only complaint used to be, ''Mary, you feed us too well, now we
will have to go on a diet when we get home.'' They weren't being
force fed, but they couldn't resist her good food.

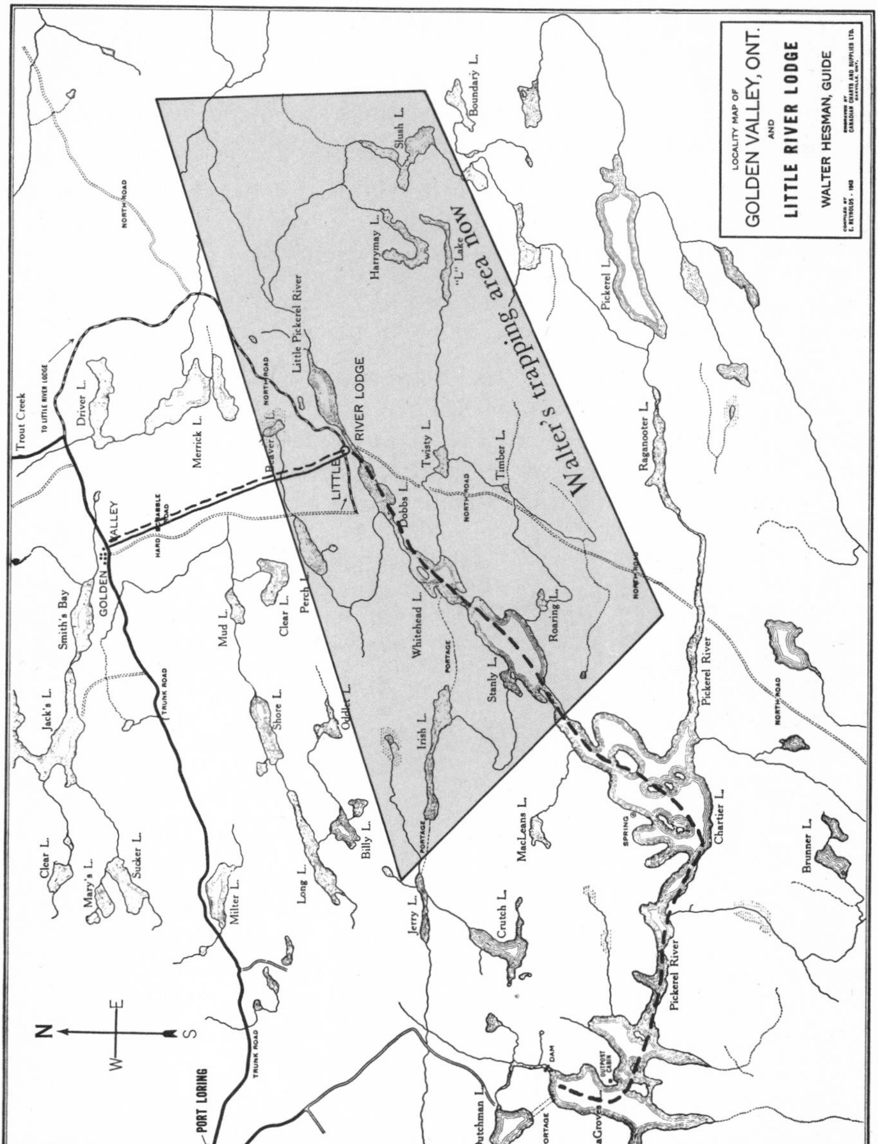
LOCALITY MAP OF
GOLDEN VALLEY, ONT.
AND
LITTLE RIVER LODGE
WALTER HESMAN, GUIDE
Walter's trapping area now
LITTLE RIVER LODGE
GOLDEN VALLEY
PORT LORING
TRUNK ROAD
NORTH ROAD
HARD SCRABBLE ROAD
TO LITTLE RIVER LODGE
Trout Creek
Driver L.
Merrick L.
Beaver L.
Little Pickerel River
Harrymay L.
Slush L.
Boundary L.
"L" Lake
Twisty L.
Timber L.
Dobbs L.
Perch L.
Clear L.
Mud L.
Smith's Bay
Jack's L.
Clear L.
Mary's L.
Sucker L.
Milter L.
Long L.
Billy L.
Shore L.
Oddie L.
Irish L.
Whitehead L.
Stanly L.
Roaring L.
Pickerel L.
Raganooter L.
Pickerel River
Chartier L.
Brunner L.
MacLeans L.
Crutch L.
Jerry L.
Dutchman L.
LaGroves
PORTAGE
DAM
SPRING
OUTPOST CAMP
N
S
E
W

Phone and Hydro Line

Boat route to dam

Mary, had a regular schedule at the lodge and through the years has still maintained it. Retiring for bed by 10:00 or 10:30 p.m. and up at 5:30 a.m. She disliked the role of acting as hostess, as she is a very quiet private person and always busy doing something. When she relaxes she is always knitting or making something with her hands. She is an excellent listener, and I am the "talker," which makes a good combination and keeps us both happy.

I fell in love with Mary and it was mutual. We lived as common-law man and wife for the next 12 years, as Lottie, due to her religion, would not agree to a divorce. Finally, I believe it was her priest who suggested she agree to a divorce and Mary and I were legally married. Now after living with Mary for over 30 years of wonderful harmony, I can truthfully say it has been wonderful. In 1969 Mary took upon herself the burden of caring for my aging mother, who was in her 80th year and lived until she was 92. The latter years were hard on Mary but she never complained and my mother worshipped her. The last year when she was in the hospital it was always "Mary" that she called for. I feel I am a very fortunate man to have found such a wonderful wife. She is someone special and I am not alone in that belief.

Mary and young Ricky.

187

CHAPTER 25

ZONE TRAPPING/WOLVES AND DEER

Up to that time I had been trapping a little every winter. Because I had no transportation, the area I trapped was limited, as I had to walk everywhere except some trapping I could do by boat during the open water. With the Jeep I was able to travel many of the log roads.

In 1948 this district was zoned and restricted to individual trappers on registered trap lines.

The far northern districts were divided into areas that drained into one watershed, as most fur bearers lived and reproduced in the one area. It was called zoning and licensed to an individual trapper to control and manage without interference from other trappers. This eliminated much quarrelling, even killing that had been going on. Finally all crown lands in Southern Ontario were zoned in the 1940's and licensed to individuals. It proved very successful, as most fur bearers increased and made for better management as each trapper was responsible for his zone. I was more fortunate than most as my area was not troubled so much with or by other trappers. My main problem was irresponsible hunters who would shoot at anything that was alive. I even had dead animals shot in a trap.

The area I was licensed for and had trapped for many years was all that drained into the Little Pickerel River watershed and emptied into Chartier Lake, which was a part of two townships.

It was always my intention to trap timber wolves, as they were killing many deer and fur bearers. Once the beaver were under the ice for the winter the wolves lived on deer exclusively. During the period lumbermen were taking logs out of this area, and as the snow deepened in the winter, the deer would gather in the logging areas to feed on the tree top browse that were felled by the loggers. The deer also took advantage of the skid trails and log roads to avoid the deep snow.

Walter and Ricky. Furs taken with bombardier equipment.

As the snow piled up, deer accummulated until there were sometimes hundreds of them in a small, logging area. On one occasion I stood on a skidway of logs and counted 160 deer in sight at one time. They had crowded into this area during the day or when the loggers were working in another area. Then at night, when the men were back at camp, the deer moved into the fresh-cut area to feed on the top browse.

The snow had become so deep surrounding the log cut the deer were practically locked in. At times like this the wovles would come into the log cut at night and it was nothing else but wholesale slaughter of the deer.

Around the end of February, the loggers would stop falling trees, as they then had to concentrate on hauling the logs out before the spring break-up. The deer quickly devoured the browse off the fallen trees and the smaller ones that could not reach as high would begin to die from starvation.

Even after the snow began to melt away the deer were like people on welfare. They had been so used to being fed all winter on the fallen trees they refused to move out and help themselves to food available elsewhere. They just kept waiting for more trees to be cut for them. They had become welfare deer.

In March of 1948 one of my hunters, Dr. Alan Secord, and the Deputy Minister of Lands and Forests, who at that time was Jim Taylor, came up to take movies of deer in one of these log cuts. We estimated over 400 deer in this particular log cut.

I would place the men with cameras on deer runways and then circle and chase the deer towards the cameras. Sometimes Jim Taylor had to duck behind a tree to avoid being over run by the fleeing deer.

Some of you readers may recall seeing some of these movies being shown on television. The King Whyte Show used to show them several times during the 1950's. I have a 400 foot reel of 16mm film of this period that I showed many times at the camp for guests.

You may also have heard wild life people say, ''Logging operations are very beneficial to deer.'' I have proved it can also be very disastrous by creating artificial feeding grounds that are suddenly stopped. The deer will starve while waiting for just one more free meal.

Walter's first wolf.

190

I caught my first timber wolf in the winter of 1946 in a snare that I had set on one of their runways between beaver ponds. The following fall I had a reservation for a group of men who wanted to do some duck hunting, so I sent Walter and Bill Driver out to set up a couple of duck blinds on Merrick Lake the last week in September. They were canoeing down the lake and just as they were passing a steep rock bluff, a large buck jumped off the bluff right beside the canoe. Before they got over the sudden shock, two large timber wovles that were chasing the buck, leaped off the rock also but they managed to get back on shore before the men could manoeuvre the canoe close enough to hit them.

The next day Walter Driver decided to put a wolf snare out on the runway between the two lakes. Before he got back across the upper lake he heard the bleating of a fawn and paddled back as fast as he could; the fawn had already broken its neck before he got there. Walter had set the snare with a pole across the runway so the deer would jump over it and miss the trap. Unfortunately, the small fawn had tried to pass under the pole. This is the reason it is so hard to take wolves around the winter deer yards without endangering the deer.

The wolves were very active that fall. One night while I was driving on our road, I spotted a wolf in my headlights. I immediately stepped on the gas and ran over it. Then to be sure I backed over it again. I jumped out of the car and grabbed it by the hind legs and gave it a cartwheel over my head and down hard onto the road. I thought it was dead so I placed it on the floor of the front seat of the car and drove out to the General Store. As I got out of the car, on the driver's side, I asked some of

191

the young fellows on the porch, "Would you like to see a wolf?" They came rushing over and when they opened the door the wolf was showing signs of coming to life again.

One of them grabbed an axe and killed it, and some of them looked at me in alarm as if I was demented and said, "What kind of crazy guy are you, driving around with a live wolf in your car?" I was a little shook myself but I grinned and replied, "I was lonely."

I recall the years I had worked for Mr. Clapperton and was in the Sagamesing hunt camp preparing for the deer hunt. We would hear the wolves howling while they were chasing deer. When they made their kill, we could hear the young ones fighting over the carcass.

With wolves as numerous as they were you would think more would be seen and shot during the deer hunt. However, they are seldom seen in the daylight.

George Brooks, one of the guides at Sagamesing, managed to shoot two on a Sunday morning when he returned to get a knife he had left when he dressed out a deer the day before. In all my years in the woods I have only seen wolves twice while carrying a gun. I had, however, seen them a number of times always at a distance crossing the ice on lakes.

Oscar Clapperton at the Outlet Cottage on Wilson Lake.

CHAPTER 26

MORE EXPERIENCES WHILE AT THE LODGE
SWIMMING WOLVES, STARVING DEER

In the spring of May, 1960, the same two guests from Dayton, Ohio, who had spent the night with me at Snow Shoe Lake in 1971 came for some walleye fishing.

I had a young local boy by the name of Don Evers that I was breaking in as a guide and choreboy. This particular morning he went down the lakes with the Dayton boys. They had their own boat with a 35 hp Johnson motor. They anchored in a channel between Stanley and Chartier Lake to fish. A short time later they heard a noise on the shore and suddenly a large doe jumped out of the brush into the river and swam by their boat.

Before they got over their surprise, a large timber wolf jumped into the river and was swimming after the deer; the wolf was gaining rapidly. Don grabbed the anchor and pulled in and they made a dash for the wolf.

When the wolf heard them coming it made for shore among the driftwood, just as the boat crashed into the driftwood. Don, at the bow of the boat, struck at the wolf's head with his oar. It turned and bit a chunk out of the blade, then clammered ashore and got away.

They were three very excited fellows when they returned to the lodge, all talking at once! They said, "Look, Walter, we have the oar to prove it!" And they did.

That same spring, at the end of June, "John Adams" from Toronto was down the lakes alone; he left Chartier Lake to return to the lodge for lunch.

As he came out of the river to Stanley Lake he saw an animal swimming across the lake. The closer he got he realized it was a huge wolf. Adams decided to try and get close enough to hit it with the oar, his only weapon.

However, each time he let go of the motor handle to strike at the wolf, the motor would swivel and the boat would circle; then he had to grab the motor and do it over again. Each time this would happen the wash from the boat would wash a wave over the wolf's head and they were gradually blowing closer to shore. When they got to shore the wolf was nearly drowned. He fell back into the lake as he tried to scramble up the steep bank.

Finally he made it and disappeared into the woods. When Adams straightened out his boat he could see Don, the guide and his party coming out of the river also on their way to the lodge. When he told Don what had happened, Don said, "Damn, if I had only been here on time, I would have got that wolf," Adams replied, "I am sure you would have, Don, too bad your timing was off."

After that experience in the spring he said, "I would have lasooed it with the anchor rope, and drowned it."

These episodes made the Dayton and Toronto papers. They also convinced everyone that wolves would take to the water when they wanted to.

One summer an Indian guide working for me was fishing in Raganooter Lake with a party when a big buck bounded out of the woods into the lake with blood showing on its side. Two wolves came out behind the buck and waded out to their bellies and stood lapping up water and looking for the buck. The buck swam right by the boat in order to get away from those wolves. He figured that was the lessor of the two evils at that moment. The party said it was lucky he didn't attempt to come aboard.

One fall, a few days before deer season, Bill Driver and I were working at the boat dock when we heard wolves down the lake. We looked up just in time to see a deer jump off from the high bank and it swam right towards us and into the boat channel. About 200 yards from us it crawled out and disappeared in the brush; as it did we saw blood on its flanks. However, this time the wolves never showed themselves.

During my years of trapping I have seen many remains of deer that have been pulled down, more than four or five times out on the lake ice, with the flesh torn out each time until they were gradually killed. Then the pack would tear them to pieces. On snow and ice it looked like a slaughter-house.

194

Lunchtime on the hunt.

A typical 'hunter's night' dance at Art Richardson's Hall, Loring, Ontario.

I often wish some of the misinformed people who want to protect wolves could see some of these tragic, bloody sights and hear a helpless deer bleating and screaming as the wolves tear the living flesh from its bones, again and again, eating it before it had died.

Unfortunately, many intelligent people have been taken in by such fiction writers as Farley Mowatt. He should be condemned for the harm he has done to our wildlife, with his fiction; in particular the book, "Never Cry Wolf."

I have never ceased to enjoy watching our beautiful white-tailed deer, and with over 50 years as trapper and guide I have had numerous opportunities to observe and admire them at close range. I will relate a few of my experiences that still stand out in my memory.

On several occasions as I paddled a canoe down the river I have spotted does along the bank, usually with a pair of fawns cavorting in exuberant play, like young lambs in the spring, just for the "heck of it." Innocent happiness personified, in every leap and movement of their beautiful speckled carefree bodies. A scene that memory stamps indelibly on one's mind, as if to say, "You will remember this!"

One stand-out scene took place as I paddled through a channel in a marsh. We came upon a doe and her two fawns; they had been standing in the water feeding on water plants.

The doe had just stepped out onto the bank; the two spotted fawns had decided it was time for their nursing, so they began. They were both going at it vigorously, one on each side of the doe, as the canoe glided into view.

The doe snorted a warning and stepped away from the fawns interrupting the ''milk bar'' momentarily; as they were more intent on getting back to her tits and nursing. She finally, to our amazement, had to put her nose under their bellies and lift them bodily away. Then she bounded away toward the cover of the brush on shore.

The look of surprise on the fawns when they saw us and how they scrambled to follow their mother I will never forget. It was both a comical and beautiful sight.

On another occasion during the winter of 1969 and 1970 the deer were having a very rough time. I had been cutting browse to feed them and had towed it behind my ski-doo when returning from trapping.

I piled the brush on the side hill just below the building where I skinned my beaver, so I could watch the deer as they fed. I soon had three or four adult deer and several fawns crossing on the river bridge daily to feed on the browse. One old buck, whose ribs were really prominent, was slow to cross the bridge and reach the browse. I noticed if any fawns were there, they would stand aside while he ate. It seemed to me in deference to his old age.

Sometimes it would take the old buck a couple of hours to nip off enough browse to satisfy him. Days that the sun was bright, the fawns would cuff the deep snow off the roots or stumps of the large pine trees near my cottages. This permitted them to lie down on the protruding tree roots and be clear of the frosty ground where their hides would not freeze; then they would chew their cud like a sheep or cow. When the sun warmed one side they would get up and stretch just like a cat, then turn and lie down with the other side facing the sun.

Deer do some very unusual things, especially during the severe winters and in recent years since snowmobile travel in our remote areas has increased to the point it is detrimental, not only to our deer and moose but also to all wildlife.

However, organized ski-doo clubs have become aware of their hazards to wildlife and are making a real effort to control the irresponsible people. Even so, there are a great many unthinking, ignorant screwballs who think it is smart to pass a deer on a ski-doo trail or worse chase one out on the ice, until the poor exhausted deer die from exhaustion. Not to mention the number of little fawns lost by does forced to plunge off ski-doo trails into deep snow.

Deer become very tame in the winter months due mainly to hunger and some probably to their instinct that it is a "safe" period. All animals have ways of communication that we don't fully understand, a kind of sign language of their very own.

As I mentioned before, they would collect together in logging areas to take advantage of the browse available on the fallen trees, and the well-beaten skid trails to travel on. Years ago when horses were used for logging, a teamster would usually pull a sleigh from the main camp back to the cutting area with his hay and oats on the sleigh rack, to feed the team at noon.

As a deer became hungrier, it was common to see them lying around in the background near the lunch area waiting for the horses to be fed at noon. Then, as soon as the men were back to work, they would crowd around a sleigh and would even fight to climb into the hayrack to pick up the spilled grain and shafe spilled by the horses.

I had many times been in the act of cutting down a tree and have several young deer approach as they heard the axe or saw. They would stand close by stamping their little hooves on the hard trail, impatiently waiting for the tree to fall. The moment the tree hit the ground they would rush in to feed on the browse, even as I was cutting the lower section into logs. There hunger stronger than their fear and some-how knowing also that no harm would befall them.

Also, during that period of using horses there was always some hay and clover seed that would sprout into growth. This not only happened from spillage but from the horse dung dropped around the logging area and on the travelled logging roads. This became another source of feed not only for the deer but other animals as well.

Partridge loved the roadside clover. All this came to a sad end when modern machinery, bulldozers, snowmobiles and such replaced the horses. Oh, all this modern equipment left behind plenty in their wake — their oil spills, fumes; their raucous noise that almost split your ear drums and that scare and scatter all wildlife out of their wits — and a few humans as well; who go there to escape from pollution and noise racket, seeking peace and quiet: those quiet sanctuaries are all being invaded by our so-called modern "progress" and to everyone's detriment.

Instead of going into the woods, like Thoreau, for a spell to sort things out, they are lying around on couches in an office of a psychiatrist, who prescribes tranquilizers along with his advice, and most end up overdosing into oblivion.

Now, how did I get from horse's dung into this?

Trails were formerly cut by axe. Axe-cut saplings and brush would develop new growth that would develop into excellent deer browse.

Now bulldozers and huge skidders rip everything out by the roots, leaving much uprooted earth to be washed away into our lakes and streams polluting the fish spawning areas with silt that sticks to the fish eggs killing them.

I have found large female pickerel dead on the spawning rapids with their gills clogged with silt and mud, after a heavy rain washed mud into the stream.

During the early period of the settlers and their clearing patches of timberland to grow crops and gardens and burning the slash, they created much deer feed with their turnip patches and seeded areas. It was common to see deer come out of the woods and feed on new grain that was just sprouting out of the ground.

In some places they were only interested in the new sprouts. They would feed repeatedly in the same areas as the new sprouts came up and would ignore adjacent areas where the growth was advanced.

I may have mentioned previously about Sank's father writing to a member of parliament complaining about deer eating his crops when he first settled here. Their reply and their only suggestion to overcome his deer problem was to shoot the deer and burn them.

Now, in the 1970's, we have a lot of well-educated biologists doing very expensive and unproductive research that has been repeated in other countries before them: to find out how to build up deer herds.

I get very disgusted with the idea of cutting the jaws and bones out of thousands of dead deer to see how old they were when they were killed or died.

Another project was the trapping of deer in wire cages, on the deer trails, to put beeper collars on them, so they could follow their movements. Everyone knows what happens when a deer gets caught in a wire fence, not to mention a cage with a steel frame. They just thrash and tear themselves to bits unless someone can quickly release them.

I have seen some of these cages stained with blood by a deer that was left for hours and even sometimes overnight, by so-called responsible personnel.

Even the wolves don't punish them that long!

A few sensible changes in our hunting regulations such as: a closed season on our does and fawns; banning the use of dogs during the hunt would help when the herd is at a low level. Also, the controlled burning of the slash areas in the spring, when only the dry surface debris will burn; allowing the new growth to sprout would be a logical way of helping to improve the deer herd.

Just yesterday, March, 1977, I heard a "Globe and Mail" reporter telling how he had accompanied George Kolenowski, a chief biologist to this area, to put beeper collars on sow bears and to tag their cubs, while still in their hibernation den.

Just some more costly, unproductive research and no doubt, most of these bears will be shot at local garbage disposals.

This same George Kolenowski was sent into Little River Lodge to see me the winter I reported the severe wolf kills of our yarded deer, after his department had made an aerial survey with a published report "that there was not one sign of wolves west of No. 11 Highway," indicating my report was not true.

That was when I cancelled my annual winter vacation to stay home and take fourteen timber wolves, where he said, "there are none."

Then the following winter, in this area, he organized a costly research program by turning some ''Beeper'' collared park wolves loose. Then hiring a six-man, radio-equipped ground crew and a helicopter at $110.00 per hour flying time to follow these wolves for days to see how they behaved or killed deer.

Any thinking person would know that any wild animal is not going to behave normally when being followed by land and air.

George was 39 years old when he and a student from Belgium spent a night with me and tried unsuccessfully to convince me after my 50 years of observing wolf behaviour: ''that in this day and age wolves were needed to control deer herds, and that they only killed sick and weak deer.''

The President of the North American Trappers' Association said, ''In 60 years of trapping wolves in many areas of the continent I have never known of a wolf to take time to take a deer's temperature, to check if it was sick before he killed it.''

However, through the efforts of Farley Mowatt's fiction and people like George, they succeeded in removing the $25.00 wolf bounty. A bounty was only paid for a dead wolf and it never came near compensating a trapper for his time and effort.

The number of beaver and fur bearers alone killed by wolves is enormous, not to mention the fact that every sheep raiser in this area was forced to give up. Even some cattle have been slaughtered by wolves.

I could relate much more on predation by wolves but it is enough to say that in this day and age we certainly do not need preditors such as wolves to keep nature in balance. Man with his modern weapons is more than capable to do the job. However, man must be subject to some control by wildlife managers, especially after severe winter kills and extreme hunting pressures.

Anyone who would sacrifice our deer for the chance to hear wolves howl, need to have their heads examined.

CHAPTER 27

OPERATING A LODGE SUCCESSFULLY:
OUTPOST CABIN

Due to the building of Legrouse Lake Dam, which improved our waterway, plus bringing in the hydro, Little River Lodge became one of the most ideal "off-the-beaten-path" hunting and fishing resorts that could be reached in the area by car, and the fact that right from the beginning, I had stocked nine lakes by my own effort with parent bass.

We were having an increasing number of prominent business people as guests. I received a great deal of publicity in the outdoor columns of both the Canadian and U.S. newspapers.

Bob Turnbull, of "Outdoor Trail" in the Globe and Mail; Jim Vipond, Sports Editor; Pete MacGillan, of the Toronto Telegram; Joe Foster; Don Buckley, of the North Bay Nugget, mentioned my name and the lodge on numerous occasions.

Also outdoor writers from New York, Pennsylvania, Ohio, Virginia and West Virginia, Michigan, Indiana, New Jersey, Maryland and Washington, D.C., wrote articles about guests from their cities and states, who returned from successful vacations fishing and hunting at the lodge, and then reported to them.

Many times I was asked, "Why do you never attend the numerous sportsmen's shows to publicize your lodge?"

I always answered, "If they ever learned that I had to attend sportsmen's shows or place ads in outdoor magazines to get guests, then they had better think twice before coming back."

My entire business had been built on satisfied guests who told their friends. I did run an ad in Outdoor Life Magazine at the request of one of their agents who roomed with me at a convention at Kenora, Ontario.

Bob Turnbull of the Globe & Mail with his wife and twin daughters during their first stay at the lodge.

I received hundreds of enquiries that cost me a great deal of time and effort to answer, and many of them were from people who had no idea where Little River Lodge was located. I don't recall that I ever received a guest from that ad. Whereas, satisfied people would tell their friends what I had to offer and could answer their many pertinent questions they would be asked. Then if they decided to make a reservation they would write or phone me. All this saved me much correspondence and time. Letter writing was never one of my accomplishments anyway.

Another thing I learned as an operator: there is a definite limit to the number of guests anyone could give personal attention to. Once my business expanded beyond the point where I had to stint on the personal "touch," some new guests never returned for their second stay. They felt cheated; because we all want to feel important, especially when you are way off in the semi-wilderness, away from your normal surroundings.

A big factor in satisfying guests is quality guides and lodge staff. A good conscientious guide could bring guests back year after year, if they were pleased with the accommodations and equipment as well.

I received many compliments from people who had spent previous vacations at other resorts. Mainly they appreciated the facilities and the service around the boat dock, as well as all the boats and equipment kept under cover when not being used.

Guests could leave all their equipment in the boats: cushions, tackle and all, and not need to carry it back and forth to their cabins.

We always replenished their fuel and bait without waiting for them to ask, and always gave them refunds for fuel not used. We had a daily chart at the boathouse to mark the charges for fuel, bait or refreshments taken from the refrigerator at the dock. This convenience meant as much to me as it did to them in time saved. I would enter all the charges to their account at night.

I learned very early that fishermen become very impatient if they have to wait for fuel to be mixed, or have to travel some distance to get it; also bait.

Many guests made it a point to tell me that my lodge was one of the cleanest, best organized camps they had ever been in.

Natural swimming pool and boat house - reflections in pool.

Boat dock scene.

Boat dock and gas supply.

205

Mary's method of planning her end of the lodge operation was appreciated by all the guests. Many men would plan to bring their family on their next trip. They would say, "Walter" I would have brought my wife, if I had known how you operated this place. She would have enjoyed it. Most women enjoyed the scenic boat ride down our chain of lakes, and in particular because these waters seldom became too rough. Also they could drive to North Bay without bothering their husbands, who preferred to fish. Another feature of our operation, the guests had a choice of taking all their meals in the lodge or only their evening meal. It was not necessary to dress special.

The natural river pool and winding river out to the lake was not only an excellent boat harbor, but a fun place for children. Those who enjoyed hiking could walk miles in several directions without a sign of habitation.

We would occasionally encounter a careless party whose boat would return each time in a terrible mess and require cleaning. The main thing was our boathouse, which I had built over the river. Not only did it protect the equipment, but it saved bailing out rain water during stormy weather.

I mentioned earlier how I built my phone lines from the lodge to Golden Valley without using a pole, and how I equiped the camp with Delco electricity.

When the hydro built the power line into the lodge, I asked for permission to hang my phone line on the hydro poles. They informed me, "Mr. Hesman, the regulations would not permit us to deal with you." They said, "If you were a registered company, we could make a contract with you."

The fact I was an individual, their insurance would not permit them to deal with me. However, one of the linemen told me confidentially, "If you were to put your wires on our poles, without our permission, that would release the hydro from any responsibility, if you should have an accident."

I got the message!

I arranged with one of my Michigan guests to purchase four miles of army surplus insulated field wire, double strand. He purchased the wire for fifty dollars, then had to pay seventy dollars to bring it across the border into Canada. Customs put their own value on it. They would not accept what we paid for it.

As soon as our hunting season was over, I had a man help me string the wire over the power line right-of-way.

Then I borrowed a safety belt and a pair of climbers to hang the wire on the poles. There were sixty-five poles from Golden Valley switchboard to the lodge.

I started to hang the wire at the switchboard; in three days I connected it to the phone at the lodge. The muscles in my legs were very sore from climbing poles, instead of hills. Believe me, there is a difference! All these little muscles have a particular job to do and when you switch them to a different job, they complain with a vengeance.

As soon as everything was connected, I gave the handle on the lodge phone a hard crank. When the operator answered, she yelled, "What did you do to me? I got a terrible shock."

I told her, "You ring me." I immediately got repaid. I also got an electrical charge that would have cured anyone of depression, blindness or whatever ailed you.

Immediately I went out to Golden Valley in the Jeep and mentioned to the lineman what had happened. He asked me, "Did you put in drain-offs when you hung your line?"

I said, "What are drain-offs?" Dumb like, which I was.

Then he explained, "Electricity from the power lines build up on the phone line, when you hung it on the hydro poles. It will be necessary to put "drain-offs" about every mile or so and ground them to drain the electricity off. Otherwise you will continue to get the full charge or shock each time you pick up your receiver at each end of the line."

He offered to make the necessary "drain-offs" and I put them on the line, about a mile apart, as soon as they were ready.

When it was completed I had a two-wire phone line that was the only private line connected to the local switchboard.

Of course I was responsible for all the maintenance required on my line. Lightening frequently burned sections.

The line worked fine for a couple of years, then we had two ice storms within a two-week period. I remember the first one came just as the deer hunt was starting. The phone line was broken off almost every hydro pole.

I managed to piece it together and put it back on the poles, but this time I had to separate the two strands of wire at each pole, as the insulation on each wire had been damaged, causing short circuits.

Shortly after this the Bell Telephone negotiated to buy the local phone company out. The contract read: "They must serve all who are connected to the switchboard." Of course this included Little River Lodge bush phone line.

This meant that I would finally be relieved of the responsibility of maintaining my own line. This had entailed an annual spring job to re-hang and splice my line, that I was only too happy to relinquish to "Ma Bell."

There were always breaks caused by trees falling or lumbermen catching the line with their jammerpoles and dragging it away. There were occasions, with my old tree line, when deer hunters cut my line and used it to hang up their deer.

I felt I really had "it made" now that I had the Bell Phone Service AND the Hydro as well, and yet still maintained my semi-wilderness status!

Both saw mills had closed down and moved out, which meant I would not have so much trouble with the six miles of road to hassle with, leading from the Valley to the lodge.

Cutting ice in river before hydro came.

Another big job that was eliminated was the former annual ice cutting and storing. It was not only a back breaking job putting the ice up, it was a heavy job digging it up and delivering it around to all the cottages all summer long.

When you look back on your life it gives you cause to wonder, "How did I ever manage to accomplish all that I did?"

The only answer seems to be, "When something is necessary, you just do it." Only later do you have time to wonder, "how you did it."

Well, anyway, we now had several freezers which enabled us to store and stock food supplies. Also guests who wanted to take fish home could freeze them in their cabin, and they did not need to be packed in ice when they took them home.

I found that by wrapping several packages of frozen fish together in newspapers then rolling them into a raincoat or old clothes, they would keep for several days. All this helped to cut down our work load.

Shortly after the dam was built, I built an outpost cabin on a point in LeGrouse Lake. We arranged many overnight fishing trips down there that everyone would remember and talk about for years.

Trophy fish.

Young Ricky calls for mother to come see the small bass for stocking the lakes.

It probably wasn't playing fair on my part, but I couldn't resist the temptation to exaggerate a little: porcupines were very numerous at that time and would wake us up at night by chewing on the cabin porch. I would tell the guests, especially to get a rise out of the women, that it was those bears.

Guests who met here at the lodge for the first time would then arrange each year to meet again. This all started with Girlie and George Schoetz from Cleveland and Byron and Margaret Henze from Windsor, Ontario. The group kept growing over the years, until they occupied most of the camp, especially during the hay fever season. Some would stay until they had a frost back home.

It was like a big happy family and in memory of those very special days and times I would like to name a few of them, as they were very special people: Dr. Arthur and June Fouke, from Dayton, Ohio; Jack Facey, of London, Ont.; Harry Tugwell, Toronto; Charles and Eleanor Stearns, Toronto; Dr. Taylor; Guy Watkins and Mr. Claude Hurley, all from Damascus, Md.; and Dan and Lou Paskey, Cleveland; Dr. Rollin and Thelma Yant, University Hts., Ohio; Harry and Eileen Genske, Novelty, Ohio.

We never had any entertaining problems, although we furnished none; they entertained us!

It became customary for them to meet at the dinner camp on Chartier Lake or at the outpost camp on LaGrouse Lake, almost every day, weather permitting, and we frequently had a fish fry.

These guests were usually in camp when our extra summer staff would leave us to return to school. The guests just pitched in by helping in the kitchen, making their own beds and tidying their cabins, even going to North Bay to do the shopping. They would do anything to help.

Usually when a new guest arrived from a particular area it would not be long until other guests would call from that same area for reservations.

Among our best fishermen were Dan Paskey, Joe Risher, Carl Mollins, Abe Powers, Harold Blair, Doc Taylor, Col. Morehouse, Bruce and Joan Wilkes. The standout woman was Joan Wilkes.

I feel very fortunate in having met all these wonderful people and I feel badly that it is too difficult to keep in touch with all of them.

CHAPTER 28

SQUIRRELS, CHIPMUNKS AND LOONS

Our squirrels and chipmunks created a great deal of entertainment for guests at the lodge. They also, at times, gave some of the women bad scares.

On one occasion we had a family with children stay two weeks in one of the cottages. The kids made pets of most of the squirrels and chipmunks around camp, to the point they had them coming into their cabin for free hand-outs; even serving them on their table.

The time came for the family to leave, and much sad and tearful good-byes as the children bade their last farewell to their new-found friends.

The next day a new party of two men and their wives arrived and moved into the cabin.

I was down at the dock preparing the boat and motor for them when I suddenly heard the women screaming.

I ran to the cabin expecting the worst and blood, just as the women burst out the door screaming, ''Get that animal out of the bedroom!''

One of the pet squirrels had come in for its usual hand-out from their little friends. I tried to explain that the children had made pets of the squirrel, but they didn't want ANY animals in their cabin while they were there.

I didn't exactly know how to get the message across to the squirrels and chipmunks, but I hoped that one squirrel would deliver it for me, with regrets.

Another time a female squirrel created entertainment and I would add, respect as well, for a group at the lodge.

We had a severe storm the night before and the guests were just coming into the lodge for breakfast. I noticed this squirrel coming down from a large poplar tree with one of her young ones in her mouth.

The storm had apparently broken a large limb off the tree exposing her young ones to the elements. Her baby (?) was almost as large as she was! She had trouble carrying it toward the corner of the lodge, as she had to pass through the long grass.

When she tried to climb the rear wall of the lodge, next to the fireplace chimney, she had more trouble slipping on the smooth-painted logs. We watched her go to where the corner logs protruded and she managed to make it to the roof.

By now her destination became obvious to all, she was trying to get her babies into the space between the warm fireplace chimney and the overhang of the roof.

As she crossed the metal chimney flange she slipped; everyone gasped as she fell free about three feet, and somehow grasped hold of the hydro lead-in cable, hanging upside down by her hind legs, yet still holding on to her overgrown baby.

Then to our complete amazement she walked the lead-in cable back to the chimney, still in her upside-down position and proceeded to deposit the baby in the warm place behind the chimney — just as she had planned in the first place.

Losing no time, she immediately reappeared and proceeded to repeat the same trip until she had her five babies safely behind the warm chimney.

On some of these precarious trips she had difficulty, as some of the guests in their eagerness not to miss anything, got into her path, trying to get pictures of her with the babies in her mouth.

Undaunted, she refused to change her route, even when she had to crawl over people's feet! Frequently she would have to lay her baby down in order to get a firmer hold and they would lay as if dead, with never a quiver from them.

Many guests remarked on how resourceful such small creatures can be, to benefit their babies' survival. Those of you who have ever watched our northern red squirrels in particular, and how they figure out ways of getting around obstructions at bird feeding stations, will understand.

In my many years of trapping I have observed many such incidents of animal resourcefulness.

In comparison, we humans in general appear rather helpless, mainly because so many of our problems are solved for us. And when you compare that tiny squirrel with a few of the human mothers, who have in dire straits, dumped their own new born flesh and blood in the nearest garbage can, it makes you wonder.

We are too much inclined to let others carry our burden and think for us, instead of thinking and planning for ourselves.

For years my interest has been attracted by the loons who spend their summers on our northern lakes raising their young. I would see them arrive as soon as the ice left the lakes; usually there would be only one pair on each small lake, until late summer when they appeared to fly in from the surrounding lakes to visit.

Sometimes I wondered if unthinking youngsters at cottages had broken up families by shooting at them. On several occasions I had tried to locate their nests, without success.

The fishing was very slow one day and the guests I was guiding suggested we make a real effort to locate the loon nest. Previously, I had often noticed as I approached a small island in Stanley Lake, a single loon became more vocal. Soon after I would see a second loon surface some distance from the island.

I reasoned that this vocal outburst was the mate's signal to his mate on the nest, which no doubt was on this small island. So we began a close-in search of the island shore line.

We were soon rewarded by finding a slippery wet looking spot in the teaberry shore brush. This indicated that something had been sliding in and out of the water regularly. I pushed the bow of the canoe in close and by spreading apart the brush with my paddle, I spotted two loon eggs.

They would have been very difficult to see even from a short distance, as they were perfectly camouflaged; the same color as the ground they were one. Actually there really was no nest material, they were just layed on the ground.

It was plain to see that the eggs were within a foot of the water's edge, to enable the loon to dive from the nest into the lake quickly, when anyone approached, without being seen and surfacing some distance away from the island and her nest.

214

Loons are unable to walk any distance on land as their legs are far back and only used for swimming and pushing themselves up on shore. Their entire life is spent in the water or flying. They require considerable distance for a running on the water start to take off, and will never attempt to fly when pursued; instead they will dive and swim under water for long distances before surfacing.

I was able to add loon nests to the many attractions to show my guests while guiding. For a while the Stanley Lake loon would vacate her nest as I approached, then she gradually came to accept the fact I meant her no harm and she began to stay on her nest and play dead with her long neck stretched out close to the water's edge.

The first time I saw this it fooled me and I reached out to touch her with my paddle. She quickly showed signs of life and snapped at the paddle. We just as quickly withdrew.

A few days after that we saw her out in the lake with her newly hatched young. As we drew near, she really became very angry and excited and put on a fantastic display of motherly disapproval by loud vocal yells and diving.

When we got too close, that was just more than she could stand and she charged the canoe. And to make it doubly impressive she added her injured bird act as well. It was quite a show!

Her babies were like jet black balls of down that gave you an instant desire to reach out and cuddle them close. Even their first day out on water, they knew enough to try and dive when their mother did; but their very fine down was so buoyant they could only duck their heads under the surface and paddle furiously with their little rear end sticking up in the air, for all the world to see. It really was very comical to watch them trying so hard to dive with the odds weighed so heavily against them. We gave them an ''A'' for effort.

Within a few days they were able to submerge themselves and gradually able to travel some distance under water. There were times I would notice one or both of them riding on their mother's back or hiding under her wing.

I have known them to be hatched so late they would be unable to fly south before the lakes froze over, and I assumed they died or were taken by predators.

215

One very unusual experience with a loon was early one spring. We had a fine group of fellows from Chagrin Falls, Ohio, who made an annual spring fishing trip to the lodge for pickerel fishing.

It was customary at this time of year for us to fish in a narrow channel just below Kimikong Falls. On this occasion there were at least six boats anchored below the falls.

Suddenly one of the older members of the group, "Chagrin's local druggist," got a terrific strike on his fly rod; and whatever it was took off down stream, making his reel spin as it peeled off line.

Finally as it came to the end of the line, he just pointed his rod in the direction and hoped his line would not break. All at once a large loon surfaced with its wings flapping.

No one was more surprised than I was as I never heard of a loon approaching under water close to a boat. It must have been the swirling waters of the falls that obscured its view of the boat under water.

By keeping his fly rod pointed directly at the loon, the druggist managed to reel it in close enough for us to get it into a large landing net, but not without a terrific struggle from the diving and flapping loon. We subdued it by tying the landing net around it. We were then able to remove the hook. We decided to leave it in the net to "show and tell" the rest of the group what had happened.

Unfortunately, there were several pranksters in the group and before I knew what they were up to they had turned the loon loose in the shower house. Their main prankster was taking a shower at the time.

This created a panic before I could catch it; no easy matter even wearing my leather gloves. When I was able to turn it loose at the boat dock, it immediately dived and it never surfaced until it reached the lake, quite a distance away.

All these animal incidents were of considerable interest to our guests and contributed to their enjoyment while staying at Little River Lodge.

216

CHAPTER 29

LOST HUNTERS: THEIR ESCAPADES IN CAMP

For a number of years we had a group of deer hunters that fluctuated between fourteen to eighteen members, usually consisting of an equal number of Canadians and Americans.

We put them up in five log cottages, surrounding the Main Lodge. Each cottage could accommodate from four to six hunters, and was considered to be deluxe accommodation for hunters. The meals Mary served them were also rated tops.

If a hunter was capable of hunting by himself, we had no objections; however, our deer hunt was conducted mainly as a group affair, with strict safety rules and hunting procedures.

For quite a few years we had very little interference from transient hunters. Each day's hunt was planned by me as to where we would hunt, down the lakes or out the roads, depending on the weather. When we had sufficient hunters, I would try to split them up into two groups.

I would place one group on watches and another guide would place the other. We would try to close off a particular area, then make our chase between the two groups, trying not to keep them standing too long on each watch. There were times it could not be avoided, if we had to follow a wounded deer, or if we had too many deer to dress and bring out.

Sometimes it would take four or more hours to complete a chase, but for years we had no trouble taking a deer for each hunter and most of our hunters would not shoot a doe or a fawn.

At lunch each day we would arrange for all the men to come together around a fire where they could toast sandwiches and make hot soup or drinks. There was always a lot of fun and pranks around these lunch fires.

217

One of our safety rules forbid a hunter to have a cartridge in his gun barrel when two or more men were together, and anyone could call for a gun check at anytime. Anyone found guilty was fined $2.00. Also, if a hunter was not at his post where I left him, when I came by to pick him up, it was understood that we would not hold the entire group up to hunt for him. It is not feasible to signal during daylight hours.

In the event a man did become lost, we would not look or signal for him until dark. We instructed them not to keep travelling when they were confused; instead they were to find a suitable high spot and gather enough wood for a fire and wait until they heard our signal shots at dark, then answer and wait until we came for him.

Over the many years we conducted the deer hunt, I can only recall three occasions that we had to go after a man after dark. Once it was due to the man talking instead of listening when I was directing them to return to camp, while the guides went after a wounded deer.

This hunter decided to get ahead of the rest, where he might chance to see a deer. In doing this he got off on the wrong trail. He did, however, do the right thing as soon as he realized he was lost, by making a fire on high ground.

Actually he was only a hundred yards off the main trail when his friend and I found him.

We called for him to come out, "You go to hell," he said, "there is no trail. Come and get me!"

We had to go to the fire to bring him out! Some of the hunters made a special trip to town and got him a cow bell to wear.

Another hunter claimed he thought we had called him to come out, then when he tried to find his way back to his post he became lost, and wandered around for hours. Eventually he found the place he had been posted and stayed there until he heard our signal shots at dark.

Then instead of waiting for us to come for him, he started across country toward our shots. When one of the guides found him, he was a mess!

He had been running and had fallen into a swamp and was covered with black muck. He never went hunting again.

The third man had left his post to follow a deer he had shot at, then he missed us when we came to pick him up. He was luckier, as he did get back to the trail and was sitting at the lake where we landed the boat.

Each year the hunters would make a "buck pool" of two to five dollars each, to be won by the man who shot the first buck. On this occasion the first shot I heard fired on opening day was at the dam.

When I came to Dave Rae's post I called and asked, "was it you, Dave, who fired the first shot?" He answered, "Yes, and I collect the $90.00 buck pool."

He pointed into a thicket where he said the deer had fallen. When I got to the deer and turned it over to dress it out, I found that it did not have the usual buck "equipment."

It was a doe with horns.

It was the custom to hold court each evening after dinner to thrash out all the day's problems and experiences, collect fines, if any, which included cutting off a shirt tail for missing a deer.

These courts were very properly conducted and created a great deal of amusement for all. Dave's doe with horns created one of the most prolonged court trials, as the defense claimed he was entitled to the pool, because the deer did have horns; and Dave would never have shot it if he had known it was a doe.

The opposition claimed that regardless of the horns, Dave should have made sure by checking to see if it had a penis. Therefore it was not buck!

They eventually split the pool with a hunter who had shot the first buck at 9:15 a.m.

Most hunters who were charged with missing a deer would put up some fine defense arguments in hope of saving their shirt tails, even to presenting deer hair that was supposedly cut as the bullet creased the deer. One hunter went so far as to cut deer hair with blood and flesh from a dead deer and claimed we should have followed his wounded deer.

On another occasion Tom Davis, who operated Dinty Moore's Tavern in Cleveland, was the official "Shirt Tail Cutter" at that time. He had been waiting a long time to get cutting John Rondina's shirt, and John on the other hand was just as

219

determined he would never give him the chance. He was going to make darn sure of making a kill before he shot.

With all his carefulness, he finally missed, when his bullet nicked a small tree and only cut a handful of hair off the buck.

That night during dinner Tom was honing his cutting knife and wetting his lips in his anticipation of finally cutting John's shirt.

When the court was finally adjourned, after John had put up a terrific defense, with all the deer hair and even the piece off the tree he had nicked, he was still found "guilty," and ordered to submit to Tom's knife.

Due to the determined and prolonged defense John had put up, Tom gleefully cut almost the whole back out of his shirt.

While Tom was still gloating over the splendid job he had done on the shirt, John stood up, pulled the shirt off over his head and handed it to Tom saying, "Thank you, Tom, for the loan of YOUR shirt!" Poor Tom was speechless. Everyone else just roared with laughter.

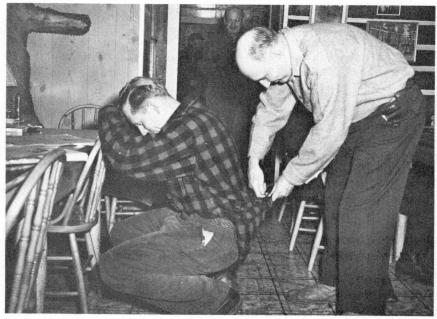

Photo: W.C. Horrigan

Dr. A. Secord of Toronto suffers the
shirttail cutting penalty for missing a deer.

One of Tom's cabin partners had given John one of Tom's shirts to wear up to "Court," so he had really cut his own shirt.

The hunters were always playing pranks, and sometimes they would go to extremes, such as blocking a cabin's chimney to smoke the occupants out.

I was the target of one of their most hilarious pranks. A dentist from Cleveland, Dr. Bill Beutel, whom I had known for many years as a fishing guest, had come up for his first deer hunt.

One evening at dinner I had not noticed him leave the lodge. Suddenly I heard the kitchen staff talking with a loud-mouth person at the back door.

When I got to the door, there was a wild-looking character with what looked like blood running down his face from under his cap. He had the most hideous looking teeth and was slobbering from the mouth as well. He shouted, "One of your damn hunters has been shooting partridge on my property and some of the shot hit me in the head."

He was trying to force his way into the kitchen with his gun and really gave me a hard time to keep him out. I was so worked up by now that I was on the verge of bopping him one, anything to keep him and his gun out.

Right then he reached up and took out his false denture and I recognized Doc and knew I'd been "had."

It is still hard for me to believe anyone's appearance could be changed so completely by a set of teeth. Knowing the "pranksters" as I did, didn't even help.

Doc pulled a similar joke on our game warden, who was also amazed that he could be fooled by a set of teeth. He asked Doc if he would put on another "performance" the next evening if he could arrange to bring his senior officer in? He would arrange it on the pretext that they were to check our deer. Doc readily agreed.

That night we sat Officer Windsor right next to Doc at dinner, so they could become well acquainted. Then just as our usual "court session" got under way, Doc slipped out to prepare his act.

Shortly after, Bill Horrigan (who was the homicide photographer for Garfield Heights Police in Ohio) went out the front door, I heard him yell, "Walter, there is some guy out here trying to cut down my buck off the pole!" Everyone rose as one and rushed outside enmass.

I got hold of Doc's leg and pulled him back down the ladder. He kept yelling, "This deer is mine, I just wounded it this morning and followed it for hours. Now I find your hunters have got it." "Calm down," I told him, "Officer Windsor will settle the problem."

Before the Officer had time to reason with Doc he scrambled back up the ladder again, yelling, "It's my deer and I am going to take it regardless of some dumb game warden."

Officer Windsor rose to the bait and shot up the ladder to pull Doc down. He did it several times and at the same time was doing his best to talk to this "lunatic."

Instead of paying any attention, Doc became very abusive; in fact, so abusive the officer took off his tunic, ready to fight Doc.

Doc figured it was high time he revealed his true identity and out came the false teeth and the officer realized it was a joke on him. Well, Doc wasn't quite finished yet and he invited the officer to come back into the lodge and have a drink. Someone then poured him a glass of cold tea.

There was no end to the various things these men concocted and one thing just led to another. I often wished that I had arranged for someone to keep notes of all the pranks and the "Court Sessions" that these normally sane men thought up and produced at the hunting season. It is difficult now for me to recall all of them. But it was a hilarious time and very few escaped being the butt of their jokes, even when you were aware of their past "performances", they were superb actors, and you fell right into their "trap."

One standout "court session" was carried out by Gib Shaw. He dressed up as a young 19 year old blonde lad in a girl's dress, and having him take the stand to testify he (she) was having a little affair with the accused, when the deer came by, causing the accused to miss the deer, and she didn't think it would be fair to cut his shirt tail.

The accused happend to be a man who operated several Beauty Salons in Cleveland and he had quite a reputation with the ladies.

That particular case was carried on for hours and everyone had tears in their eyes from laughing so hard and so long. Those days were great fun as well as good hunting. I will always have fond memories of the many fine individuals of our hunting group, which included a number of prominent Canadians and Americans. Returning year after year, we became very close.

While I got a lot of satisfaction and fun from our successful hunts, I always was under a great deal of pressure and much responsibility, which gave way to relief when each hunt was ended.

Swapping stories after the hunt.

223

The management of our wildlife, or rather the mismanagement by our so-called experts, has troubled me for years. There were periods we had a closed season, or a very short one on partridge, when in fact, they were abundant. Then when they really became scarce and were under much more hunting pressure, the season was extended from early September to December 15th. It has never changed to this day!

Our deer management has been a disgrace.

There has been no change in our deer regulations for many years, regardless of the big increase in hunters and hunting pressures, not to mention the severe predation by wolves and dogs plus severe winter kills.

Worst of all is the permission given for the use of dogs to chase these beautiful creatures, and the abolishment of the wolf bounty.

The continued killing of the doe's and fawns, when we should be trying to build up the deer population.

About the only thing our Life Department has done in recent years is to constantly increase their Personnel Department and Equipment, to carry out the many unproductive and useless research projects, by young career biologists who have little or no practical experience, which really is the only knowlege worth a damn!

It is just another "do nothing" division of our Ministry of Natural Resources, who have changed ministers a number of times but never changed their programs.

"My gawd, five dollars!"

CHAPTER 30

WHERE DID THEY ALL COME FROM?
REGULATION HEADACHES: LODGE FOR SALE

Dr. Yant was one of my first guests in 1934, and over the years I would say he was directly responsible or indirectly responsible for at least 50 per cent of all the guests that ever came here, until I sold out.

Doc never missed coming up for fishing or hunting, from two to four times every year, until he had a stroke in 1965.

Through the years I had guests from nearly every state in the United States. A couple from South American countries, the British Isles, Japan and Germany. It has been my pleasure to entertain hundreds of wonderful people, including some very prominent well-known guests.

Unfortunately, time and age catches up with all of us and I gradually thought of selling out before I reached the point of not being able to carry on — I have probably worked harder since my retirement, but at my own leisure.

If I waited until something happened, I was afraid Mary would be left to settle our affairs on her own. Actually, had it not been for her I would have quit when Lottie and I separated. There is only so much one person can do, and I feel without Mary's help, I'd have never made it in those trying times.

Another reason that made me consider selling was the help problem, which worsened each year. The government, as well, kept making more and more demands and kept interfering with small enterprises such as ours. They demanded almost as much bookwork from us as they did for businesses that could afford an office staff.

For a period we were employing as many as seven on our staff besides ourselves. At that time the bureaucrats increased and took over the Unemployment Insurance, Workmen's Compensation, Sales Tax, plus many more government departments.

Hired help learned to take advantage of the Unemployment Insurance and leave us in mid-season. We were gradually forced to cut down to one middle-aged woman to help Mary — and we had no guides.

Men who were capable of guiding could work for the Highway Department for higher wages than my guests could afford to pay, plus the former guides only had to put in an eight hour day and five days a week. They were free also at 4:00 p.m. and no one would expect a full day's work out of them. They were paid for holidays and were given welfare, higher than I could afford to pay, just to stay home. "Why should anyone want to work?"

The Department of Labour notified me of several minimum wage regulations and the compulsory eight hour day. I was obliged to pay any of my staff, who had to remain over 40 hours a week on the lodge premises, double time as well as filling out reports to explain why. All this takes time. It almost required more help to take care of all this paper work. If you go that route then you are in the same mess as the government itself: more staff, more paper work, more expenditure of money that no one can afford, and "there goes the budget." A vicious circle that eventually consumes itself.

As a result, I had a number of people who suggested they would work for me if I would not report them or take off any deductions or Unemployment Insurance.

In desperation, I did it with one. She quit later and married. Her husband black-mailed me into over-paying her. I hired what I thought was a good cook to relieve Mary.

She was here three days and Mary gave her the afternoon off, the day before our first of the season guests arrived. She went down to our outside root cellar to get a cold beer. She slipped on the pine needles and broke her ankle.

I was away fixing the frost holes on our road when Mary came out to get me. I found the cook crying because she had broken her ankle while she was off duty and didn't know what she was going to do, as she had a pregnant daughter at home.

Naturally, I felt sorry for her. I assured her I would arrange for her to get Workmen's Compensation. I drove her to the

Burk's Falls Hospital. She was on compensation until the fall, then returned with her daughter to spend a week on us. Then she developed back trouble, which she claimed was due to her fall.

It took two years and three visits from the Workmen's Compensation Inspectors before they took her off compensation, not to mention the considerable correspondence and forms to fill out. All this for a couple of days work!

I was compelled to neglect my guests when they arrived, as I was frantically running around trying to get help for Mary. Being so isolated made it extra difficult to keep young help.

The new regulations (labour) were almost impossible to comply with in this type of business. No way could we regulate the time of arrival of our guests. We had no problems with our "regulars," they knew what to expect; as long as we had their cabin or unit ready they could look after themselves. However, with new people we had to be prepared to greet them and direct them — even if they arrived at midnight, as they frequently did, or 5:00 a.m., which was even worse.

If they had not eaten, Mary had to feed them, as we had no handy coffee shop or lunch counter within thirty miles or more, if it was open?

How the government expected a business that catered to the public and tourists in remote areas to operate within their regulations is beyond me.

So I advertised Little River Lodge FOR SALE. I received 65 replies in 1969. A number of prospective buyers came in during that summer.

I finally agreed to sell to a Windsor couple, Lilly and Irwin Parkins, and the deal was closed in February, 1970.

For Mary and me I purchased a Glendale Palace (my first Palace) Mobile Home and located it close to the lodge, at the rear of the lodge property. I planned to carry on each year with my trapping as long as I was physically able.

This was centrally located in my trapping zone and I kept myself busy during 1970 putting our "palace" on permanent foundation and closing in all around the bottom.

Then I built a double garage and combination fur house with four rooms above to store the many things we had accumulated at the lodge and wanted to keep. One room made a nice guest bedroom and another a sewing room for Mary.

A few guiding trips were done for some of the old guests at the lodge and in between I managed to start a garden plot. I had little time to agonize over ''retirement blues.''

Mary also was keeping busy. Besides getting our new home in order, Mary's form of relaxation was competing with several bears while picking berries, something she always liked to do. We have the most scrumptious blueberries you will ever find, fat and juicy, and worth the risk of bears as competing competitors.

One thing that struck me, I noticed I felt much more relaxed while guiding when I didn't HAVE to worry about other important things at the lodge, especially on some of the ''fly in'' trips that I made to Snow Shoe Lake. I had stocked this lake in 1962 with a few parent bass, and they had multiplied rapidly.

Dr. R. Yant of Cleveland, Ohio became a regular at Little River Lodge.

CHAPTER 31

DUCKS AND DUCKLINGS; THE BEAR HUNTER; A SPECIAL DAY

You will note by the map there was a mill pond and marsh on the river above the lodge that drained passed the lodge and cottages, through our pool and boat house and on out to the first lake. This was a good feeding area for ducks.

However, any ducks foolish enough to stay there all night were easy prey for predators. It was not unusual to hear fussing and quacking as they were attacked.

I noticed some broods gradually disappear as the predators killed them off. Also it became obvious to me that those who survived soon learned how to avoid the predators.

I have watched mink running along the bank trying to get as close as possible before diving under water, intending to come up under the ducklings to snatch one. In most incidents the parent duck would detect them in time to warn their ''babies'' and they would take off running on the water with wings flapping to the opposite shore and out of danger.

Some of the mother ducks, after feeding in the pond all day, would bring her brood over the mill dam, down through the swim pool and work their way among the boats in the boat house, then make a fast run past the dock and on out to the middle of the first lake.

There she would collect her little family into a small group and they would spend the night safely, far from shore and predators.

The next morning at daybreak we would see her reverse her trip back to the feeding grounds, her little family intact.

During the years I was personally making and guiding trips I was able to observe many unusual and interesting animal in-

229

cidents that rivaled human ones. I will relate them as they come to my mind.

There were two prominent gull rocks or small islands in the centre of Chartier Lake. They were almost bare of any growth except weed seeds that took root in the crevices of the rock.

It was very apparent to me that the same gulls made their nests on these rock islands year after year. Also on the larger islands with heavy brush and tree growth, ducks and loons made their nests.

Frequently their nests and eggs were destroyed by mink, otter and racoon, or sometimes by hawks, owls and even eagles if their nests were not well hidden.

This particular incident, something had destroyed a black duck's nest. She had become on friendly terms with the gulls; probably to ease her sense of loss and spent her lonely nights roosting with them on the gull rock to avoid the danger of shore predators.

I would usually see her flying from the feeding marsh and landing on the "gull rock," as I paddled back to the lodge just before dark. She would waddle up on the rock to settle down next to the nesting gull for the night.

Each time I saw her coming I was able to accurately predict to my guests what she would do. I had it all down pat! However, she really surprised me (don't all women?) early one morning, when I saw her sitting on the gull's nest as I passed.

Apparently, while the gull was away feeding, she felt it was only fair that she keep her friend's nest safe and warm in her absence, and at the same time nurture her own thwarted mother instinct.

The next summer, I am sure it was the same duck, who had no "racial prejudice," with her brood of ducklings, I saw swimming from the marsh and taking her brood up onto the gull rock for the night and safety with her friends.

This took place one spring when I went down to my island cottage to open it for the first party coming in. I found the interior in a mess and a dead black duck in the kitchen.

It was very apparent it had come down the brick chimney and had knocked out a chimney clean-out plate, then it had flown around inside until it killed itself. What made it come down the chimney no one knows.

Another spring I was guiding for a bear hunter from Brooklyn, New York. I had previously put out several bear baits on the Pickerel River and the Kimikon River above Chartier Lake, where the bear had been travelling along the banks and breaking into beaver and muskrat dens.

As the hunter and I came to a fresh beaver dam, I noticed a large beaver swimming toward us. I motioned to him to crouch down below the dam, where we could not be seen. I told him, "Get your movie camera ready, if you want a close-up of a beaver."

The beaver kept diving and slapping with its tail until the hunter ran out of film.

By that time it dawned on me that it was trying desperately to drive us away from the pond as it no doubt had kits.

When we stood up and proceeded to walk around the pond the beaver swam along shore slapping its tail until we were about half way around the pond.

Suddenly, it charged up out of the water, hissing like an old gander; just as it reached me, it whirled and hit my leg with its tail then dived back into the pond. It returned and kept charging at a pole I had picked up to ward it off. It still continued to follow us along the shore until we reached the end of the pond.

I have been around beaver all of fifty-two years in this area and I never have seen one behave like that beaver before or since. Later, I did have one charge my boat, trying to drive me away from its house and babies.

Mothers the world over are revered and the mother in the wild and the extent they go to, to protect their young, is a beautiful and humbling thing to see.

The hunter was beside himself, because he had not taken time to put another film in the camera, as he missed all this action by the beaver.

He did put another film in before we proceeded up the river to where I placed the bear bait. I had also spread some fermented honey from our local apiary on the tree trunks around the bait.

I could see that a bear had found the honey but had not taken the suckers. His trail coming and going from the bait was plain to see. I picked out a suitable place for a blind where we could sit and watch for the bear.

We were not settled in it long before several muskrats swam by hauling some green browse for their young. Also, several red-headed fish ducks, diving to catch minnows as they passed.

The hunter could not resist taking pictures of this action. But as soon as the ducks heard the sound of the camera, they took off quacking loudly which was not the best way to attract a bear!

A short time later, I spotted a wood duck coming down the stream with five ducklings, three of them riding on her back. They were having quite a time doing a balancing act, trying to stay on, as the overhanging alders knocked them off. Also, each time she had to dive under fallen trees, they would then rush like mad to catch up and it was so funny to see them in their struggle, as to which would succeed in climbing on her back again, while she serenely coasted along, seemingly oblivious to the ''rat race'' behind her.

My hunter was as busy as the ducklings trying to get this beautiful scene on film.

We spent a couple of hours in the blind and I was sure at one time I had heard the bear coming, but we never saw him.

The hunter was not really disappointed, he said, ''I feel I have some very unusual movies of the beaver and ducks; also a good picture of a very large moose track in the mud, plus I have the feeling of walking most of the day on a piece of this earth where few others have ever trod.''

Not one shot was fired that day to disturb the busy sanctuary that still lives to this day on film and in memory.

CHAPTER 32

RETIREMENT; FLY-INS; KEEPING BUSY; FANTASTIC FISHING

I flew in a canoe at Snow Shoe Lake and also had access to a fiberglass boat at the Snowshoe Hunt Camp. The fishing was fantastic!

The bass I had stocked developed very fast, as the lake was full of food fish and crayfish, their main food. It was almost impossible to drop a line into the lake without a bass striking it at once.

Word like that travels fast; soon two other lodges began flying in their guests and they flew lumber in on the pontoons and built a flat-bottom boat and anchored it in the middle of the lake, so they could unload right from the plane.

In 1971 Don Odorizzi, who owns the sawmill at Golden Valley, and has a Cessna 185 Skywagon Plane, offered to fly enough lumber into Snow Shoe so I could build a boat and leave it there. I brought the lumber home first and precut every piece I needed.

With my son Ricky I had Don fly us into the lake early one morning. We were not quite finished when Don came for us that evening. Don offered to bring me back the next day. Mary came back with me and she painted the boat while I finished putting in the seats and last-minute details.

With togetherness, we finished early and caught a good string of bass for Don and ourselves. With the job completed and food to take home we felt it was a very satisfying day.

A few days later Don flew me back with two old maid school teachers from Pennsylvania. They had been coming to the lodge for two years and I knew they were both very good at fishing.

We landed on the lake and taxied over to where I had built the boat. Don helped me launch it. It leaked a little, but I knew that pine lumber would soon swell up tight.

Don Odorizzi with the Floatplane.

L. to R. - Harry Gensky, Ab Powers, Joe Risher, D. Perkins, Tom Moore.

With my Ted Williams Motor, which I had brought along, we cruised over to the nearest island. I put the motor in reverse and throttled it down until it just barely moved the boat.

On one teacher's line I put a Heddon tiny torpedo surface lure; on the other line a small Repalla, with only two hooks. I instructed them to "Cast as close as possible to shore, without getting your lines tangled up on shore."

A bass hit the first plug just as it hit the water, before she started retrieving. The second teacher made her cast and a bass took her plug and came right out of the water with it. However, she was so shocked and excited she plum forgot to set the hook and the bass threw the plug and dived for safety.

I turned to land the first bass for the other lady and suddenly the second teacher exclaimed, "I don't believe it!"

Apparently, as her first bass threw its plug, another struck when it fell back into the water and hooked itself.

To top that, the next time it surfaced there were two bass on one plug. Pandemonium set in fast, and you can imagine the excitement and utter confusion probably better than I can now write about it. With two old maid teachers to boot, it was hilarious; their excitement was contagious and I came down with it as well!

I just shut the motor off and drifted as they continued to catch and lose bass in rapid succession, until number one teacher put her rod down to rest and light up a cigarette. She said, "Walter, I have heard you tell of this kind of fishing and I have even read about it, but truthfully, I never thought it would ever happen to me after thirty years."

When it came time for lunch I took them over to the mainland and they both took a necessary walk back in the bush while I prepared to get lunch from our lunch kit. We had brought sandwiches and thermoses, as they felt time would be too short for a shore dinner. Time was limited as Don was due to pick us up at 4:30.

After lunch I said, "I will fillet the fish and I suggest you two stand at the stern of the boat and fish. If you catch anything larger than we have, then we will exchange them and release what we have. Try using sinking lures as it is deep off the stern." We all went about our business.

But before I could get started on filleting, I had to climb into the boat and remove a few small bass. I told them, "I will never get my fish clean if you keep me removing fish, how about casting farther out from the shore and let it sink deeper." This worked briefly, and I managed to start the fish cleaning.

This did not last long; the cleaning came to a full stop as soon as they yelled, "Where's the landing net?" Apparently a school of larger bass had come along and began to take the worms. As I went to net one that was not through fighting, I could see several more large ones darting around it.

Finally, as much as I hated to be a spoil sport, at 4:00 p.m. I told them, "You girls, will either have to stop or look after your own netting."

One of them who was getting weary said, "Well, our wrists are sore anyways." So they stopped.

I finished filleting the ones we caught and packed them up.

We took the boat into a protected bay, where I anchored it.

Immediately we saw Don winging over the end of the lake. Don is an excellent float plane pilot. He usually glides down into the water without a bump, like a sea gull landing.

The "girls" asked me, "Could you bring three of the younger members of our party over the next day?" Before I could reply she continued, "We would pay for the trip as we want the young ones to have the experience of a fly-in trip."

The plane trip was $25.00 each way and I charged them $30.00 for guiding, which was ten times more than I received in 1936.

Don said, "Sorry, I can't make it tomorrow, but how about the following day?" Both of them agreed that would be fine. "In fact, we need to rest up after today."

When the teachers got through telling the other guests about Snow Shoe Lake, I could not take care of all the requests I received.

Sometimes I took as many as seven over. Don, of course, had to make two trips, and we used the hunt camp boat. This went on season after season until 1975. The only bad trips were a couple of times when storms came up that interfered with Don flying. He never took chances; so, we were compelled once to stay in the old hunt camp overnight. It was always understood with Don that we would be okay if he felt flying would be the least bit dangerous.

On one occasion I was on a two-day stay at Snow Shoe, with two men from Dayton, Ohio. We were fishing out of a canoe.

The first day was perfect and we stayed overnight in the hunt camp. One of the men was sleeping in an upper bunk; naturally, we expected we would have to put up with a few bush mice, but I woke up during the night and found the lad, with his mattress and him, sleeping on the floor.

I asked him, "What happened?"

"I felt something move in my bed and when I turned on my flashlight, I discovered a family had joined me." Sleepily, he added, "A family of snakes had curled up beside me, so I decided to let them have the bunk."

Even at that hour I couldn't resist telling him, "Well, I have heard of men being away so long that they will sleep with anything that comes along, but NEVER with snakes."

When we left camp next morning we loaded all our duffel in the canoe and took it across the lake where Don would pick us up in the afternoon. It turned out to be a very hot day. Later in the afternoon it clouded over and became quite blustery.

Suddenly I noticed the black clouds racing in two directions at different altitudes in the sky. I told my guests, "We had better get off the lake and QUICKLY."

We just made it to shore and I propped the canoe upside down in a thick spruce tree, when "bam" the storm hit!

For protection, we got under the canoe and it took the three of us to keep it from blowing away. We could see the wind pick up large sheets of water off the lake surface and just slam it over the tree tops across the bay. It only lasted about ten minutes, but we never could have kept afloat had we stayed on the lake. This was followed by a couple of heavy downpours of rain. I told the men, "We had better load our canoe and make an attempt to get back to camp between showers, as I am sure that Don will not be out to pick us up."

We made it into the bay where the camp was, but a cloud-burst hit us as we were gliding into shore. When the bow of the canoe hit that shore, the two men jumped out and like a streak of lightning they raced for the camp. I grabbed a poncho and spread it over our sleeping bags and got under it, well, as much as I could.

The storm again passed quickly and the men came out to help carry in our duffel. Just then I heard a plane; but it was coming from the wrong direction.

Suddenly it swooped over the camp and circled the bay. I could see it was Don. The men were really happy to know we were not going to spend another night in camp with goodness knows what.

When Don taxied into the landing I told him, "We certainly never expected you to show up." He said, "Well, I was already in the air over my mill when I got the report on the radio, advising anyone in the air about the freak storm and how to avoid it. So I went up several thousand feet and flew around it and then came in behind it."

By the time we had tied the canoe onto the platoon and loaded our gear the sky was clear and the sun shining.

On another trip in 1974, I was guiding a couple of my favourite guests, Bruce and Joan Wilkes, from Charleston, West Virginia. Both were terrific fishermen. Joan could handle a spinning tackle better than most men.

The first time they came to the lodge, Joan, after unpacking, walked down to our swim dock at the natural pool. It was apparent she was going to get in some practice casting as she carried her rod with her. I was at the boat dock gassing up motors. Several men were standing around, as people will do when someone is working. One of them poked me in the side and motioned toward Joan, and said with apparent scorn, "watch."

They expected to see a woman embarrass herself in front of these experienced fishermen, and they were anxious to scoff at first and then rush to offer their expertise.

Well, the minute she prepared to make her cast, I knew she was no novice. She was using an ultra-light artificial worm tied directly to her line, about the most difficult bait to cast any distance.

238

Bruce Wilke's record walleye.

Some sportsmen brought everything but the kitchen sink.

239

When her rod came back to make her cast the lure sailed out beautifully, clear across the pool. I heard one of the men say, "She certainly has done that before!"

The strange thing was that Joan was allergic to fish. If she ate them her throat would swell up and break out in a rash. But she still loved the sport of fishing. Her husband, Bruce, was among the best sports fishermen I ever met.

Bruce worked for the Union Carbide in Charleston. He was a research chemist. They had a very active sportsmen's club at the plant. About thirty-five of their employees were regular guests at Little River Lodge. Dr. Yant's nephew worked there and he was responsible for them all coming to the lodge. Every one of them were excellent sports fishermen.

To get back to my trip with Bruce and Joan. It had been customary each year for me to spend several days at a couple of the feeder lakes I had recently stocked with small mouth bass. They preferred small mouth.

Bruce made up his own artificial worms and he usually had two hundred with him. The worms had an action when pulled slowly through the water, like I never saw on regular artificial worms.

They had never fished Snow Shoe Lake, as Bruce was not very anxious to fly. However, with persuasion, I convinced him how careful Don was and he decided to make the trip. It was the last week of June, 1974.

Don flew us in one morning. I told him, "I want to try and take some bass from Snow Shoe over to Harrymay Lake this evening when you come back for us."

We started to keep bass on stringers about 3:00 in the afternoon. By the time Don was due to pick us up we had forty-six bass on our stringers. Each time I filled a stringer I would hide them from the turtles among the alders along the shore.

The plane was late coming, and when it did, it was not Don. Instead, it was a young student pilot from Orillia Air Services in North Bay. They had rented Don's plane during the day to take a large party up the French River some place.

Don had told them to fly direct from the French River and pick us up at 5:30, so this young pilot didn't know anything

240

about our plans to take our bass into Harrymay Lake. Furthermore, he didn't even know where it was. He agreed to take us there if I could direct him.

We loaded everything first, then put the bass in two large plastic fertilizer bags, and off we went. As soon as we were taxiing to the take-off section of the lake, I knew Bruce was not happy with our pilot, as he casually informed us, "I just got my license!" Naturally, he was proud of the fact, but this left Bruce skeptical of his ability.

The pilot was short and had to stand at the controls to see where he was going. This did not add any assurance to the doubts Bruce already harboured.

With me directing it only took fifteen minutes to get to Harrymay Lake and circle it. The pilot appeared to be concerned about landing, due to the wind being in the wrong direction. I said, "Just circle once more and we will make an air drop of the bass, if you can swoop low over the lake."

When he banked suddenly and dropped lower he really gave Bruce and Joan a scare; and when I opened the side window to drop the bass, the wind pressure coming through the open window at flying speed, didn't improve Bruce's feelings one bit. We made the drop with no casualties and circled again to see if the bass were getting out of the plastic bags.

We could see a few on the surface. I could only hope they would revive and swim away and find a new home. I planned to check on them next summer to see if I could catch any bass.

Bruce was just glad the whole operation was over so he and Joan could return to the lodge and have themselves a good stiff drink.

During the past forty-one years I have stocked nine different area lakes with parent bass that only had rough and panfish in them before. In every case, the bass multiplied so fast they soon dominated the lake. Some fantastic fishing took place in these lakes and was enjoyed not only by my guests but many local people.

This stocking effort on my part was the main reason for the popularity of Little River Lodge with so many of the sports fishermen. They felt assured of having action when they came.

After twenty-four years a guest returned. It was in 1953 I received a reservation from Dr. Raymond Currie, from Washington, D.C., who runs an animal clinic. He took care of all Arthur Godfrey's stock and horses at that time.

Dr. Alan Secord, of Toronto, one of our regular guests, had recommended me to Dr. Currie and he was coming with two of his sons and bringing Micheal Godfrey, Arthur's youngest son. The boys were all under 12 years of age.

Dr. Currie was an ardent fly rod fisherman and Dr. Secord had mentioned to him how I had stocked Irish Lake with small mouth bass and how they had increased to the point of over-population, making an excellent place to fly fish. Exactly the kind the Dr. wanted to do.

Some lucky guests.

242

I will not go into detail of how pleased Dr. Currie and the boys were with fishing, other than to say the boys were beside themselves with excitement of having fish strike on almost every cast. They vied with each other as to who caught and released the most fish.

In 1975 Dr. Currie and his wife spent another week at the lodge and I took them to two more lakes I had stocked; one with large mouth bass and another with small mouth.

Again they had excellent fishing. He informed me that his son Gordon, who was with him in 1953, was now a partner in his clinic.

Then in June of 1977, Gordon made a reservation at the lodge for August 13th to the 20th and wanted me to the same thing for him and his son as I had twenty-four years earlier with his dad.

Gordon, his wife with their six year old son and a three year old daughter, arrived and I took Gordon and the boy to what shows on my map as Dorothy Lake, which I stocked in 1958.

Gordon had his dad's ultra lite bamboo spinning rod and reel. It was the first time I had been to Dorothy Lake in over eight years. I must mention here that Gordon is over six feet tall. As we were going to fish out of a rather tippy canoe I had both him and Junior sitting in the bottom as I paddled out about one hundred and fifty feet from the landing and anchored. I baited their lines with a green frog on Gordon's and a dew worm on Junior's.

For the next two hours they had the most fantastic bass fishing that I have witnessed in my fifty-two years, and I have seen some fabulous bass fishing over those years.

I had to help Junior, as his little arms became so tired he could not handle them alone. He pleaded, "Oh, Walter, help me!"

Gordon was fighting three to four and a half pound bass continuously with his ultra-lite bamboo rod, from five to ten minutes on each bass. He prayed volubly they wouldn't break his rod. Many times his only recourse was to point the rod at them and let them take the line out on the drag. He only lost one, and that managed to get him caught in the weeds.

Finally we went back to shore to have our lunch and I cleaned the fish, as they were too heavy to carry back whole. We had a two mile portage to cover.

243

We did however take pictures first. As Gordon said, "Who would ever believe this mess of fish?" It was formidable.

Around three-thirty we went back out and tried several other spots, duplicating our morning catch, then took their picture and released them.

At one time I picked up Junior's rod and made a cast and hooked one of the largest for the day. At the same moment, Gordon got one on his rod.

16½ lb. walleye caught by Joe Risher.

The fish managed to get our lines crossed as we fought them. Without a doubt, it was the most exciting fishing I can recall. That is saying a lot after all these years, but it is true.

On Tuesday, I had to go to Sudbury, and it rained on Wednesday. Thursday I arranged with Don Odorizzi to fly us into Snowshoe Lake. When Don came back to pick us up, he surprised us as he had Gordon's wife and daughter with him. Don wanted to show Mrs. Currie the lakes we had fished from the air.

When they were leaving to return to their home in Maryland, Gordon laughingly said, "Well, I am sure that dad will understand when he see the pictures and the filets we took off all those bass." He was referring to the slight warp I had noticed in his dad's bamboo rod.

"I expected good fishing, but Walter, certainly nothing like we have had. Really it has just been amazing."

Junior, his eyes sparkling said, "That was really fun!" It probably made a confirmed fisherman out of him. His dad remarked, "It is a trip Junior and I will never forget, right son?" Son, looking smug, nodded vigorously.

A number of my guests who came to the lodge during my early years have returned with their sons and also grandsons. This made me feel very good.

The most recent was Carol Emery, who formerly came with her husband, now deceased. Carol and her new husband, the Reverend Hal Emery, came with their sons in August. I spent a few days fishing with them, which included a fly-in trip to Snowshoe, where they developed sore wrists reeling in the fish.

Carol brought back many memories of the fishing incidents in former years I had with her and Jim.

Another of our early guests was Bill Leightner, who frequently was the first guest to arrive on opening of fishing season. Bill was from St Clairsville, Ohio. He was associated with the Dix Publishing Co. They published three southern Ohio newspapers. Bill was considered to be a specialist at setting up and maintaining those complicated printing presses. The company president valued Bill's services a great deal, and frequently included Bill on some of his annual fly-in Arctic fishing trips. Bill always brought back fantastic pictures and tales of fishing where the sun never sets. However, he said that a few days of that barren country was enough. He missed the sound of the wind in the pines and scenic beauty of our area. Bill came to Little River Lodge two and three times a year. He brought his family when they were very young and after they were married, he would arrive in Camp with his gransons, who felt they had the greatest grandfather in the world.

I could write another complete book about the wonderful people who were guests of Little River Lodge and like Bill Leightner, they came with their families and eventually their grand children. They helped to make me feel that the life I chose has been worthwhile, and a very interesting one. Many have passed away, others in their late years retired to distant places. Since I retired I have managed to visit a few of them, and spent many pleasant hours reminiscing and looking at the many pictures they took during their stay at the lodge.

Guests relaxing with ice cream on the porch.

246

CHAPTER 33

WALTER AS A TRAPPER

I started to write this to tell how I became a trapper and so far I have given you details of how I also became a successful resort operator. However, all this time I continue to be a trapper whenever I have time to do so. So there were naturally a great many instances that I related and will relate as I remember them and not necessarily in sequence. So please bear with me.

Trapping has always been fascinating to me; also a challenge. There were many years when fur prices were very poor and trappers who had to depend on trapping for a livelihood had problems. Even when fur prices were considered good, a trapper's income never really compensated him for the effort required.

However, the area I trapped was finally zoned. This gave me a chance to permit my zone to build up without someone interfering during the period I was not trapping.

Trappers were gradually striving to become organized. I was active in our local district and established a local Trappers' Council, and at one stage I was President of the North East Parry Sound District Trappers' Council.

Some of our main problems were the proper and uniform preparation of our pelts for sale, and how we could receive fair market value for our furs. In the past we had been at the mercy of many travelling buyers. They would take every advantage they could of trappers who were unable to know what the fur market value was at that particular time.

To begin with I had for years sold my furs to a buyer by the name of Cohen in North Bay, mainly because I could take my furs directly to him. If I was not satisfied with his offer, at least I could turn it down. I also learned that a number of the travelling buyers were selling their furs to him.

One year when I considered I had a substantial amount of fur, I took them to Cohen. I told him I would only give him one bid, and it better be his best, as I would not accept a second bid, regardless if it was higher.

This worked satisfactorily for me for years. Then one year, not knowing what the actual market demand was, I turned down Cohen's offer and later took my furs to Sudbury. I was offered less money everywhere I tried to sell.

Finally, I sold them for a few dollars less than Cohen had offered, as I had no intentions of taking them back to him.

Later that spring, however, I met Cohen on the street in North Bay and he said, "Walter, why did you accept less money for your furs than I offered you?" I knew then that he controlled most of the buyers in Northern Ontario. How did you know, I asked? He then paid me a compliment, "You prepare your beaver pelts better than most trappers and I recognized your furs when they came in."

I was more determined now to organize the trappers so we could find better outlets for our furs.

Cohen passed away shortly after that and the Hudson Bay Company that had a branch there became more active when he was gone.

Glen McConnel was the manager of the North Bay raw fur buying. The Hudson Bay Company had earned a bad reputation as fur buyers in many areas, due to the way some of their Northern factors had taken advantage of Indian trappers.

Many trappers were compelled to purchase all their equipment and supplies on credit from the Hudson Bay factory in their district, and in turn were compelled to bring all their furs to them to pay off their debt. In many cases they were never permitted to get free of debt to the company.

Our local Trappers' Council delegated me to try and make a deal with McConnel at Hudson Bay, I approached him the same way I had with Mr. Cohen. I arranged certain dates in the coming season when all our local trappers would bring their furs to one trapper's home. McConnel was to come in and meet us there and buy our furs.

The idea was that this would mean that all council members would know what each member received for his furs, if he accepted McConnel's bid. This worked satisfactorily for all concerned for several seasons; council members could compare the quality of each other's furs. It also benefited the Hudson Bay Company, as they could be assured of a decent volume of furs. McConnel could also show trappers why one trapper's fur was worth more than the other, due to better handling.

One time after he had bought our mink pelts he sent each trapper an extra $2.00 per pelt, as the mink market had improved. This increased our confidence in him as you can imagine.

I wanted to leave for Florida one year on the first of February, so I took my furs to the warehouse in North Bay.

McConnel and his boss were there and they both looked my furs over, which consisted of thirty-three beaver, seven mink, an otter and a wolf.

They offered me $465.00 for the lot. I said, "No." I began to gather my furs to leave, when the boss said, "Well, maybe we could come up a few dollars." I told him exactly what I thought of him as a fur buyer and left.

At that time we had a new conservation officer or game warden sent to our area, Frank Saunders. Frank happened to be staying at my lodge until he could find a house for his family. When I brought the furs back he told me, "Ralph Bice, from Kearney, is also endeavoring to get all the Ontario trappers organized and he has arranged a convention and fur auction at the Empire Hotel in Huntsville for January 20th. I suggest you take your furs to that auction, Walter."

At first I hesitated; it was too close to my Florida departure date. Finally, I decided to do just that!

Once I had made a decision, I called Russell Eckford, a trapper at Restoule and also a camp operator; we arranged to go and room together at the convention. The hotel arranged a storage room for our furs in their basement. Only twelve or fifteen buyers attended that auction.

Ralph Bice conducted the fur auction the third day. Each trapper's furs were to be sold separately as one parcel. It turned out that my parcel of furs, that the Hudson Bay company had offered

249

$465.00, brought the highest bid; and was sold to Mr. Jack Salter and Mr. Greenspoon of Toronto for $1,000.00 even!!!

To add to my utter joy, Glen McConnel and his boss were among the buyers bidding!

Their comment regarding the great difference in their offer to me and the $1,000.00 I received, they said was, "In the time that has elapsed, the market has improved." I said, "How come, a large company like the Hudson Bay Company did not bid my furs in?"

Their reply, "Now, Mr. Hesman, you know that Mr. Salter is going to lose money on them."

I had to get to the bottom of this and when I told Mr. Salter what had been said, he reassuringly replied, "I could have even bid higher and still made money on quality furs such as your parcel is." That proved to be the end of the Hudson Bay Company from buying from all our council members, except for the usual shiftless wino-trapper, who just caught enough furs to enable them to purchase enough wine to keep them happy and stoned.

It became very obvious to me at the auction that the only way trappers could hope to successfully carry on with these fur auctions was to have sufficient volume of furs to permit each species to be sold separately, after being graded as to quality and size.

It was plain to see that some buyers at this first auction only wanted beaver or mink or other specific fur, but were compelled to buy everything in each parcel.

This proved to be exactly what happened at the next auction in Huntsville. It turned out to be a flop. As well, there was definite collusion between the few buyers who were present.

After that second auction, Mr. Jack Grew, of the Wildlife Department, who was in charge of the trappers' affairs, helped us successfully organize the Ontario Trappers' Association Raw Fur Auctions in North Bay. This has now turned out to be one of the most prominent in the world.

Our sales last year reached $15,000,000.00 — 1982 sales reached $24,000,000.00.

Mary has been so very tolerant and uncomplaining; I know I have given her plenty of reason to be otherwise. I would become so involved in my trapping that sometimes I would be miles from the lodge when darkness came. (It gets dark early in mid-winter, about 5:00 p.m.)

This early darkness seems to come so quickly and I would stay on rather than make an extra trip, using my flashlight and ski-doo headlights to check my remaining traps in that area.

Occasionally, due to unexpected problems such as bad slush on the ice, or ski-doo breakdown, caused me to walk and arrive hours late at home.

Some trapping and hunting equipment.

I know Mary worried but she continued to be tolerant. Even I realize I should not expect to continue working such a large trap area alone at my age. So I MAY quit or at least give up part of my zone. This will even be harder perhaps than it was for me to sell the lodge. I have been too active all my life to suddenly retire to a rocking chair, no matter how old in years I become!

I have had numerous close calls during my many years of guiding and trapping, even though I did learn not to take unnecessary chances. For example: on one occasion when the temperature was fifteen below zero, I was chopping through eighteen inches of ice to check an under-ice beaver trap. When my axe cut through, the water gushed up to the surface, making further chopping difficult, as it splashed water on me that froze.

So I took a chance, a chance I had taken frequently, luckily without an accident. I rolled up my sleeve and shoved my arm down the hole where I could feel the bait sticks and feel my way down to where the trap was set.

In my hurry, I forgot where my thumb pointed — it sprung the trap! When I tried to pull the trap to the surface, it would not come through the small hole. I saw my axe was out of reach, but by laying full length on the ice I was able to reach it with my foot.

With my right arm stuck down the hole it was difficult to try and chop the hole larger with my left hand, very difficult as the water splashing on me froze immediately.

With a great deal of effort I got the trap up through the hole, only to find the chain was too short to allow me to bring it to the surface!

By this time I was becoming desperate and seriously considered cutting my thumb off.

That was the last thing I wanted to do and as a last resort I tried one more thing; by sitting stradle of the hole, I was able to depress one trap spring with one foot as I pried the other spring with my axe. I freed my thumb!

I had to run about a half mile across the ice to my truck and as the frost was coming out of my arm the pain became excruciating. You can be sure I never took that chance again.

Another close call happened about four years ago, also in sub-zero weather, five miles from home. My double track ski-doo broke through slush ice on a beaver pond. I was loaded down with five large beaver.

I buried the beaver under the snow and felled a spruce tree to use the limbs to make a trail off the ice and to support the ski-doo. While standing in a foot of slush I managed with a hand spike pole to pry the machine up onto the spruce boughs. After digging enough ice out of the tracks I was able to head for home, where it took over an hour to remove my frozen boots and clothing.

Mary said, "Now, can you see why I worry about you out there all alone."

During a Huntsville convention I was telling Russell Eckford about the wolves killing the deer every night in a log-cut near

Stanley Lake. Russell was considered a wolf trapper. After I explained that I could not figure out how to set snares for these wolves without the possibility of killing deer instead, he said, "If it does not require too much walking I will come in and look things over." In reply I assured him, "I will escort you into the log-cut with my Jeep." Russell thought that would be fine.

When we got there two of the men that were falling trees said, "We will take you where the wolves killed two deer just the night before, and the worst part is they have only partially eaten them."

After driving around a few of the log roads Russell remarked, "Walter, I have seen enough." On the way back to the lodge he told me, "Tomorrow, put on your snowshoes and try circling outside the log-cut until there are no more signs of deer tracks. Continue in a widening circle until you find the runway where these wolves are coming in and out of the log-cut at night. The wolves are not staying inside the log-cut, where the men are working during the day."

I followed his instructions, and once I was clear of that log-cut, I did find the runway the wolves were using. The snow was about thirty inches deep so they really had to travel in that one runway. I placed four snares on poles against trees where the runways passed close to the trees. As I left I was careful to brush out my snowshoe tracks from their runway.

Due to a bout of flu it was a week before I went back to check the snares. I found a wolf in three of the four snares. To say the least, I was elated that Russell's system worked. As they came down the runway the first wolf had got into the first two snares and the other two wolves had been caught in the others. There were tracks of two more that had got by the snares after the first three were caught.

I no doubt could have caught more had our spring break-up not started early, but I was determined to make an effort from then on to take more wolves.

The following season I felt sure that many of the wolves that were invading our deer yards were coming from Algonquin Park; they were protected there from trappers and multiplying.

When I first came to the Golden Valley area, back in the mid-1920's, every homesteader and farmer was raising sheep.

The main predation on sheep at that time was by bears and dogs; then the wolves increased suddenly. That was the end of sheep raising around here.

This could have been due to several factors. The devastating forest fires in the northern area and the increase in breeding in the Algonquin Park area. Also, there had been an increase in deer and predators during both World Wars, fewer hunters and trappers were in the field.

The wildlife managers refused to increase the bounty on wolves enough to warrant trappers to spend the time and effort to control them. Instead, they began a costly and unproductive research program on wolves, AND ACTUALLY TRIED TO CONVINCE THE PUBLIC THAT WOLVES NEEDED PROTECTION! This was ONE of the most ridiculous programs ever conceived by that department. This finally led to the abolishment of the wolf bounty.

They established what is known now as the PREDATOR CONTROL DEPARTMENT, with many salaried chiefs. They now hire trappers in many areas and supply them with four-wheel drive vehicles, ski-doos and all the necessary equipment to take wolves. They collect their salary regardless whether they take a wolf or not; whereas, with the bounty system the trapper would always have to produce a dead wolf before he could collect his $25.00. It may have cost that trapper hundreds of dollars before he caught him.

Some of the wolves taken now by the present PREDATOR CONTROL DEPARTMENT has cost taxpayers over $1,000.00 each.

The MINISTRY OF NATURAL RESOURCES tells us they can make accurate aerial counts of wildlife while flying over the area, and if that is so they can also control predators by using aircraft or choppers.

Many people were taken in by Farley Mowatt's book, "Never Cry Wolf," that has since proven to be fiction; but the damage Mowatt had done with that piece of fiction will take a long time to overcome. There are still many who accept it as fact.

In 1974, two federal wildlife biologists spent two months in the barren ground caribou country and reportedly counted over 2,240 caribou calves that had been slaughtered by wolves, leaving some partially eaten. The survey was made because the natives complained that the caribou were becoming scarce. Then in May, 1976, they announced on CBC National News that the wolves were killing off the buffalo herd that so much money had been spent to establish.

I get very provoked when I hear or read about misinformed people saying, "Those are endangered species," when actually wolves have been spreading over areas of Ontario where they have not been seen for many years, and they are killing domestic livestock.

In the fall of 1967 Mary and our son Ricky had gone to North Bay. On the return trip, coming in on our six-mile road, they suddenly saw a wolf as they came around a bend. Ricky yelled, "Hit it mother!" and before she had time to think she stepped on the gas and ran over it. In the dark they couldn't see what damage they had done to the wolf so they drove to a place where she could turn around. They arrived in time to see the wolf drag itself into the bush.

Naturally, both were excited and Mary would have never done it had she taken time to think; she would never kill anything if she could help it. However, they came home and drove into the garage. Ricky was still so excited he never noticed me in the garage. He ran to the lodge yelling, "Pop, Pop, Mom killed a wolf!"

I finally got the story from Mary and Ricky assured me he could show me the place where the wolf had left the road. I took my shotgun and flashlight and he and I drove about three miles when he said, "It was right here, Pop."

I turned the car crosswise so my headlights covered the area. As we got out of the car we heard wolf howls in several directions. Each time Ricky would say excitedly, "There he is dad." I finally convinced him there was a whole pack of wolves and they no doubt had made a kill of a deer or beaver, probably just before Mary had hit the one on the road.

They were now howling in an effort to regroup themselves after being disturbed. We started in the direction the injured wolf had taken and it wasn't long before I could hear it struggling through the brush ahead. Rushing on with the gun in one hand and my flashlight in the other, we caught up with him and I finished his misery.

255

It had an injured back and could only pull itself ahead slowly. That episode was the beginning of a very exciting winter for me. I would try to eliminate as many of them as I could, as they were killing many of my beaver. They killed the beaver as they ventured away from the water to cut their winter feed.

I put out a number of wolf snares where they were crossing on beaver dams and managed to catch two more before the deer hunt. Then I had to lift up the snares until the deer hunt was over. I didn't want to catch any deer or dogs.

After the hunt I proceeded to put out more snares and by Christmas I had four more wolves. I saw a number of places where they had killed deer at open water at the beaver dams, where the deer had come to drink.

One day while I was in North Bay I met a reporter from the Nugget, Don Buckley. I told him, "You know, the wolves are killing more deer than the hunters." He reported this in his column. It started quite a few "Letters To The Editor" from other trappers who also reported more kills, and a number of hunters who were pressing the "wildlife managers" to increase the wolf bounty.

To counter all this publicity on wolves, our Minister of the then, LANDS AND FORESTS, Kelso Roberts, had a report published in the prominent newspapers informing the public that he had ordered an aerial survey from the Algonquin Park Headquarters and they concluded: "there was not one wolf west of Highway No. 11." This indicated my report, by Don Buckley, was not true.

Many of us were in a position to really get a true and factual knowledge of our wildlife and we felt Roberts was not a qualified Minister of the Department.

By him saying my report was false, this made me mad as hell! Especially, as I had just come across two groups of wolf tracks that very day. One of five wolves had just killed a large buck on Twisty Lake and another group of four, travelling in my ski-doo trail, which made walking easier for them.

Normally, I would trap each season until mid-January. By then I felt I had all the fur I should take or harvest from my trap zone. Most animals were past their prime pelt period anyway, so I would quit and prepare to go south for the balance of the winter.

256

However, when the LANDS AND FORESTS concluded I had lied about their wolf problem, I made up my mind to stay home that winter and concentrate on taking as may wolves as I possibly could.

I took fourteen wolves by spring, as well as losing several that chewed and broke snares and got away. This was not only a record for me but also for the entire area. I proved my point and it made me feel a hell of a lot better, in spite of the fact I had sacrificed my winter in Florida to do it.

Don Buckley felt the same as I did about Kelso Roberts and Dr. Clark's survey, so he was happy to come in and take pictures of my wolf catch. Then he gave it "front page" coverage on his paper. By the time our Trappers' Convention convened, there was a real controversy going on in the North Bay Nugget and the Globe and Mail between hunters, trappers, and a number of misinformed naturalists and biologists, who still insisted treating the wolf as an endangered species.

I will insert here a few of the many articles I clipped at that time. The main thing the biologists were trying to do was to have the wolf bounty of $25.00 removed. They kept publishing the amount of the taxpayers's money being paid out annually for bounty. What they did not publish was the huge amounts of taxpayer's money being wasted by the department on unnecessary and unproductive biological research, surveys and experiments. I managed to get access to one of the departments expenditures reports for one year ending March 1965 as follows;

Supervision (Dist. Biol. & Supervisors)	$ 692,643.45
Management	1,321,199.84
Enforcement	829,320.80
Hatcheries	631,135.32
Equipment	240,942.99
Training	62,249.34
Grants	17,300.00
Wolf Bounty	59,997.00
RESEARCH	795,045.65
Surveys	9,743.65
Administration	725,569.00
Construction	205,324.69
TOTAL $	5,590,471.73

It is my opinion that a much bigger portion of this money should be made available to increase the wolf bounty. It would tend to keep this predator under control and increase revenue from hunters and trappers.

There are increasing reports from Southern Ontario, as far as Essex County (Windsor), of predation by wolves on livestock and an increase in rabies, which in 1980 is still increasing.

Just in my last mail, I received word from Howard Norman, down in Elgin County, outside St. Thomas, that wolves had been seen in groups of six or seven at a time near farms. One farmer near Lethbridge had lost forty sheep and he had actually killed the wolf that was after his sheep, so he had proof.

Wildlife biologists and other bureaucrats continued their propoganda re bounty, until they succeeded in having the bounty removed entirely. They ignored all the complaints from sheep and cattle raisers, who in many cases were forced to quit raising sheep in many areas.

They told the farmers and sheep raisers that they were going to establish a "Predator Control Department," and they hired a noted "wolf trapper," Ken Clark, to teach the control men, how to take wolves. All these men were not only on salary but they were also supplied with all the equipment necessary, including transportation! These same men were paid regardless whether they caught any wolves or not.

It is a known fact that some of these wolves that had been taken cost as much as $3,000.00. I feel safe in saying that average cost of EACH wolf cost them $1,000.00 at least.

The Wildlife Department has not made any changes in our deer hunting regulations for many years, even though we have a terrific increase in hunting pressure since 1945, as well as severe winter kills. Also, Ontario, Canada, is the only place I know of where dogs are permitted to run deer. Each year there are many dogs lost and left to become deer killers, until someone catches them or shoots them.

In all of the many years that I operated a hunting lodge and guided for hunters, I noted in particular, the majority of does and fawns are shot — when dogs are used. During the deer season, which is also the mating and rutting season, bucks are usually with the does and fawns, when you can find them.

258

When a deer hound starts them, the doe and fawn always take off in the lead. If she is in heat, that buck is only interested in following her. Naturally, with a dog on the trail, the doe and fawn are the first to come out to the hunters watching; and most hunters start to shoot. The buck trailing along behind gets enough warning to permit him to slip away from the gunshots. This was proved to me over and over again.

After more than fifty years of hunting, and several years at Little River Lodge, I convinced my hunter guests to shoot only bucks. Some disagreed with me until we proved time and time again that letting does and fawns go by, they still had an opportunity of shooting a nice large buck, and not to panic.

In areas of our hunt, where we had no interference from other hunters, we found we could flush out three or four bucks along with seven or eight does and fawns. If we shot only the bucks, we frequently could go back there a couple of days later and find new bucks with those same does. In areas where there were no does left, we could see where the buck's tracks travelled right through and kept on going, without even stopping. No wonder, what did he have to stop for, he certainly wasn't interested in the scenery. If he was, he was making fast tracks to find a lady friend to share it with.

I used enjoy deer hunting with old Sank, when we still hunted on our own. I considered Sank the best "still" hunter I ever met. He taught me more things about "still" hunting than ten so-called experts ever could have. He knew more about what a deer would do (that wasn't being chased by dogs) than anyone.

I truthfully can't say I enjoyed hunting the way we had been hunting at the lodge. The hunts conducted there actually did not give the deer a chance. If I had twenty or more hunters with me and a couple of good guides, we could shut off an entire area in such a way that deer could not be chased out of there without going by one of the hunters. However, this was the only logical way to conduct a hunt with a group.

Now that I have sold the lodge, I am not interested in hunting anymore; in fact, I seldom carry a gun while trapping, as shooting a fur bearer usually ruins the pelt.

Naturally, I've had many unusual and sometimes comical experiences with hunters over the years. Not only hunters do funny things when they are excited; I believe it was some of my fishing

259

guests who displayed the most excitement and funny reactions when they caught a good size fish.

I will tell about one on old Sank. He, like most of the original settlers, fished and hunted mainly for food. Sport hunting really never entered into it. When Sank went fishing his equipment usually was a ten-foot pole he had cut in the bush with some heavy chalk line, strong enough to land a one-hundred pound fish fastened on the end. When he hooked a fish he heaved it into the boat. In trolling, he just let out a hand line.

On this occasion, after I had started the lodge, Sank and John Odorizzi drove in one day and asked me to take them fishing. John had a short, stubby steel-trolling rod. I supplied Sank with a good all-purpose rod and reel.

We were trolling over a good shoal in LeGrouse Lake and we were catching some nice walleyes. Sank could not get used to the reel, so I had to put the break on so his line would not run out if he forgot to hold it. Several times when he hooked a fish he just dropped the rod and pulled the line in hand over hand. All of a sudden he thought he had a big one and I was sure he was going

Walter and Mrs. Anita Curry, Washington D.C.

260

to break the line or the rod before I could stop the boat. So I shouted, "Let it go, Sank, let it go!" Before I could make him understand that I only meant for him to release the line, he threw rod and reel overboard.

Of course Sank was not the only one to do this. I have had several women guests do exactly the same thing. I remember one who threw her rod into the lake when I went to net the fish; she didn't want the fish in the boat.

Many people don't realize that fishing with inexperienced people can be dangerous. I consider myself lucky, after all these years guiding, to have my eyes and ears still attached to my head. I learned very early in my career not to have a guest sit beside me while they were casting, especially when they used a side-arm cast.

One of the most annoying problems is when a guest will insist on bringing the fish all the way in, right to the tip of the rod, when I am trying to remove the hook, especially when they have not played the fish out enough.

In the begining, the way I learned was by close observation of the expert fishermen, that I had the pleasure to guide for. In fact, all I know I learned from my guests.

In 1978 I decided to take on a trapping partner. His name was Robert Lampman, a taxidermist at Port Loring. We agreed to trap on a percentage basis, until such time that I decided to quit, then Bob would take over. During the next three years fur prices increased, especially all long-hair species, such as fox, racoon, and lynx; even wolf and bear became worth the trouble and time to take. For years most of these long-hair furs were not worth skinning. Many were shot and wasted by inconsiderate hunters, who feel if you see something, shoot it. This type of hunter continues to waste these fur bearers even now when they have become very valuable. Good quality red fox sold as high as $190.00. Fisher females, $296.00. Iowa Raccoon $160.00. Lynx, over $400.00. Even quality Beaver sold as high as $140.00. Of course trappers' costs also went sky high. These high prices already are dropping. As far as the trapper is concerned, it is the average price he is concerned with. It has turned out that taking Bob as a partner was the best thing I could have done. He is not only a good trapper and taxidermist, but also a fine individual. I could not have found a more suitable person to turn my area over to. I plan to turn my trap area over to Bob next season, with the understanding he permits me to do a little trapping as long as I am capable. If I was to consider all the hard work and hours I have put in trapping, not to mention the hazards and danger working alone, I doubt if I have earned much over fifty cents an hour. But there is a challenge that keeps a trapper trapping year after year; also he accumulates many memories.

After fifty-eight years of observing wildlife and watching how they can adapt to changes in the environment, I am convinced they can survive legal methods of trapping, as long as their food supply is maintained and not contaminated, or that we never revert back to using poison, that completely eliminated several species of fur bearers as well as destroying a great number of eagles and ravens, that in turn flew away miles spreading poison over large areas. Most of this poison was used in the early settlers' days. However, it was again used by a misinformed group who decided it was the best way to kill wolves, but very few wolves ever eat anything they have not killed themselves; in fact, where game is plentiful they seldom return to a previous kill. They just kill again. On one occasion I am aware of the Federal Wildlife Dept. authorized the dumping of many tons of poisoned horse meat from aircraft over the barren ground caribou country, and never returned to see the results.

Dr. Bill Beutel, one of the many fishermen and hunters
from the United States, who came to Little River Lodge.

262

CHAPTER 34

FISH-SPAWNING AND RESTOCKING

I first became acquainted with restocking fish the years I worked at Camp Caribou, as it was done by our fish and wildlife department at that time. It became very obvious their main efforts were in stocking trout; other species were given only secondary consideration. They were netting pickerel (walleye) for this area from Lake Nipissing to strip the spawn and fertilize the eggs before taking them to the Skelton Lake hatchery near Huntsville to hatch. They would be ready to distribute as soon as the two eyes were visible in the eggs. They were then put on wet cotton trays and packed in special ice packed boxes that was supposed to delay hatching until the eggs were placed in water at their final destination. Each tray had several thousand eggs. When they reached their destination on the hatchery truck, the trays were emptied into tubs or other containers of water to be spread around the lakes by those who requested them. My first experience to distribute pickerel spawn in my lakes, I had to meet the hatchery truck at Golden Valley with a team and wagon, as our seven mile road was not in shape. The men on the hatchery truck emptied the two trays of eggs into my tub of water, and told me I had 50,000 eggs. I learned later it was more like 10,000.

By the time I reached my lake most of the eggs were hatching. I then spread them by boat in three lakes. I did this for several years, until I noticed a couple times I had received some dead spawn, due to the hatchery truck running out of ice during delivery. On one occasion all spawn remaining on the truck was dead due to it being stuck before reaching here. So I discontinued applying for fish stock. By this time I had learned some very interesting facts about pickerel spawning themselves in the Little Pickerel River, right in front of the lodge. I was able to observe them closely and noted the many different predators that fed on the spawn before and after it hatched. I watched female

263

pickerel (up to fifteen pounds) with several males swimming close to her, as she expelled her eggs, depending on the currents to fertilize her eggs by chance. At the same time a school of minnows manoeuvering behind the female, feeding on her eggs as they were expelled. I learned also there were many other predators that fed on the spawn, such as ducks, birds, catfish, trout, perch, and many kinds of water bugs and crayfish that thrive on spawning areas. A large female pickerel can expel as much as 800,000 eggs each year, and soon after she spawns will begin to form next year's eggs. Not only predators destroy the eggs, silt caused by heavy rain will muddy the waters and stick to the egg. I have found large pickerel dead with their gills plugged by mud and silt on the area after a storm. I've also picked up large pickerel floating in the lakes that apparently died from being spawn bound, unable to expel the spawn due to age.

From information I received from some West Virginia guests, who were connected with a hatchery, I decided to set up my own small hatchery. I dammed up the overflow from my spring well to furnish my water supply for my gallon pickle jars that would contain the fertilized eggs. I then used a landing net to take a couple male pickerel, and put them in my bait tank, until I could locate a female that was in the process of expelling her eggs. When I did, I stripped her of as many eggs as would come out freely, into a large plastic pail, then by pressing a male's side, I fertilized the eggs with male sperm, by stiring it in the pail with a ladle, then I washed the eggs with clean water until they were clear, placed them in my jars below the dam where I could keep the eggs rotating just enough to prevent congealing. They were supposed to hatch within ten to fifteen days and as soon as the two eyes were visible in the eggs, they were ready to distribute around the lake. But this did not happen and the eggs began to turn white. When I inquired why this was happening, I learned that my spring water was too cold, so I immediately spread them around the lake.

The next year I established my hatchery on the river dam just above the pickerel spawning area. I had special copper tubing made to permit me to regulate the water pressure to rotate the eggs until they began to hatch. This worked well, but it did take considerable time and effort daily to check and remove defective eggs from the jars. I soon decided I could accomplish what I wanted with less effort by spreading the fertilized eggs as soon as I had them washed. By spreading them on suitable shallow places around the lakes away from the usual predators, a much larger percentage would survive. Also no silt after a storm to coat the eggs. If our conservation officers would carry a pail and do this while they are policing the many spawning areas, I am sure it would do much good. There is much harm done by many people curious to see the fish spawning, by disturbing them with flashing lights, separating the males away from the female, leaving many eggs to miss being fertilized. Another problem is, before the pickerel are off the spawning area, thousands of suckers come in to do the same thing, and if there is no barrier to stop them, suckers will continue going upstream as far as possible, and struggle over obstacles that stop other fish. Many people say suckers destroy pickerel spawn. I have never seen proof of this, as they are up on the spawning area to spawn too. But they come up in such great numbers and make such a commotion they stir up silt that can spoil pickerel eggs. Once the pickerel and sucker spawn hatches, the young fry is very fragile and depends on the stream currents to gradually float it out to the lakes. Much of the young fry is devoured or swallowed up by predators on the way. In the natural pool in front of the lodge, once the young fry becomes visible, schools of perch would make the water boil with the activity of them chasing the fry to devour them until fry developed enough to escape.

The reproduction of the bass family is different than other species. Bass do not leave the lake to spawn. Instead the male and female will pair off together and clear off a nest in the gravel in a shallow sunny location. A mature bass will produce approximately only 2,000 eggs, but the big difference is bass will guard their nest until it hatches, chasing any predator that threatens or comes near the nest. When bass find a likely place for the nest, they clean the area off by fanning with their fins and tail until all silt is removed. The female then deposits her eggs and the male fertilizes with sperm, then both hover over the nest and areate the water by fanning with their fins. On several occasions, while guiding a fisherman, bass have struck at a lure that came too close to its nest. One time a large bass broke the line and took off with the lure, a few days later I was in the area with another guest. I had told him about losing the plug and said I would like to try and get it back, not for the value of the plug but because if the bass still had it I would like to remove it. So I put a meps spinner on his line and told him where to cast. Sure enough the bass struck the lure before it actually hit the water and after a good fight we landed the bass and removed both lures and released it so it could continue to guard the nest. I should mention here a method of removing plugs from bass and lessen the danger of getting hooked yourself due to the bass struggling. Take hold of the bass by the lower jaw with your thumb and forefinger. (or pliers), bend the jaw down slightly, and the bass will be unable to struggle while you remove the lure. Regarding the fish in these waters, bass fishing was by far the most sport with light tackle, and pickerel much the best for eating.

It doesn't always take big fishermen to catch big fish!

CHAPTER 35

FREDDIE THE COOK

One hunting season I received reservations from a group of Cleveland, Ohio, deer hunters, while at the same time I still had my usual Group of Ontario hunters.

I decided to conduct the deer hunt with the two groups, by accommodating the Cleveland bunch at my island cottage and the Ontario group from the main camp.

This made it necessary to obtain a male cook to handle the island group. I advertised in the North Bay paper and I received several replies to my ad. After interviewing all but one, who was out of town making some additions to a poultry house, I was finally convinced by his wife, "You should not decide on any one until you have talked with my husband."

She was so positive, I decided to take her advice.

His name was Fred Jeannault, and when I found the chicken farm, I was directed to a two-story poultry house. I called out Fred's name and the man who climbed down the ladder was really a sight to behold.

He was short and was covered from his hair to his feet with the kind of dust, a straw chaff, found in chicken houses. My first thought was to terminate the interview as quickly as possible and get out of there.

Freddie never gave me the chance. He informed me he WANTED to cook in my hunt camp, regardless whether I paid him or not! Well, I listened. He proceeded to convince me that among his references was the fact he had cooked two winters in St. Joseph Hospital, when carpenter work was scarce. I told him to come in, and I kept my fingers crossed.

It turned out I had no need to worry. Freddie arrived on Friday, just as meat for the hunt came in: half a beef and pig.

While I was considered good at skinning fur, I had never mastered the art of cutting meat. When I mentioned this to Freddie he said, "Just leave that to me."

Saturday morning came and we loaded the supplies for the island, and my wife came along to make up the beds. When we landed at the dock, Freddie insisted that we leave him to carry in the supplies, "so he will know where everything is." Well, that made sense.

My wife and I proceeded to make up the beds. When we came downstairs, he not only had all his supplies in place, he had his chef's cap and apron on, and was rolling out pie crusts!

I expected him to complain about the stove, as it was a small four lid, with a very small oven. His only comment was, "I will come to the lodge and cut up the meat as soon as I get these pies done."

He came to the lodge and cut up the meat and it looked like a professional job. The hunters arrived on Sunday. Most of them were successful business men, one, Ike Martin, a Hall of Famer, who had played with the famous Jim Thorpe, now in the Sports Hall of Fame.

I sent one of the guides to help with the chores at the island, but it was soon apparent Freddie would have the chores done while the guide was still thinking about them.

I conducted the hunt by combining the two groups, as it enabled me to have enough men to cover all likely outlets for the deer. Also, most of the men had agreed not to shoot does or fawns.

The first day the island group met us at the lodge and we hunted the road area. I asked them if they were satisfied with Freddie's cooking? They all said, "The best food we ever had in a hunt camp, but we aren't happy with his poker playing."

He had shown such interest in their game, they finally invited him to sit in. He won most of their money!

The second day I took the lodge group down to the island and we made some lake shore drives. When we were returning in mid-afternoon, I saw Freddie out fishing. My first thought was "how can he have time to fish and still take proper care of his group?"

However, the hunters were quick to assure me that he not only caught pickerel for them to eat, they said, "He also made a rack to dry all their clothes and boots."

Before the hunt ended they praised Freddie for all the extra service. He even baked them birthday cakes! They told me he was very anxious to get out on some of the hunts. So I told him to bring one of the boats so he could come back to the island after the first drive in time to get his work done. Somehow Freddie would manage to be on hand wherever there was a deer to dress out. He was incredible.

That was the only time I used the island cottage for the Cleveland group, as we had such good relations between the two groups, they decided to stay together at the lodge for all future hunts.

Freddie continued to hunt with us for years. During those years, I was to learn that he was the most versatile individual I ever knew; a cook, carpenter, brick and block layer, expert on floor tile; in fact, he would take on any project and do a good job. On one occasion, he even moved a complete house several miles. However, one cottage got away on him and landed in Trout Lake.

Another thing for sure, he kept the breweries in business with his beer drinking. Something that somehow never seemed to interfere with his prodigious accomplishments in the kitchen and elsewhere.

Cook and 'jack-of-all-trades', Fred Jeannault was an exceptional individual.

Ike Martin dressed for the annual "Hunters Dance."

CHAPTER 36

ABOUT THE AREA I SPENT THE
PAST SIXTY YEARS IN

The past sixty years of my life has been spent in the area of North Parry Sound District of Ontario, in an area that takes in part of four Townships — Pringle, Mills, Ferrie and Lount. I did spend three of the early years in Wilson and Hardy Townships. Most of this area water shed drained into the Pickerel River and Georgian Bay. Much of this area is considered wilderness area, especially the part I have been involved in for sixty years, and did much to develop.

I have seen many things happen to our timber and wildlife that I have been critical of, especially The Ministry of Natural Resources. We have had Natural Resources Ministers changed more than six times, several of them were well aware of what was needed in the north to correct problems. But decisions are made for votes, not for what is right or wrong. When I first came to this area in 1924 it was a pleasure to walk on bush trails. Today it is a disgrace and very difficult, even impossible in many areas. Where we used to have fire trails and portage trails maintained by the rangers, they are now slashed or cut up by all terrain vehicles. Their budget — personnel and equipment — have increased annually, while improvement and good management slows. After the main logging was finished, a program was started to girdle all remaining trees left by chopping a deep girdle around all mature trees so they would die gradually over a few years. Once they stopped producing leaves and died the woods became a dense jungle of brush, then the dead trees began to fall, adding to the mess. It was dangerous to walk in the woods. It will take many years to overcome.

These four townships were well forested with a good variety of Canadian timber. Cutting rights to large areas of timber was leased to several lumber and logging companies during the 1800's, and they continued to control these leases for years until about 1960. Even after they had stopped operating themselves and began to sublet cutting rights to small jobbers, who paid them a fee. The companies took the pine out first, and by building a series of dams on headwater streams, they were able to float (drive) the pine all the way to Georgian Bay. When they opened these head water dams to flush the logs down stream, the logs gouged out banks and everything along the water way, and eventually depositing it in ponds and small lakes, filling them with earth and debris, especially at the head of lakes.

About this time, or late 1880, ninety settlers were granted homestead land in this area, only to learn later that most of this area land was not suitable for farming, but not before they had felled and burned much valuable timber to clear the land they eventually had to abandon, and move elsewhere. Instead of attempting to reforest these abandoned lands, they were left to grow weeds and brush until they eventually reforested themselves with second growth timber. Much more timber was burned by runaway fires. This mismanagement of our resources continues to this day by our politicians who don't know or don't care.

EPILOGUE

I have written the story of my life from my school days up to my leaving Little River Lodge.

It includes the many and varied experiences and activities during that time, and mentions the many incidents that were directly responsible for changing the course of my life, and maybe you will agree with me has turned out to be a life style that many men envy. It has not been dull, at times exciting and very fulfilling.

Never was it an easy life without setbacks or discouragement. However, by hard physical labour and determination, plus encouragement I received from numerous wonderful people who became regular guests of Little River Lodge, plus my good fortune in having met and married Mary, who really brought harmony into my life and gave me a wonderful son, Rickey, I managed to make a success of my life.

Since bringing my first guests in by pack horse in June, 1934, I have contributed a great deal to the development of the Little Pickerel River area, without disturbing the ecology; by improving the access road, the water way, the stocking of nine feeder lakes with game fish, bringing in the hydro and telephone, managing a large trapping area and ridding the area of numerous timber wolves.

Because of Little River Lodge, Golden Valley and the area became known to many people all over Canada, U.S.A. and a few from Europe and South America. It was the money left in this area by satisfied guests that made this possible.

I have learned a great deal, during my life as a trapper, observing animals and their fitness to survive the changing environment. I know we continue to learn as long as we live; also, that experience is really the only teacher, however, many times an expensive one.

It has been a good life and only recently have I left trapping. In August, 1985, Mary and I left Golden Valley and moved to our present home.

Our consolation is: memories require no packing and yet they go right along with you, to ease the departure.

Walter Hesman
Sundridge, 1989

273